PARCC ELA/Literacy Assessments

Grades 9-12

Dennis M. Fare, M.Ed.
Assistant Superintendent
Mahwah Public Schools
Mahwah, New Jersey

Research & Education Association
Visit our website: www.rea.com

Research & Education Association
61 Ethel Road West
Piscataway, New Jersey 08854
E-mail: info@rea.com

PARCC ELA/LITERACY ASSESSMENTS, GRADES 9–12

Published 2015
Copyright © 2014 by Research & Education Association, Inc.
All rights reserved. No part of this book may be reproduced in
any form without permission of the publisher.

Printed in the United States of America

Library of Congress Control Number 2013936855

ISBN-13: 978-0-7386-1167-9
ISBN-10: 0-7386-1167-0

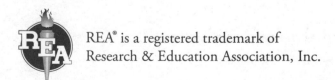

REA® is a registered trademark of
Research & Education Association, Inc.

Dear Student,

Let's be clear…

The Common Core assessments you'll soon be taking are unlike any tests you've ever seen.

These tests are known in many states as "PARCC" assessments. For the record, PARCC stands for the Partnership for Assessment of Readiness for College and Careers, which should give you a strong hint about what this is all about. PARCC is one of two major groups that states organized themselves into for the sake of developing next-generation exams to assess the Common Core State Standards being introduced into classrooms across most of the nation.

From here on, the way you LOOK AT and INTERACT with standardized testing will need to change.

Gone are the days of filling in answers on a bubble sheet. The new tests place more emphasis on your ability to *think*, not just memorize stuff.

For example, the new tests don't treat reading and writing skills separately, as, say, the SAT test, does. Blended together, reading and writing become a so-called JOINED SKILL. And guess what? This kind of skill is central to the very type of thinking that's most prized in college and in the workplace.

Put another way, you need to be able to evaluate information and use it to your advantage. And that's something you've never been asked to do on a high-stakes test before.

Key questions the PARCC assessments will force you to face include: What is credible? What will work for my source?

To succeed on the PARCC assessments, you need to become a mini-researcher or mini-lawyer, *reasoning through an argument*—not merely answering a series of plain-old multiple-choice questions testing your recall of seemingly disconnected facts.

The way the new tests are built also means your score will mean a lot more to you and to your future. Now, your score will follow you in a continuing quest to increase your personal growth and allow you to relate to the larger world with greater impact.

This test will be focused on the way students MAKE CONNECTIONS. How does one piece of information relate and link to another? In the days before Common Core, students like you were asked to look at pieces of information independent from anything else. Those days are over: Now you'll have to put the pieces together, CRITICALLY THINK, and make it all make logical sense.

This is no easy task, but with the right preparation, and the conscious choice to change the way we all think and PROCESS information, it's all very doable.

Let us show you how!

Dear Teacher,

You and your students are part of a historic shift in American education.

The adoption of the Common Core State Standards marks the first time in the history of the nation that most of our states have opted to set the bar for K–12 education by ambitiously collaborating on setting and meeting internationally-benchmarked standards.

What does this mean to you?

Well, for one thing, tougher tests.

You likely live in a state that chose to become a member of one of two Common Core assessment consortia. This book was developed to address the English language arts/Literacy assessments for the PARCC* consortium, whose members span 19 states, the District of Columbia and the U.S. Virgin Islands. Altogether, PARCC states educate about 22 million public K–12 students.

You've probably seen your share of screaming headlines about the Common Core, but now the big headline for you is that next-generation assessments are coming—and soon. So it's time to get ready.

There are plenty of books on the market that cover the theory behind the Common Core, as well as the curriculum that brings it into your classroom. This is not one of them. Instead, this is the first *practical* guide to Common Core *assessment*. It's a bracing tour of what makes the new assessments tick, brimming with test tips and carefully crafted standards-aligned practice—a workout, really—that reveals what your students most need to know to succeed on the new PARCC assessments for grades 9-12.

Your tour guide is author Dennis Fare, a veteran language arts supervisor and teacher in one of the nation's top school districts.

This is not test prep as you've come to know it because, truth be told, there's never been a battery of tests quite like the PARCC assessments.

Now, let's tackle the tests together.

---

* PARCC stands for Partnership for Assessment of Readiness for College and Careers.

Contents

Chapter 3: Narrative Writing Task

Chapter 4: Literary Analysis Task

Chapter 5: The Research Simulation Task

Chapter 6: Research Simulation Task: English

Chapter 7: Research Simulation Task: History

Chapter 8: Research Simulation Task: Science

Chapter 9: Research Simulation Task Practice Questions

Chapter 10: Final Thoughts

Bibliography

Acknowledgments

Appendices

About the Author

Dennis M. Fare holds a B.A. in English Writing and an M.Ed. in English Education. In 2014, Mr. Fare was named Assistant Superintendent of Mahwah (N.J.) Public Schools. Mr. Fare formerly served as the Supervisor of English Language Arts, Grades 6–12, for the Mahwah district, where he developed curriculum and supervised English Language Arts teachers. He taught English for many years at Hackensack (N.J.) High School and has also taught at the college level. Mr. Fare holds supervisor, principal, and superintendent certifications. He served as an AP reader for the AP English Language and Composition exam for the College Board and was also a rater for the SAT test. Mr. Fare's presentations to College Board conferences include: *AP Open Enrollment: From Theory to Practice; AP Online Curriculum*, and *AP Vertical Teaming: Working from the Ground Up.*

 # Author's Acknowledgments

I would like to thank the following people for their invaluable input and support throughout this project: Dr. C. Lauren Schoen, Superintendent at Mahwah Public Schools; Christine Zimmermann, Director of Curriculum at Mahwah Public Schools; Brian Miller, Principal of Ramapo Ridge Middle School; Suzanne Straub, Assistant Principal of Ramapo Ridge Middle School; John P. Pascale, Principal of Mahwah High School; Linda Bohny, Assistant Principal of Mahwah High School; and Dominick Gliatta, Miriam Lezanski, Roger Pelletier, Danielle Poleway, Patricia Reinhart, and Kristen Trabona, all instructional supervisors at Mahwah Public Schools.

Further, I would like to acknowledge my parents, Dennis (Sr.) and Lois Fare. I would also like to thank Caseen Gaines for his help during the proposal phase of this project.

About REA

Founded in 1959, Research & Education Association is dedicated to publishing the finest and most effective educational materials—including study guides and test preps—for students in middle school, high school, college, graduate school, and beyond.

Today, REA's wide-ranging catalog is a leading resource for teachers, students, and professionals. Visit *www.rea.com* to see a complete listing of all our titles.

REA Acknowledgments

Publisher: Pam Weston

Vice President, Editorial: Larry B. Kling

Senior Editor, PARCC Series: Alice Leonard

Managing Editor, Frontlist: Diane Goldschmidt

Copywriter: Kelli Wilkins

Cover Design: Christine Saul

Page Design: Claudia Petrilli

Copyeditor: Anne McGowan

Proofreader: Ellen Gong

Typesetter: Kathy Caratozzolo

Permissions: Katherine Benzer, S4 Carlisle

The PARCC Assessments At-a-Glance

Because PARCC is a new assessment system that is in development, not everything about it has been finalized. Based on the most recent guidance from the PARCC consortium, the following information is available.

The PARCC assessments in English Language Arts/Literacy (the content basis of this book) and Mathematics are designed to measure the degree to which students have learned the critical knowledge, skills and abilities essential for college and career success. While this guidebook focuses on grades 9–12, PARCC assessments will be administered in grades 3 through high school beginning in the 2014–2015 school year. The assessments for each grade will be based on the Common Core State Standards for that grade level.

Structure of the Tests

To effectively implement the PARCC design, assessments in both ELA/Literacy and Mathematics will be administered in two parts, a **performance-based assessment (PBA)**, administered after approximately 75% of the school year, and an **end-of-year assessment (EOY)**, administered after approximately 90% of the school year.

Each grade level of the ELA/Literacy PBA will include three tasks: a narrative task, a literary analysis task, and a research simulation task. For each task, examinees will be asked to read one or more texts, answer several short vocabulary and comprehension questions, and write an essay that requires examinees to gather evidence from the text(s). Each grade level of the ELA/Literacy EOY will consist of 4–5 texts, both literary and informational (including social science/historical, scientific, and technical texts in grades 6–11). Short-answer vocabulary and comprehension questions will also be associated with each text.

Administration of the Tests

PBA and EOY assessments will be administered in a total of nine sessions. The PBA for each grade level will be administered in five sessions, three for ELA/Literacy and two for mathematics. The EOY for each grade level will be administered in four sessions, two for ELA/Literacy and two for mathematics. Individual examinees will be involved in testing sessions for both the PBA and EOY over a period of five to nine days. Refer to the following tables for a graphic representation of test components and times by grade(s).

Performance-Based Component

	ELA/Literacy			Math		
	Literary Analysis	Research	Narrative	Session 1	Session 2	Total
Grades 9–10	80 min	85 min	50 min	50 min	50 min	315 min
Grade 11	80 min	85 min	50 min	65 min	65 min	345 min

End-of-Year Component

	ELA/Literacy		Math			
	Session 1	Session 2	Session 1	Session 2	Total	Summative Total
Grades 9–10	70 min	70 min	65 min	65 min	270 min	9 hours, 45 minutes
Grade 11	70 min	70 min	55 min	55 min	250 min	9 hours, 55 minutes

Test Results

Results of the ELA/Literacy assessments will be reported in three categories: (1) ELA/Literacy; (2) reading and comprehending a range of sufficiently complex texts independently (reading) and (3) writing effectively when using and/or analyzing sources (writing). ELA/Literacy results will be based on a composite of the examinees' reading and writing scores. Students will receive both a scaled score and performance-level scores for ELA/Literacy, and scaled scores for the reading and writing categories. Performance-level scores will be reported according to five levels.

In order to be deemed "CCR" (or "College and Career Ready"), students must earn a "4" or a "5" at the end of eleventh grade.

Readers should be aware that some materials used in this book—including contemporary articles and broadcast transcripts—are sourced from the United Kingdom and thus use British spellings and punctuation. We have included this content because it's considered fair game by developers of the PARCC assessments.

CHAPTER 1

Introduction

The Common Core State Standards Initiative

This book gives you what you most need to know about the PARCC assessments for English language arts/literacy.

In doing so, it proceeds from these five basic principles:

1. We believe in the PARCC assessments.

2. We believe in the Common Core Standards, which inform how the PARCC tests are being developed.

3. We believe the PARCC test battery assesses the very skills today's students most need to succeed in college and the workplace.

4. We believe in affording today's students the best possible shot at success in college and their chosen career.

5. We believe the PARCC assessments need the no-nonsense, practical perspective of the schoolhouse—and that's exactly what you'll find in this study guide.

The foundation for the PARCC tests lies in the Common Core State Standards. Adopted by the vast majority of U.S. states, the Common Core achieves for the first time in American history a near-common curriculum for the nation as a whole.

In essence, the PARCC is designed to assess whether or not students are making progress toward achieving the benchmarks set forth in the Common Core.

Thus, our book is closely aligned with the PARCC, and, by extension, the Common Core. For instance, most of the readings you will find in our book are taken from the reading suggestions from the Common Core (please see Appendix B of the Common Core: *http://www.corestandards.org/ELA-Literacy*). By using these reading suggestions and the curricular guidelines set forth in the Common Core English language arts document, we are giving you an advantage in taking the PARCC exam. Why, you might ask? The answer is simple: The more familiar you are with the literary and nonfiction texts of the Common Core, the better prepared you will be to take the PARCC assessment.

While there are certainly a lot of standards, keep in mind that two standards will always be in play, regardless if the task involves reading or writing. They are:

- Reading Standard One (1): Use of Evidence
- Reading Standard Ten (10): Complex Texts

Therefore, we are supremely confident that the reading exercises and the activities within this book will help you on the PARCC exam.

Reading the Standards

Throughout this test prep guide, we have aligned each task to the Common Core standards. This is a natural alignment, as the test and Common Core standards are interlinked. The following chart shows how the standards are denoted.

Standard Strand	Title
RL	Reading Literature
RI	Reading Information
L	Language
W	Writing
SL	Speaking/Listening
RH	Reading History/Social Studies
RST	Reading Science/Technology

Overview of the PARCC

PARCC stands for *Partnership for the Assessment of Readiness for College and Careers*. We know—it's a long title! Throughout this guidebook, though, we will refer to the test by its widely known acronym: PARCC.

The nature of the test makes it unlike any test you have ever taken. Three things make this so:

- The test is given on computer.

- The test is actually a series of tests given throughout the school year.

- What's on the test will require you to think in new and stimulating ways—both because of the content itself and the way it's presented.

So, how will the testing schedule look? We have broken down the PARCC's various assessments so that you can easily see that this is a test that will not be taken on just one day of the school year, but actually will be taken several times *throughout* the school year. Check out the timeline below:

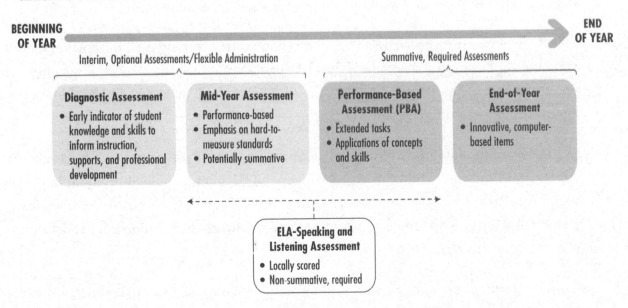

As shown above, you will be required to take the "Performance-Based Assessment" and the "End-of-Year Assessment." The "Diagnostic Assessment" and the "Mid-Year Assessment" are optional depending upon the state in which you live. The Performance-Based Assessments (PBAs) consist of reading activities and three writing activities based upon the reading: (a) a narrative essay, (b) a literary analysis essay, and (c) a research-simulation task. This book will address the reading skills you will need as well as the writing skills for these three types of writing assessments.

Because this test will be taken on the computer, your results will be returned to you much faster than with pencil-and-paper exams you have taken. It is also very important to look at these practice questions in the context of keyboarding your responses. If you do not yet feel comfortable with keyboarding, it is time to practice these skills on your own!

Now that you are familiar with the structure of the PARCC, let's look over each of its question types together.

Introduction to Interactive Reading

In every other test prep book you've ever read, or any English language arts classroom you've ever been in, you've most likely worked on strategies to engage with a printed text. While these strategies should not be forgotten, it is important to begin thinking of them in the context of brainstorming and working with a text on a computer.

Many of you surf the Web daily. At this point, you're probably used to casually skimming, scanning, and reading texts online. If this isn't part of your daily, or even weekly, routine, then you should start. Since the PARCC is administered entirely on computer, it is time to think about this test in a different way.

The reading skills you will learn in Chapter 2 will help you on the "Performance-Based Assessment" and the "End-of-Year Assessment." In Chapter 2 you will begin looking at how to appropriately read and take notes from a screen. You will learn how to take what you've learned in your English language arts classes and modify these techniques for the purposes of preparing for this test.

Most students are familiar with reading comprehension sections that appear on any state test or even the SAT. Generally, you would read the passage or selection, and then answer a series of multiple-choice questions and/or open-ended questions. The PARCC, however, will assess reading in a more interactive manner. Often, you will answer questions *as you read*, as opposed to answering those questions after you've read.

You will need to electronically highlight text in relation to questions. You will also need to address how the reading selection raises specific points to support the writer's viewpoint or argument. As you read, you'll have to interactively investigate. While this sounds complicated, it is actually quite doable. The key is to be prepared, which is why you're using this guidebook in the first place!

As you read through the question types during the interactive reading chapter, be sure to review our "Thought Process" (a feature utilized throughout this book) as we navigate through the questions. This should serve as a model for you as you complete the interactive reading questions on your own.

This is the only chapter in which we focus our attention on multiple-choice questions with regard to the PARCC. All performance-based assessment chapters (narrative, literary analysis, and research simulation) concentrate on the prose-constructed response, using overarching literacy skills to enable you to confidently approach and complete each.

Throughout your reading of this chapter, pay careful attention to the ways in which close reading is modeled. If you are not aware of the language of authors in relation to their purposes, the questions will be more difficult to answer accurately. Think about how writers craft their viewpoints and project a desired effect upon the reader. You'll find that many of the question types in this particular chapter look closely at how you, as the reader/test-taker, can recognize how writers put together their viewpoints or arguments. This is what close and active reading successfully will clarify as you develop your understanding.

Also, according to PARCC requirements, the following word counts apply to all reading selections:

Grade Level	Word Count
Grades 9–11	500–1,500 words

The PARCC requirements also assign a complexity rating for each text, which follows this protocol:

Grade Level	PARCC "Complexity" Determination
Grades 9–10	1050–1335
Grade 11	1185–1385

The balance of texts on the Performance-Based Assessments and End-of-Year Assessments will shift by grade band.

Grade Level	Types of Texts
Grades 9–11	Approximately thirty (30) percent literary texts Approximately seventy (70) percent informational text

Criteria for Selection of Authentic Texts

One goal of the PARCC is for students to be exposed to texts that are content-rich and challenging. These will be actual, authentic texts, not texts merely created for the test itself. Thus, throughout this test prep guide, we have utilized texts specifically suggested by the Common Core.

Criteria for Selection of Paired or Multiple Texts

As you work through the various tasks, you will notice that you will encounter questions that involve paired or multiple texts. These texts purposefully expose students to the domains of English language arts, science, history/social studies, technical subjects, and the arts. Through multiple texts, students will be able to analyze larger themes while also addressing informational validity and reliability.

Special Education/Accommodations

As you read through each of these chapters, be mindful of the accommodations that will be available to students with disabilities. As detailed in the *PARCC Accommodations Manual*, embedded electronic supports will be available to all students to use, including features like font magnification, highlighting tools, bolding, and underlining. The PARCC assessment will also include a computer-delivered system that provides features that are made available at the discretion of school-based educators, including background/font color and answer masking. Further accommodations exist to increase access while maintaining a valid and reliable student score, including braille form, extended time, small-group testing, and a word-to-word native language dictionary. Paper-and-pencil tests will be available for students who need this specific support.

Keep in mind that, according to the *PARCC Accommodations Manual*, even students who are not classified may still be eligible for test accommodations. This will be determined by the school building's principal or the principal's designee, as per data collected by the student's teacher(s) or administrator(s). Once it is determined that a student may need accommodations for the PARCC, a Personal Needs Profile (or "PNP") will need to be completed.

As teachers instruct students with regard to PARCC-related skills, differentiating instruction (by focusing on targeted instruction through different modes of learning) will help all the different students/learners in our classrooms to access these different assessment types. Computer-based keyboarding experiences should be occurring regularly, and the accommodations above should also be made available to students so that the practice-testing environment mirrors that of the PARCC assessment as closely as possible.

Introduction to Chosen Texts

Since the Common Core Standards call for students to work with a variety of complex texts, this range will also be mirrored in the PARCC assessment.

Examples of Literary Text Types:

- Poetry
- Drama

- Fiction
- Multimedia (in the form of film, radio, etc.)

Examples of Informational Text Types:

- Literary non-fiction
- History/social science texts
- Science/technical texts
- Multimedia (texts that have both words and audio/video)

More specific informational text examples:

- Advertisements
- Agendas
- Autobiographies
- Biographies
- Company profiles
- Contracts
- Correspondence
- Essays
- Feature articles
- Government documents
- Histories
- Interviews
- Journal articles
- Legal documents
- Magazine articles

- Memoirs
- News articles
- Opinion/editorial pieces
- Political cartoons
- Product Specifications
- Product/Service descriptions
- Recipes
- Reports
- Reviews
- Science investigations
- Speeches
- Textbooks
- Tourism guides
- Training manuals
- User guides/manuals

Please note that we have utilized this range of texts across our question-types.

Introduction to the PARCC'S Performance-Based Tasks

- Narrative Writing Task (Performance-Based Assessment; 50 minutes)

- Literacy Analysis Task (Performance-Based Assessment; 80 minutes)

- Research Simulation Task (Performance-Based Assessment; 85 minutes)

Each of the three main writing tasks of the Performance-Based Assessment will assess very different skills. In order to work through these skills, it is crucial that you first become familiar with the setup of these types of questions. Don't worry, though, as we have mapped out the steps in tackling each of these questions for you!

Before we begin to discuss these three writing tasks, let us be clear on one very important point: Reading and writing on PARCC's Performance-Based Assessments are inter-connected and cannot, nor should they be, separated from each other. For instance, on the "Literary Analysis" task, you will write an analytic essay **based upon your reading** of the literary texts presented on the task. This fact completely distinguishes the PARCC from a test like the SAT. **In essence, on the PARCC, how well you write will depend upon how well you read.** We emphasize this point now and in most every chapter of this book.

Be sure to utilize the graphic organizers provided throughout this guidebook. They will help you to organize your thoughts. Remember that when you are sitting for this test, the brainstorming and pre-writing stage is particularly essential to your success. When you take this exam, you should be able to mentally visualize these easy-to-follow graphic organizers to manage your thinking with ease.

Many students become nervous and anxious about thinking "on their feet." The setup of this guidebook will give you the confidence and skills needed to have the structure of the essays already pre-planned, and will give you the necessary foresight to predict what the PARCC test will ask you.

If you think you're a weak reader and writer, which many students do, you need to start seeing these tasks as doable, regardless of your training in your former English language arts classes. In fact, even if you consider yourself a naturally strong reader and writer, each of the three main tasks of the "Performance-Based Assessment" may still be difficult simply because they are unfamiliar at first. Look closely at the steps that we have clearly defined for you. If you can follow these steps, which we know you can, then you can map out a well-thought-out response.

We have already mentioned that these performance-based tasks will be new exercises for you. So, do not let the title of this assessment, "English Language Arts," fool you. Not everything you write will be based solely on what you've learned in your English class this year. These writing tasks are meant to be cross-curricular, which means that various subjects will be integrated into these writing tasks.

With each of these three reading and writing tasks, you will need to use the writing process in conjunction with your own content knowledge. This may require you to access your knowledge of different subject areas, including social studies, science, and art, along with reading and writing skills from your English language arts classes.

Introduction to the Narrative Writing Task
(Performance-Based Assessment)

Now that you have been introduced to the structure of the test, and the purpose and philosophy behind the PARCC assessment, it is important to introduce you to each of the reading and writing tasks.

The narrative writing task has a 50-minute testing time and will require you to organize your thoughts in ways that are both easy to follow and interesting to read. When students think of a narrative, they instantly think of a story. This is understandable, but it can be so much more. Don't forget about other subjects as you tackle this component of the test. Writing a story is just one of the various possibilities that might need to be completed.

Most simply, this task may require you, as the test-taker, to complete a story. The PARCC will provide you with an introduction, usually consisting of a few sentences, and you will need to take elements from that introduction and remain faithful to those details while completing the story independently, *in your own words*. There is a delicate balance that needs to be mastered—through utilizing the details presented in a meaningful way throughout the presentation of your own narrative.

In this task, we will look at brainstorming strategies and graphic organizers that will help you organize and manage your thoughts. We will look closely at using language in a purposeful manner to create a desired effect upon the reader.

As discussed earlier, not only will you need to create a short story rich in figurative language, but the possibility also still remains that this task may require you, as the test-taker, to complete either the organized description of a scientific process or historical account. We will explain how to structure your thoughts and use language effectively to prepare your response.

By integrating separate content areas, you will not only need to know how to organize your thoughts, but you will also have to use your content knowledge to accurately complete the scientific process or historical account. We will address each of these possibilities, helping you to structure and prepare such a response, while maintaining your control of language throughout any writing situation.

Introduction to the Literary Analysis Task
(Performance-Based Assessment)

The literary analysis task has an 80-minute time limit and will be difficult to organize at first, but with some practice, you'll find that writing this essay can be an interesting experience. Once you are comfortable with the format of this question, all other pieces will fall into place. You will need to use many of the helpful strategies from the interactive reading chapter to help master the literary analysis task.

The goal here is to look at *two* different types of literary texts. These writings could consist of any of the following genres: poems, story excerpts, play excerpts, famous speech passages, nonfiction article excerpts. These reading selections can be from a variety of content area backgrounds, but most likely will be brief. Regardless of the situation, you will gain a great deal of practice looking at a wide assortment of different reading excerpts.

After you have read each of the two reading passages, you will need to compare and contrast the two excerpts. This task will require you to look deeply at the content of the reading selections, along with its use of language. When looking at this writing task, we will look closely at the purposeful usage of rhetorical and literary devices. Not only will we master the definitions of widely used devices, we will also analyze how each device is most prevalently used for specific desired effects. Having this prerequisite knowledge will help you in mastering this writing task. We have created a quick reference guide for you to use in doing this.

The content of these selections will vary. Selections will not only be English-based, but rather, may be related to social studies, science, or any of your technical subjects. It is your duty to make connections between these two texts, and to consider how they are both similar and different.

This may be the most difficult writing task for you to organize easily, but we will review an outline that will make the process that much more seamless in arranging your ideas. This will take a lot of practice, especially when you have to compare and contrast the usage of language.

After you have looked at both content and language closely, you will have to connect the two together in your essay. You will be introduced to a framework to put these items together in a way that simplifies the drafting process.

Introduction to the Research Simulation Task
(Performance-Based Assessment)

Initially, the Research Simulation Task, with an 85-minute time limit, seems daunting, as it is supposed to mimic the skills that students often use to draft a traditional "research paper." Dreaded for years by students of all ages, the research paper requires a certain set of processes in order to become confident in putting all of its pieces together.

In the research simulation task, you will be given a variety of different sources pertaining to a certain topic. This particular reading and writing experience is similar to a persuasive or argumentative essay, except you will be using information from the sources given to support claims in a written essay.

The subject of this task could pertain to any particular topic, from a contemporary social issue to an issue related to any of the content areas. Like the other two writing tasks, this essay will ask you to become familiar with a wide array of information in order to adequately respond to the writing prompt.

In this chapter, we will look closely at how to analyze a source. The sources are not all traditional texts, but rather may be considered "non-print" texts, from which you will be able to extract information from a photograph, chart, graph, survey, painting, or advertisement in order to bolster or support the main thesis of your essay.

Not only will you learn how to organize your thoughts, as will be the case with structuring all other essays, but you will also review how to weigh the credibility of a source to choose relevant information as support. You will be required to take this information and weave it together; we will discuss how the sources should "have a conversation with one another." This will contribute to the flow of your essay, and will serve as a reasonable alternative to what many of you have known as the "research paper" that you have perhaps worked on in your English classes.

So, as you can tell, there is a great deal of detail that will go into framing your research simulation task. Not only do you have to be able to analyze each type of source in great detail, but you will also have to string the sources' information together in order to create a solid argument or viewpoint, while also keeping the power of language in mind throughout this experience.

With regard to the multimedia sources integrated into these chapters, we have made sure to include summary information and to address potential access issues that you may have. These sources require you to access websites in order to fully experience the information's delivery.

We have found that many students, when having little to no experience with writing the research simulation task, will avoid many visual sources to support their written points because they are not comfortable with how to analyze these types of sources. Also, students often do not know how to make convincing connections between sources that are, initially, seemingly unrelated to one another. In the upcoming chapters, we will address these areas of concern.

Introduction to Speaking/Listening Task

Based on released information, we expect that the Speaking/Listening assessment will be much like a research simulation task, where students will utilize multiple sources to support their claims and perspectives through oral presentation. Keep this in mind as you work through the various RST chapters throughout this guidebook.

We do know that students will be required to complete this Speaking/Listening Assessment inside the classroom, but this will not be included in their summative scores. This component will be locally scored.

Performance Level Descriptors (PLDs)

After you complete the PARCC assessment, you will be provided with your performance level descriptor, or "PLD." This will indicate your level of college and career readiness, according to the standards of the PARCC. A student's PLD is based on his/her performance that relates to level of text complexity, range of accuracy, and usage of quality of evidence.

When reading the charts that follow, consider the following criteria—text complexity, range of accuracy, and quality of evidence.

Text Complexity

PARCC uses two components for determining text complexity for all passages, including quantitative text complexity measures and qualitative judgments from rubrics.

Accuracy

"Accurate"—The student is able to accurately state both the general ideas expressed in the text(s) and the key and supporting details. The response is complete and the student demonstrates *full* understanding.

"Mostly accurate"—The student is able to accurately state most of the general ideas expressed in the text(s) and the key and supporting details, but the response is incomplete or contains minor inaccuracies. The student demonstrates *extensive* understanding.

"Generally accurate"—The student is able to accurately state the gist of the text(s) but fails to accurately state the key and supporting details in the text or to connect such details to the overarching meaning of the text(s). The student demonstrates *basic* understanding.

"Minimally accurate"—The student is unable to accurately state the gist of the text(s) but is able to minimally state some of the key or supporting details with accuracy. The student does not connect the specific details of the text to the overarching meaning(s) of the text. The student demonstrates *minimal* understanding.

"Inaccurate"—The student is unable to accurately state either the gist of the text or the key and supporting details evident in the text.

Quality of Evidence

"Explicit evidence"—The student shows how the explicit words and phrases (details) from the text support statements made about the meaning of the text.

"Inferential evidence"—The student shows how inferences drawn from the text support statements made about the meaning of the text.

The levels follow the criteria below:

Grade 9

Level	Level of Text Complexity	Range of Accuracy	Quality of Evidence
5	Very complex	Accurate	Explicit/inferential
	Moderately complex	Accurate	Explicit/inferential
	Readily accessible	Accurate	Explicit/inferential
4	Very complex	Mostly accurate	Explicit/inferential
	Moderately complex	Generally accurate	Explicit/inferential
	Readily accessible	Accurate	Explicit/inferential
3	Very complex	Generally accurate	Explicit/inferential
	Moderately complex	Generally accurate	Explicit/inferential
	Readily accessible	Mostly accurate	Explicit/inferential
2	Very complex	Inaccurate	Explicit
	Moderately complex	Minimally accurate	Explicit/inferential
	Readily accessible	Generally accurate	Explicit/inferential

Grade 10

Level	Level of Text Complexity	Range of Accuracy	Quality of Evidence
5	Very complex	Accurate	Explicit/inferential
	Moderately complex	Accurate	Explicit/inferential
	Readily accessible	Accurate	Explicit/inferential
4	Very complex	Mostly accurate	Explicit/inferential
	Moderately complex	Accurate	Explicit/inferential
	Readily accessible	Accurate	Explicit/inferential
3	Very complex	Generally accurate	Explicit/inferential
	Moderately complex	Mostly accurate	Explicit/inferential
	Readily accessible	Accurate	Explicit/inferential
2	Very complex	Inaccurate	Explicit
	Moderately complex	Minimally accurate	Explicit/inferential
	Readily accessible	Mostly accurate	Explicit/inferential

Grade 11

Level	Level of Text Complexity	Range of Accuracy	Quality of Evidence
5	Very complex	Accurate	Explicit/inferential
	Moderately complex	Accurate	Explicit/inferential
	Readily accessible	Accurate	Explicit/inferential
4	Very complex	Mostly accurate	Explicit/inferential
	Moderately complex	Accurate	Explicit/inferential
	Readily accessible	Accurate	Explicit/inferential
3	Very complex	Generally accurate	Explicit/inferential
	Moderately complex	Mostly accurate	Explicit/inferential
	Readily accessible	Accurate	Explicit/inferential
2	Very complex	Inaccurate	Explicit
	Moderately complex	Minimally accurate	Explicit/inferential
	Readily accessible	Mostly accurate	Explicit/inferential

In order to be deemed "college and career ready," students must achieve at least a level "4" on the grade 11 PARCC ELA/literacy assessment. PLDs are further explained below:

Level	Policy-Level Performance Level Descriptor
5	Students performing at this level demonstrate a **distinguished command** of the knowledge, skills, and practices embodied by the Common Core State Standards assessed at their grade level.
4	Students performing at this level demonstrate a **strong command** of the knowledge, skills, and practices embodied by the Common Core State Standards assessed at their grade level.
3	Students performing at this level demonstrate a **moderate command** of the knowledge, skills, and practices embodied by the Common Core State Standards assessed at their grade level.
2	Students performing at this level demonstrate a **partial command** of the knowledge, skills, and practices embodied by the Common Core State Standards assessed at their grade level.
1	Students performing at this level demonstrate a **minimal command** of the knowledge, skills, and practices embodied by the Common Core State Standards assessed at their grade level.

End-of-Year (EOY) Assessment

The End-of-Year Assessment will consist of two 70-minute sessions during which students will infuse all skills relevant to their work through the Performance-Based Assessments. Students will need to read and write in relation to narrative, literary analysis, and research simulation tasks, just as they have practiced throughout the chapters of this guidebook.

The literacy skills found in each of these chapters, including the analysis of text and the working with text, will be helpful when ultimately completing the End-of-Year Assessment. As we will discuss further, reading and writing skills work hand-in-hand, which is a similar relationship between the skills needed for the Performance-Based Assessments and the End-of-Year Assessment.

Essentially, the reading and writing exercises that students complete throughout the Performance-Based Assessments will be ideal preparation for the End-of-Year Assessment.

 ## Looking at the Acronyms

It seems as if the PARCC labels a lot of its components by abbreviations or acronyms, which is nothing new in the world of education. We wanted to put all of the acronyms in one place to help in clarification and explanation, as we understand that this will be a new language for all of us.

Acronym	Actual Title	Explanation
PARCC	Partnership for Assessment of Readiness for College and Career	The name of this particular assessment's consortium of states.
ELA	English Language Arts	This refers to the literacy skills used throughout these PARCC assessments.
CCR	College and Career Readiness	In order for students to be deemed as "college and career ready," they will have demonstrated the academic knowledge, skills and practices necessary to enter directly into and succeed in entry-level, credit-bearing courses in College English Composition, Literature, and technical courses requiring college-level reading and writing.
CCSS	Common Core State Standards	The standards with which the PARCC assessments are aligned.
OWG	Operational Working Group	The groups of professionals formed to work forward and to revise assessments.
PLD	Performance Level Descriptor	A student's level determined by his or her performance on each assessment.
PBA	Performance-Based Assessment	This label is used for the three assessments you will take throughout the school year before the End-of-Year assessment. These include the narrative PBA, the literary analysis PBA, and the research simulation PBA.

(continued)

Acronym	Actual Title	Explanation
MYA	Mid-Year Assessment	This assessment is taken in the middle of the school year.
EOY	End-of-Year Assessment	This assessment is taken at the end of the school year.
PCR	Prose-Constructed Response	The larger writing task that you will complete with each performance-based assessment.
EBSR	Evidence-Based Selected Response	When a second question on the PARCC is dependent on a student's answer to the first question.
TECR	Technology-Enhanced Constructed Response	A task that requires the student to use technology to show student comprehension, including the following tasks: drag and drop, cut and paste, shade text, move items to show relationships.
WHST	Writing History, Science, and Technical Subjects	The interdisciplinary writing standard.
RST	Reading Science and Technical Subjects	The interdisciplinary reading standard.
RST	Research Simulation Task	The synthesis performance-based assessment that asks students to use information from a variety of sources to support their opinion.
PNP	Personal Needs Profile	An accommodation plan for a non-classified student or classified student

CHAPTER 2

Interactive Literacy

Introduction

(Performance-Based and End-of-Year Assessments)

Some people say that technology—especially the way that teens use it today, with its interactive features and touch screens—has changed the world. Certainly it has with the PARCC assessment. Students and teachers who use this prep book are undoubtedly familiar with the "old way" of taking an exam. Take, for instance, the SAT. On that test, students read a passage, mark it up with a pencil if they are so inclined, and answer the multiple-choice items that follow. The PARCC, however, is quite different. This exam requires students to interact in ways with the text that were not possible even a few years ago. This chapter is designed to help you perform well both on the *Performance-Based* and the *End-of-Year* assessments.

This chapter is aligned with the following Common Core standards:

Range	CCSS Standards
RL.1–8; RL.9–10	RL.1: Cite strong and textual evidence.
	RL.2: Determine two or more themes.
	RL.3: Analyze the impact of the author's choices.
	RL.4: Determine the meaning of words and phrases.
	RL.5: Analyze how an author's choices contribute to its overall structure.
	RL.6: Analyze a case in which grasping a point of view requires distinguishing what is directly stated in a text.
	RL.7: Analyze multiple interpretations of a work.
	RL.9: Demonstrate knowledge of foundational works of American literature, including how two or more texts from the same period treat similar themes.
	RL.10: Read and comprehend complex texts.

Range	CCSS Standards
RI.1-7; RI.9-10	RI.1: Cite strong and thorough textual evidence to support analysis.
	RI.2: Determine two or more central ideas of a text.
	RI.3: Analyze a complex set of ideas or sequence of events.
	RI.4: Determine the meaning of words and phrases.
	RI.5: Analyze and evaluate the effectiveness of the structure an author uses.
	RI.6: Determine an author's point of view or purpose in a text.
	RI.7: Integrate and evaluate multiple sources of information.
	RI.9: Analyze U.S. documents of historical and literary significance.
	RI.10: Read and comprehend complex texts.
L.1-6	L.1-2: Demonstrate command of the conventions of standard English grammar and usage.
	L.3: Apply knowledge of language to understand how language functions in different contexts.
	L.4: Determine or clarify the meaning of unknown and multiple-meaning words and phrases.
	L.5: Demonstrate understanding of figurative language, word relationships, and nuances in word meanings.
	L.6: Acquire and use accurately general academic and domain-specific words and phrases.

To begin, let's clarify exactly what we mean by the term *interactive literacy* so that we can be prepared for the types of activities you will encounter on the PARCC. First, *interactive literacy* denotes the specific reading and writing skills that are tested by the PARCC Performance-Based and End-of-Year assessments. These literacy skills include, but are not limited to, four areas we'll explore in greater depth later on: inferring, interpreting, analyzing, and critiquing. Second, the term *interactive literacy* implies that the test-taker of the PARCC will use a computer interface to click on and manipulate the text as part of the reading process. So, in various ways, you will apply your literacy skills using a computer-based interactive approach.

Let's see how you will utilize these literacy skills by examining a short excerpt from the passage below. This selection is taken from a *New York Times* article, written by Justin Gillis, entitled "An Alarm in the Offing on Climate Change":

> The natural conservatism of science has often led climatologists to be cautious in their pronouncements about global warming. More than once they have drawn criticism for burying their fundamental message—that society is running some huge risks—in caveats and cavils.
>
> To judge from the draft of a new report issued by a federal advisory committee, that hesitation may soon fall by the wayside. The draft, just introduced for public comment before it becomes final, is the latest iteration of a major series of reports requested by Congress on the effects of climate change in the United States.
>
> I caution that it is a draft, so we don't know what final language will make it into the report. I am always hesitant to give too much credence to drafts that could change substantially, but in its current form, the document minces no words.
>
> "Climate change is already affecting the American people," declares the opening paragraph of the report, issued under the auspices of the Global Change Research Program, which coordinates federally sponsored climate research. "Certain types of weather events have become more frequent and/or intense, including heat waves, heavy downpours, and, in some regions, floods and droughts.

The passage above is typical of a PARCC reading passage for grade 10. With words such as "credence," "pronouncements," "fundamental," "caveats," and "cavils," the passage presents some tough vocabulary. When a student interacts with the passage by inferring the meaning of these words and by analyzing the main idea and purpose of the text, the PARCC assessment will test this understanding through manipulation of test questions. We'll see how in a moment.

Let's look at the following question in order to illustrate one way in which the PARCC will require you to interact with the text on the computer screen:

Below are three claims that one could make based upon the article we just read, "An Alarm in the Offing on Climate Change."

CLAIMS	There is still time to mediate the effects of climate change.
	The effects of climate change will most severely be felt in terms of warmer and erratic weather.
	The preliminary findings of the draft report, while not finalized, paint a grim future of the effects of climate change.

PART A

Highlight the claim that is supported by the most relevant and sufficient evidence within the article.

PART B

Now let's move to Part B. What two supporting details in the text would you select to support the claim in Part A?

As you can see, with Part A and Part B, the PARCC requires that you find answers to the questions posed by going back, reading through portions of the text, and using the mouse to highlight segments of the passage that pertain to the answer that you previously identified as correct in the Claims box.

What did you choose for the correct answer in Part A? The claim that is supported by the most relevant and sufficient evidence is in the third box, "The preliminary findings of the draft report, while not finalized, paint a grim future of the effects of climate change." What about PART B that asks for the two supporting details within the text? You guessed it: 1.) "The draft, just introduced for public comment before it becomes final, is the latest iteration of a major series of reports requested by Congress on the effects of climate change in the United States." and 2.) "I am always hesitant to give too much credence to drafts that could change substantially, but in its current form, the document minces no words."

So far, we've had just a peek at how the test will assess your ability to read, infer, interpret, analyze, and critique difficult text. The next section of our book will review the specific literacy skills you will need to succeed on the exam.

Key Literacy Skills: Vocabulary and Context

One of the aims of the PARCC is to assess your ability not only to know vocabulary but to understand how context is used to create or influence the meaning of a specific vocabulary term. A good way to approach this aspect of the test is to think of it as solving a puzzle. Each word is a piece of the larger puzzle, or context. And all of them have to fit together to allow you to solve the puzzle. So, two skills are being assessed: 1.) To infer the meaning of a word based upon context, and 2.) To identify the specific textual evidence used in the passage that gave rise to the meaning of the term. Whew! Do not worry! This is not as difficult as it may first appear.

Let's look at a passage from the previously quoted article, "An Alarm in the Offing on Climate Change":

To judge from the draft of a new report issued by a federal advisory committee, that hesitation may soon fall by the wayside. The draft, just introduced for public comment before it becomes final, is the latest *iteration* of a major series of reports requested by Congress on the effects of climate change in the United States.

Here is the way PARCC will present a vocabulary question:

PART A

What does the word *iteration* mean in the text, "An Alarm in the Offing on Climate Change"?

a. assignment	b. report
c. reason	d. mistake

PART B

Which words from the lines of the text best help the reader understand the meaning of *iteration*?

a. The draft . . . is the latest	b. requested by Congress
c. climate change	d. public comment

TEST-TAKING STRATEGY: For Part A, the most effective and easiest way to go about answering the questions is a two-step approach:

1. Read the sentence in the passage while inserting each letter for *iteration*. For example, insert "a. assignment" for *iteration* and see what happens. You get: "The draft, just introduced for public comment before it becomes final, is the latest *assignment* of a major series of reports requested by Congress." It is clear that "a. assignment" does not work, which leads us to step

2. Use the Process of Elimination to mentally "cross out" answers that do not work.

The only answer that works for Part A is "c. report." Now that we got the correct answer, you need to be aware of something crucial when answering vocabulary items. Experienced teachers can attest that many students answer vocabulary items on standardized tests **without** reviewing the text and considering the context. That is a *major* error. Here's the reason why: The term *iteration*, if looked up in the dictionary, means, "the act of repeating; a repetition." Notice that not one of the answer choices looks anything like the term *repeating* or *repetition*. The reason: The PARCC does not necessarily care for the dictionary definition of terms! Instead, the test is designed to assess your ability to think! Test writers want you to understand vocabulary as dynamic and alive, filled with meaning from the word choices that authors make. Now, let's move on to Part B to consider the literacy skills necessary to get that answer correct.

The first thing you will need to notice about Part B is that the correctness of its answer hinges entirely on getting the correct answer to Part A. Fair or not, that's the way the test is designed, all the more reason to get you to consider the context when deciding on vocabulary choices.

So, for Part B, we just have to think backwards. And thinking backwards requires back-solving. Here's how it works: When you decided that "reports" was the correct answer for Part A, what specifically in the text steered you toward that answer? Once we ask the question this way, all we have to do is complete the process of elimination again. Did "a. the draft . . . is the latest" lead us to *report*? Did "b. requested by Congress" lead us to report? This process should be completed until we have eliminated all the answer choices that do not make sense. In this case, answer "a. the draft . . . is the latest" was the first and correct answer. Even so, it would be a good idea to check the other choices just in case.

To summarize, we have discussed and illustrated the two-step process to answering vocabulary items on the PARCC most effectively. 1.) Use the context in the passage to identify the correct answer choice, and 2.) Identify the specific terms in the context that directed us to that answer. Next, we will go through more excerpts from "An Alarm in the Offing on Climate Change" so that you can practice your newly sharpened vocabulary skills.

Vocabulary Practice 1

Excerpt from "An Alarm in the Offing on Climate Change":

"Climate change is already affecting the American people," declares the opening paragraph of the report, issued under the *auspices* of the Global Change Research Program, which coordinates federally sponsored climate research.

PART A

What does the word *auspices* mean in the text, "An Alarm in the Offing on Climate Change"?

a. disguise	b. formality
c. alarm	d. sponsorship

PART B

Which words from the lines of the text best help the reader understand the meaning of *auspices?*

a. climate change	b. issued under
c. American people	d. federally sponsored

Answers:

Part A: "d. sponsorship"; Rationale: Using the process of elimination, "sponsorship" substitutes best for *auspices.*

Part B: "b. issued under"; Rationale: The phrase "issued under" implies that the Global Change Research Program "sponsored" the report.

Vocabulary Practice 2

Excerpt from "An Alarm in the Offing on Climate Change":

> For some reason, the government put out this draft without the usual advance notice to journalists that accompanies major federal reports, so I confess I have not yet had time to read all 1,193 pages. But I did spend Monday *trolling* through big sections of the report.

PART A

What does the word *trolling* mean in the text, "An Alarm in the Offing on Climate Change"?

a. passing	b. fidgeting
c. funneling	d. browsing

PART B

Which words from the lines of the text best help the reader understand the meaning of *trolling?*

a. through	b. But I
c. the report	d. spend Monday

Answers:

Part A: "d. browsing"; Rationale: Using the process of elimination, *browsing* is the only term that logically fits.

Part B: "a. through"; Rationale: The term *through* implies that the reader read at least portions of the report.

Vocabulary Practice 3

Excerpt from "An Alarm in the Offing on Climate Change":

I caution that it is a draft, so we don't know what final language will make it into the report. I am always hesitant to give too much *credence* to drafts that could change substantially, but in its current form, the document minces no words.

PART A

What does the word *credence* mean in the text, "An Alarm in the Offing on Climate Change"?

a. power	b. questioning
c. truth	d. deterioration

PART B

Which words from the lines of the text best helps the reader understand the meaning of *credence?*

a. too much	b. substantially
c. minces	d. current form

Answers:

Part A: "c. truth"; Rationale: Using the process of elimination, *truth* is the only term that logically fits.

Part B: "a. too much"; Rationale: The term *too much* implies that since the report is in draft form, it must not contain much truth.

Key Literacy Skills: Reading Comprehension and Comparative Thinking

Unlike other standardized tests that treat reading and writing as separate activities, the PARCC views the two (reading and writing) as one literacy event. For example, those familiar with the PSAT and the SAT know that those tests have a "critical reading section" and then an essay at the end. It's as if the tasks of reading and writing weren't related to each other! This is why the PARCC, in our opinion, is a far superior and *fairer* assessment of reading and writing skills.

As you will see throughout the course of this section, reading and writing are treated as interconnected activities; hence, we need to have a new outlook on how the PARCC, as a standardized test, treats the two as one. Lets consider why this is so.

The PARCC assessment tests literacy skills through three domains. These include:

    a.   The Literary Analysis Section,

    b.   The Narrative Writing Task, and

    c.   The Research Simulation Task.

In this part of our book, we will cover and practice the literacy skills you will need to be successful on all three parts. In later chapters, we will take you through a detailed explanation of each section. For now, our intent is to prepare you for the general literacy skills required to attack the PARCC successfully.

The Literary Analysis Section: Literacy, Language Choices, and Comparative Thinking

In the Literary Analysis section of the PARCC, you will be faced with two thematically connected texts that you typically would associate with your English class. You will read works of "high literary value" from such greats as Shakespeare and Twain. For purposes of our preparation for the PARCC, we will consider an excerpt from Shakespeare's play *Othello*, and William Blake's poem "A Poison Tree." These two works will be treated under the theme of *deception*.

To begin, you will read an excerpt from the character Iago in the play *Othello*. While you read, you should focus acutely on the language choices contained within the text. For instance, you should ask yourself questions like these while you read: "What figurative language did the author use and why? "What word choices within the text are repeated and why?" "What imagery and other literary devices did I notice and what is the connection of these literary devices to the text?"

The major point that you should take away: **PAY ATTENTION TO THE LANGUAGE CHOICES WHILE YOU READ!** The makers of the PARCC want you to make the connection between the author's language choices and how those choices shape the meaning of the text. OK, so here we go.

In order to practice the type of critical reading where language choices become the basis for interpretation, we will give you the excerpt side-by-side with the thinking process. On the left is the text; on the right are examples of what you should be thinking about **WHILE** you read. **PAY ATTENTION TO THE LANGUAGE CHOICES**:

Excerpt from *Othello*	Thought Processes
IAGO: O, sir, content you; I follow him to serve my turn upon him: We cannot all be masters, nor all masters Cannot be truly follow'd. You shall mark Many a duteous and knee-crooking knave, That, doting on his own obsequious bondage, Wears out his time, much like his master's ass, For nought but provender, and when he's old, cashier'd: Whip me such honest knaves. Others there are Who, trimm'd in forms and visages of duty, Keep yet their hearts attending on themselves, And, throwing but shows of service on their lords, Do well thrive by them and when they have lined their coats Do themselves homage: these fellows have some soul; And such a one do I profess myself. For, sir, It is as sure as you are Roderigo, Were I the Moor, I would not be Iago: In following him, I follow but myself; Heaven is my judge, not I for love and duty, But seeming so, for my peculiar end: For when my outward action doth demonstrate The native act and figure of my heart In compliment extern, 'tis not long after But I will wear my heart upon my sleeve For daws to peck at: I am not what I am.	• "Serve my term upon him" means Iago has an agenda against someone. • True leadership is rare. Iago wants to be in charge. • "knee-crooking knave" and "obsequious bondage" connote that Iago is not a follower. • "Master's ass" conveys a very negative connotation. Iago has a poor impression of those who follow. • There are those who follow as part of a "duty." • Duty-bound individuals are focused on "themselves." • Duty-bound individuals put on a show for their leaders but really serve themselves. • Iago is speaking to Roderigo here and admits to him that he (Iago) serves himself: "In following him, I follow but myself." • Key term here is "seeming so"; Iago pretends to be something he is not. • Iago pretends to "wear his heart upon his sleeve"; he is fake. • Paradox: "I am not what I am"; Iago has evil in his heart.

Our reading of the sample above, captured in the notations in the right side of the box, leads to an overwhelming theme. Can you infer what it is? Yes, you are correct! The answer here is any term or word similar to "deception." While the notes in the box above might seem lengthy and unnecessarily drawn out, we are showing you, in slow motion, the thought processes necessary for you to excel on the Literary Analysis section of the test.

Next, let's look at some test questions that you will encounter when taking the Literary Analysis section:

PART A

Which of the following sentences best expresses a theme about human nature present in the excerpt from Shakespeare's *Othello*?

    a. Leadership is a noble quality that most people can achieve.

    b. Those who follow should not be frowned upon.

    c. Duplicity and deception are means, even if evil, to get ahead.

    d. Everyone should have a chance to be a leader.

So, how do we go about answering a question like this? The answer is straightforward and simple: If you take the time to outline the passage, as shown above, taking note of the key words and phrases in the text, the answer emerges: c. Duplicity and deception are means, even if evil, to get ahead. Through a process of elimination, you can see that none of the other choices even come close. It's a no-brainer.

Ah, but let's be clear: We are not suggesting that you outline and summarize the texts that you find on the PARCC assessment in the manner that we have. The chart above is a way for us to show you the kind of thinking you will have to do in order to answer these kinds of questions correctly. When taking the actual PARCC, you will not have the luxury of indefinite time. Therefore, you will have to practice this type of close reading time and time again with your teachers.

Now let's move on to Part B of this literary analysis section. Review the question below:

PART B

Select three pieces of evidence from Shakespeare's *Othello* that support the answer to Part A.

    a. "We cannot all be masters, nor all masters / Cannot be truly follow'd."

    b. "Whip me such honest knaves."

    c. "You shall mark / Many a duteous and knee-crooking knave"

    d. "For, sir, It is as sure as you are Roderigo,"

    e. "For nought but provender, and when he's old, cashier'd:"

    f. "I am not what I am."

    g. "O, sir, content you;"

    h. "And, throwing but shows of service on their lords,

    i. Do well thrive by them and when they have lined their coats"

Well, you might be thinking to yourself at this moment: "If I get the answer on Part A incorrect, then I will also get Part B incorrect." Unfair as it may seem to be, the answer is "yes, as we've established." This is all the more reason that you should heed our advice that when reading the passage, you must consciously and deliberately focus on the language choices in the text and think about the connection of these choices to the overall meaning of the work. To illustrate this point, let's look at the answer choices to Part B:

In walking through our analysis of the excerpt from *Othello* above, the language choices in the passage led us to infer correctly that the major theme of the excerpt dealt with deceit and duplicity. Iago, it seems, has his heart bent upon doing damage to someone and he will accomplish this nefarious end through deception. Knowing this about the excerpt, our answer choices in Part B become clear. Take a look above at the choices and eliminate those that do not fit with the theme of deception. What's left will be the correct answer choices. Did you get it? Yes! You are correct. The only logical choices are *a.*, *f.*, and *h*.

Up to this point we have shown you how to interact with a difficult literary text by focusing on language choice so you can properly analyze the multiple-choice questions correctly. Whew! That was a lot but we are not yet done! Remember, on the Literary Analysis section, the PARCC will give you to *two* texts so that you can engage in some comparative thinking.

Let's look at our second excerpt. It is a poem from the highly regarded Romantic era English poet, William Blake. As with the *Othello* excerpt above, we will use a chart to show you the type of thinking you should be doing in order to be successful on the PARCC assessment. The left column shows the poem; the right one focus on language choices and their connection to meaning.

William Blake's "The Poison Tree"	Our Thought Process
[*Past tense*] I WAS angry with my friend: [*anger*] I told my wrath, my wrath did end. I was angry with my foe: [*friends*] I told it not, my wrath did grow. [*began to cry*] And I water'd it in fears, Night and morning with my tears; And I sunnèd it with smiles, And with soft deceitful wiles. And it grew both day and night, Till it bore an apple bright; And my foe beheld it shine, [*angered in the past*] And he knew that it was mine, And into my garden stole When the night had veil'd the pole; In the morning glad I see My foe outstretch'd beneath the tree.	• Key word here is "told"; being honest is healthier than "hiding" anger. • Wrath, over time, will get worse. Fear has a way of making lies worse. • The speaker in the poem is feeding this wrath with "smiles" that are deceitful. • Wrath grew until it manifested in something tangible and real, that is, an apple. • The foe took the apple and died. • Apple might be an allusion to the Genesis story. • Blake might be suggesting that closed-off and pent-up anger could very well be deadly. • The narrator of the poem is "glad" to see his foe dead.

OK, so, what have we learned about Blake's poem through completion of an analysis of the language choices? "Wrath and anger, if held inside, can ultimately be deadly. Wrath grows over time, becoming more and more powerful. Deception and wrath, if left unchecked, are a means to eliminate one's foe. There can be satisfaction in seeing one's foe dead."

You should be starting to see the literary and thematic connection between "A Poison Tree" and the excerpt from *Othello*. What those connections are will be dealt with in a moment.

You should now be able to see how intertwining the reading and writing tasks actually plays to the advantage of the test-taker. Here's how: If you can adequately and competently read the texts from the literary analysis section in the manner that we have demonstrated above, then the written portion of the exam shouldn't be that difficult at all. Next, we will show you just how you can use the reading selections to your advantage when tackling the writing activities.

Comparative Thinking

The skill of comparative thinking—put another way, comparison and contrast—represents a very high level of competent literacy activity. To be able to compare and contrast two texts that are of high literary value is quite an accomplishment. The good news here is that writing a successful comparison contrast essay is something *all* students are capable of doing if given the right tools and the right know-how.

To begin showing you the tools and knowledge necessary, let's attack a typical literary analysis essay question that you will encounter on the PARCC. We'll use our *Othello* and "A Poison Tree" texts as the bases of analysis. On the actual PARCC, the test-creators have labeled this question a "Prose Constructed-Response." Here's what such a question will look like:

Prose Constructed-Response Essay Question

Use what you have learned from reading the excerpt from *Othello* by Shakespeare and "A Poison Tree" by William Blake to write an essay that provides an analysis of how deception is treated in the two texts.

As a starting point, you may want to consider what is emphasized, absent, or different in the two texts, but feel free to develop your own focus for analysis.

Develop your essay by providing textual evidence from both texts. Be sure to follow the conventions of Standard English.

As any good English teacher will tell you, the strongest guarantee to a successful essay is the pre-writing step. The PARCC is no different. Next, we will show you how to use a very simple graphic organizer with which to write a successful comparative thinking essay. This organizer will allow you (a) to record quotations that show the diction, tone, and intended effect of each literary selection, and (b) to record your thinking about these quotations. Both items (a & b) are absolutely essential for your success on the written portion of the literary analysis essay. Our thoughts appear in italics under the quotation. Lastly, the bottom row of the graphic organizer is reserved for our judgments about the theme of deception in each work.

Top Hat Graphic Organizer for Prose Constructed-Response

Shakespeare's *Othello*	Blake's "A Posion Tree"
Key Phrases: diction, tone, intended effect	

"I follow him to serve my turn upon him:" "In following him, I follow but myself;" ? leader *Iago's deception of him (Othello) is self-serving.* "You shall mark hard worm Many a duteous and knee-crooking knave, love That, doting on his own obsequious bondage, Wears out his time, much like his master's ass," *Those people who serve others are mere servants;* *they are just like slaves in "bondage."* "Heaven is my judge, not I for love and duty, But seeming so, for my peculiar end;" *Iago's serving of Othello might seem good in* *"heaven's judgment" but he really serves himself.* "I am not what I am." *This is perhaps the summary of Iago's speech. His* *outward appearance will belie his inner-emotions* *and reality.*	"I WAS angry with my friend: I told my wrath, my wrath did end. I was angry with my foe: I told it not, my wrath did grow." *Key terms here are "told/not" and friend/foe."* *Blake's use of parallelism tells reader that wrath* *is something that can build over time.* "And I water'd it in fears, And I sunnèd it with smiles" *The narrator's wrath continues to grow; outward* *appearance belies true emotions on the inside.* "Till it bore an apple bright; And my foe beheld it shine," *The narrator's wrath emerged into an actual* *plan; an outward reality.* "In the morning glad I see My foe outstretch'd beneath the tree." *Key word is "glad"; the narrator takes delight* *in the death of his foe. Negative/evil tone to the* *work. Revenge is somehow justified.*

How exactly is deception treated in both works? In Shakespeare's *Othello* and William Blake's "A Poison Tree" deception is a rationale for revenge. Implicit in both works is an air of immorality through the justification of deception and revenge. Both works justify the end of personal gain through nefarious (evil) means.

We have successfully broken down and analyzed a passage from a play and a poem. Now that we have come to a conclusion about the role of deception in each, let's take a closer look at the essay question itself: *Write an essay that provides an analysis of how deception is treated in the two texts.* With the top-hat graphic organizer this seemingly difficult task is made more manageable. The last box of the organizer contains the beginnings of a solid thesis statement for the essay. We just need to play with the words a little bit. Here's one example of a thesis statement that satisfies the essay question: *In Shakespeare's* Othello *and William Blake's*

"A Poison Tree," *deception and immorality serve as rationales for personal revenge.* As you can see, a lot of work was done to get to this point:

a. the initial active reading and analyses of the works

b. the completion of the top-hat graphic organizer

c. our development of a solid thesis statement

The PARCC assessment is not meant to be an easy test. However, if you follow the steps outlined here, you will be equipped with a series of tools and strategies to succeed. Our next item of business is to provide you with more practice by using new texts so that you can do well on the Literary Analysis section of the PARCC assessment.

Literary Analysis: Independent Practice

The two works that will serve as the basis of this sample literary analysis are an excerpt from Edgar Allan Poe's narrative poem, "The Raven," and Emily Dickinson's traditional work, "A Bird Came Down the Walk." To begin, we will give you the excerpt of "The Raven" placed in a two-column chart so you can begin your literary analysis, just as we modeled earlier. After you complete the chart, you will face two reading comprehension questions. Finally, you will encounter a Prose Constructed-Response for the two literary works, which will be accompanied by the top-hat graphic organizer.

Remember: Focus on the author's language choices and how these choices lay the basis for the meaning of the work.

Reading Selection #1

Excerpt from "The Raven"	My Thought Processes
ONCE upon a midnight dreary, while I pondered, weak and weary, Over many a quaint and curious volume of forgotten lore,— While I nodded, nearly napping, suddenly there came a tapping, As of some one gently rapping, rapping at my chamber door. "'T is some visitor," I muttered, "tapping at my chamber door; 5 Only this and nothing more."	• A tretourous event at night • rethink of myself • heard something that woke me • Knock on the door •
Ah, distinctly I remember it was in the bleak December And each separate dying ember wrought its ghost upon the floor. Eagerly I wished the morrow;—vainly I had sought to borrow From my books surcease of sorrow—sorrow for the lost Lenore, 10 For the rare and radiant maiden whom the angels name Lenore: Nameless here for evermore.	• Dreary season • Scary wish it was over
And the silken sad uncertain rustling of each purple curtain Thrilled me—filled me with fantastic terrors never felt before; So that now, to still the beating of my heart, I stood repeating 15 "'T is some visitor entreating entrance at my chamber door, Some late visitor entreating entrance at my chamber door: This it is and nothing more."	• Mocking continues • scared • Try to get the fear out of you don't overthink it.

(continued)

Excerpt from "The Raven"	My Thought Processes
Presently my soul grew stronger; hesitating then no longer, "Sir," said I, "or Madam, truly your forgiveness I implore; 20 But the fact is I was napping, and so gently you came rapping, And so faintly you came tapping, tapping at my chamber door, That I scarce was sure I heard you"—here I opened wide the door:— Darkness there and nothing more.	Fear went away To leave my dwelling asleep the noise continued continued knocking
Deep into that darkness peering, long I stood there wondering, fearing, 25 Doubting, dreaming dreams no mortals ever dared to dream before; But the silence was unbroken, and the stillness gave no token, And the only word there spoken was the whispered word, "Lenore?" This I whispered, and an echo murmured back the word, "Lenore:" Merely this and nothing more. 30	wonder who was at the door calling of his name
Back into the chamber turning, all my soul within me burning, Soon again I heard a tapping somewhat louder than before. "Surely," said I, "surely that is something at my window lattice; Let me see, then, what thereat is, and this mystery explore; Let my heart be still a moment and this mystery explore: 35 'T is the wind and nothing more."	fear for myself This will go away don't think about it.

(continued)

Excerpt from "The Raven"	My Thought Processes

Open here I flung the shutter, when, with many a flirt and flutter,
In there stepped a stately Raven of the saintly days of yore.
Not the least obeisance made he; not a minute stopped or stayed he;
But, with mien of lord or lady, perched above my chamber door, 40
Perched upon a bust of Pallas just above my chamber door:
   Perched, and sat, and nothing more.
 	
Then this ebony bird beguiling my sad fancy into smiling
By the grave and stern decorum of the countenance it wore, —
"Though thy crest be shorn and shaven, thou," I said, "art sure no craven, 45
Ghastly grim and ancient Raven wandering from the Nightly shore:
Tell me what thy lordly name is on the Night's Plutonian shore!"
   Quoth the Raven, "Nevermore."
	looked out the window
	
	Out the window their stood a raven
	
	The bird flew in and stayed ontop of my front door

PART A

Which of the following best expresses the tone in this excerpt from Poe's "The Raven"?

a. witty and unforgiving

b. serious and illustrative

c. solemn and haunting *(circled)*

d. evil and dire

e. *haunting and annoyed (handwritten, circled)*

PART B

Select three pieces of evidence from Poe's "The Raven" that support the answer to Part A.

- (a.) "Ah, distinctly I remember it was in the bleak December"
- (b.) "From my books surcease of sorrow—sorrow for the lost Lenore, For the rare and radiant maiden whom the angels name Lenore"
- (c.) "Thrilled me—filled me with fantastic terrors never felt before;"
- d. "But the silence was unbroken, and the stillness gave no token,"
- e. "Soon again I heard a tapping somewhat louder than before."
- f. "Surely," said I, "surely that is something at my window lattice;"
- g. "Tell me what thy lordly name is on the Night's Plutonian shore!"
- h. "Open here I flung the shutter, when, with many a flirt and flutter,"

Reading Selection #2

Emily Dickinson's	My Thought Processes
A Bird came down the Walk— He did not know I saw— He bit an Angleworm in halves And ate the fellow, raw, And then he drank a Dew From a convenient Grass— And then hopped sidewise to the Wall To let a Beetle pass— He glanced with rapid eyes That hurried all around— They looked like frightened Beads, I thought— He stirred his Velvet Head Like one in danger, Cautious, I offered him a Crumb And he unrolled his feathers And rowed him softer home— Than Oars divide the Ocean, Too silver for a seam— Or Butterflies, off Banks of Noon Leap, plashless as they swim.	

Prose Constructed-Response: "The Raven" and "A Bird Came Down the Walk"

Use what you have learned from reading the excerpt from "The Raven" by Edgar Allan Poe and "A Bird Came Down the Walk" by Emily Dickinson to write an essay that provides an analysis of how each bird is depicted in the two poems.

As a starting point, you may want to consider what is emphasized, absent, or different in the two texts, but feel free to develop your own focus for analysis.

Develop your essay by providing textual evidence from both texts. Be sure to follow the conventions of Standard English.

Top Hat Graphic Organizer for Prose Constructed-Response

"The Raven"	"A Bird Came Down the Walk"
Key Phrases: diction, tone, intended effect	
Scary dreary affect bird is dictating the story	happy friendly affect • Together with the bird. • wonder of the bird as it prospers in life.

How exactly is deception treated in both works?

The difference of how the bird affects the person.

Write your Prose Constructed-Response Essay in a notebook or on loose-leaf paper.

The Narrative Section: Tested Literacy Skills

As we discussed and have shown in the previous section, the PARCC treats reading and writing as one literacy event. The Narrative Task portion of the exam is no different, and, in fact, many of the literacy skills transfer easily from the Literary Analysis section. These skills include your ability to a.) define vocabulary in context, b.) identify terms that give rise to the meaning of vocabulary, c.) infer personality and character traits from narrative text, and d.) analyze characters' motivations and desires. Last, the Narrative Section culminates in some form of creative and/or speculative writing.

Below is an excerpt from F. Scott Fitzgerald's *The Great Gatsby*, Chapter 8, which will serve as the basis of the Narrative Section skills that we will practice. As before, the text will be given in a two-column chart to show you the literacy skills in action that you will need to be successful on the narrative section.

When reading the narrative excerpt, you should focus on the ways in which the author presents and develops the main character. You should also focus on the underlying desires and motives of that main character. In our excerpt from *The Great Gatsby*, we will model these reading skills for you. Later on in this chapter, there will be another text with which you can practice independently.

The Great Gatsby, excerpt from Ch. 8	Our Thought Process
I couldn't sleep all night; a fog-horn was groaning incessantly on the Sound, and I tossed half-sick between grotesque reality and savage, frightening dreams. Toward dawn I heard a taxi go up Gatsby's drive, and immediately I jumped out of bed and began to dress—I felt that I had something to tell him, something to warn him about, and morning would be too late.	• Something is upsetting the narrator; he cannot sleep. • The narrator is very eager to see Gatsby. • Got dressed to go to Gatsby's party
Crossing his lawn, I saw that his front door was still open and he was leaning against a table in the hall, heavy with dejection or sleep.	• Going to the great Gatsby house.

(continued)

The Great Gatsby, excerpt from Ch. 8	**Our Thought Process**
"Nothing happened," he said wanly. "I waited, and about four o'clock she came to the window and stood there for a minute and then turned out the light."	• Gatsby was waiting all night to talk with someone. Gatsby is anxious like the narrator is.
His house had never seemed so enormous to me as it did that night when we hunted through the great rooms for cigarettes. We pushed aside curtains that were like pavilions, and felt over innumerable feet of dark wall for electric light switches—once I tumbled with a sort of splash upon the keys of a ghostly piano. There was an inexplicable amount of dust everywhere, and the rooms were musty, as though they hadn't been aired for many days. I found the humidor on an unfamiliar table, with two stale, dry cigarettes inside.	• The emptiness of the house parallels the empty feelings of Gatsby. • Ghostly piano and dusty rooms are also symbolic of Gatsby's and the narrator's emotions. Clean them.
Throwing open the French windows of the drawing-room, we sat smoking out into the darkness.	
"You ought to go away," I said. "It's pretty certain they'll trace your car."	
"Go away now, old sport?"	
"Go to Atlantic City for a week, or up to Montreal."	
He wouldn't consider it. He couldn't possibly leave Daisy until he knew what she was going to do. He was clutching at some last hope and I couldn't bear to shake him free.	• Gatsby feels an incredible longing for Daisy. Something terrible has happened between him and Daisy.
It was this night that he told me the strange story of his youth with Dan Cody—told it to me because "Jay Gatsby" had broken up like glass against Tom's hard malice, and the long secret extravaganza was played out. I think that he would have acknowledged anything now, without reserve, but he wanted to talk about Daisy.	• Gatsby reveals to the narrator that he is not who he seems. His image had "broken up like glass."

(continued)

The Great Gatsby, excerpt from Ch. 8	Our Thought Process
She was the first "nice" girl he had ever known. In various unrevealed capacities he had come in contact with such people, but always with indiscernible barbed wire between. He found her excitingly desirable. He went to her house, at first with other officers from Camp Taylor, then alone. It amazed him—he had never been in such a beautiful house before, but what gave it an air of breathless intensity, was that Daisy lived there—it was as casual a thing to her as his tent out at camp was to him. There was a ripe mystery about it, a hint of bedrooms up-stairs more beautiful and cool than other bedrooms, of gay and radiant activities taking place through its corridors, and of romances that were not musty and laid away already in lavender but fresh and breathing and redolent of this year's shining motor-cars and of dances whose flowers were scarcely withered. It excited him, too, that many men had already loved Daisy—it increased her value in his eyes. He felt their presence all about the house, pervading the air with the shades and echoes of still vibrant emotions.	• Gatsby falls in love with Daisy. She, however, seems to be from a world that is not reachable for Gatsby.

Loved the aura of the house |
| But he knew that he was in Daisy's house by a colossal accident. However glorious might be his future as Jay Gatsby, he was at present a penniless young man without a past, and at any moment the invisible cloak of his uniform might slip from his shoulders. So he made the most of his time. He took what he could get, ravenously and unscrupulously—eventually he took Daisy one still October night, took her because he had no real right to touch her hand. | • Gatsby was in Daisy's house because of a colossal accident.

• "He had no real right to touch her hand." Gatsby and Daisy were from separate worlds. They did not "belong" together. Seems to be a "class" issue. |

(continued)

The Great Gatsby, excerpt from Ch. 8	**Our Thought Process**
He might have despised himself, for he had certainly taken her under false pretenses. I don't mean that he had traded on his phantom millions, but he had deliberately given Daisy a sense of security; he let her believe that he was a person from much the same stratum as herself—that he was fully able to take care of her. As a matter of fact, he had no such facilities—he had no comfortable family standing behind him, and he was liable at the whim of an impersonal government to be blown anywhere about the world. But he didn't despise himself and it didn't turn out as he had imagined. He had intended, probably, to take what he could and go—but now he found that he had committed himself to the following of a grail. He knew that Daisy was extraordinary, but he didn't realize just how extraordinary a "nice" girl could be. She vanished into her rich house, into her rich, full life, leaving Gatsby—nothing. He felt married to her, that was all.	• Gatsby "tricked" Daisy into falling in love with him—primarily through his "phantom millions." • Gatsby was at the mercy of the government. Was he in the military service? • Daisy is compared here to a "grail." She is sacred in his eyes. Daisy retreats back into her wealth, leaving Gatsby with nothing.

We have now read and paid close attention to the language choices within the narrative passage, particularly the ways in which the narrator's and Gatsby's characters are developed and the underlying motivations of each. Now it's time to look at the type of reading comprehension questions the PARCC will ask.

Narrative Section: Sample Questions

PART A

Based upon the excerpt from *The Great Gatsby*, what can you infer about Gatsby's relationship with Daisy?

a. They were once passionately in love with each other.	b. Their relationship is on hold for the moment.
c. Gatsby left their relationship to serve in the military.	d. Gatsby and Daisy belong to separate social worlds, and therefore have no business being together.

PART B

What excerpt from the passage best supports your answer from Part A?

a. He found her excitingly desirable. He went to her house, at first with other officers from Camp Taylor, then alone.	b. He was liable at the whim of an impersonal government to be blown anywhere about the world.
c. She was the first "nice" girl he had ever known. In various unrevealed capacities he had come in contact with such people, but always with indiscernible barbed wire between.	d. He might have despised himself, for he had certainly taken her under false pretenses.

After you have chosen the correct answer for each of the items above, we want to make one point explicitly clear: If you read the sample selection with a critical eye—focusing on character development and character motivations—then the questions the PARCC throws at you are really not so hard.

The annotations we have used above were an excellent aid for us to answer these narrative questions. Let's look at Part A: Through a process of elimination, the only viable choices are letters *a* and *d*. Letters *b* and c should have been discarded as not applicable. Choice *a* is also incorrect. There is no proof within the text that Daisy shared in the same love that Gatsby had for her. This leaves us with our only possibility: choice *d*. Great job! Now, turn your attention to Part B. Which answer choice best supports our choice of *d* in Part A? You guessed it; answer *c* is correct because of the references to Daisy as the "nice" girl and the "barbed wire" that stood between him (Gatsby) and girls like Daisy. Let's look at another type of narrative question PARCC will feature:

PART A

Choose one word that describes Gatsby's personality as shown through the excerpt from *The Great Gatsby*. There is more than one correct choice listed below:

    a. dejected

    b. exuberant

    c. ambitious

    d. fleeting

    e. stunned

    f. duplicitous

    g. empty

    h. reactive

PART B

Find a sentence in the passage with details that support your response to Part A. A computer based test would say, "Click on that sentence and drag and drop it into the box below." Here, please write the sentence in the box.

> But he had deliberately given daisy a sense of security

Find another sentence in the passage with details that support your response to Part A. Again, on the computer-based PARCC test, you will be directed to click on that sentence and drag and drop it into the box below. (See note on page 49.)

> I tossed half sick between grotaque, reality, and savage.

As you can see from the passage above, the PARCC is giving you more options. And with more options come multiple correct responses! Let's look carefully at our Part A and consider our commentary on *The Great Gatsby*. Through a process of elimination, we can mentally cross out these choices: "exuberant," "ambitious," "fleeting," "stunned," and "reactive." If you consider our comments in the two-column chart above, you will clearly see that Gatsby is none of these choices.

So, we are now left with *a—dejected*, *f—duplicitous*, and *g—empty*. While any of these choices might seem to work with the excerpt from *The Great Gatsby*, we have to consider the example that best provides us opportunity to utilize proof from the text to support our answer. Since choices *a* and *g* are pretty close in meaning, we should go with choice *f—duplicitous*. There is ample evidence from the text that would support such an answer. Here are some sentences that you could choose:

> He might have despised himself, for he had certainly taken her under false pretenses.

> It was this night that he told me the strange story of his youth with Dan Cody—told it to me because "Jay Gatsby" had broken up like glass against Tom's hard malice, and the long secret extravaganza was played out.

> He let her believe that he was a person from much the same stratum as herself—that he was fully able to take care of her.

Excellent work! Now, let's consider the last portion of the Narrative Task section of the PARCC: creative/speculative writing.

Prose Constructed-Response from Narrative Writing Task

We've now firmly established that the PARCC considers reading and writing to be one literacy event. Moreover, we've proven that this facet of the exam plays to your advantage as a test-taker. Consider, for a moment, the annotations about the selection of *The Great Gatsby* that we showed earlier. This type of reading—where you question the qualities and motivations of characters—is essential to your success. Let us show you another reason why this is true. Let's look at a sample Narrative Selection writing task:

 Narrative Writing Task

In this excerpt from *The Great Gatsby*, the text ends with Daisy "vanish[ing] into her rich house, into her rich, full life, leaving Gatsby—nothing. He felt married to her, that was all."

Think about the character Gatsby as developed through this selection. Write an original story, **_from Gatsby's point of view,_** to continue where the passage ended. In your story, be sure to use what you have learned about Gatsby when you write from his point of view.

Since the focus of this chapter is to show you the literacy skills you will need to be successful in such a narrative writing task, let's take a moment to engage, as we did in the previous Literary Analysis Section, with some prewriting.

The task at hand here basically requires two things from you: 1.) You need to write a story from Gatsby's point of view about Daisy, and 2.) You need to make sure that your original story is based upon the characteristics of Gatsby as derived from your reading of the excerpt. *Whew!* Let's break it down into bite-size chunks. This is where our annotation of the excerpt comes into play again. We have learned all we need to know about Gatsby; we just have to create a story around these characteristics.

Consider the simple graphic organizer that follows. It is set up to reveal Gatsby's defining characteristics. On the left side, we will identify Gatsby's defining personality traits. On the right, we will provide evidence from the text. Just to note: We need not concern ourselves with so much detail about the textual evidence. Although quoted material is required by the narrative task writing response, the PARCC does not need to see quotations in your original narrative.

Textual Evidence	Gatsby's Characteristics
He couldn't possibly leave Daisy until he knew what she was going to do. He was clutching at some last hope and I couldn't bear to shake him free.	Absolute dedication to Daisy
But he knew that he was in Daisy's house by a colossal accident. However glorious might be his future as Jay Gatsby, he was at present a penniless young man without a past, and at any moment the invisible cloak of his uniform might slip from his shoulders.	Gatsby has a real sense of inferiority. He doesn't belong to the same "class" as Daisy.
He took what he could get, ravenously and unscrupulously—eventually he took Daisy one still October night, took her because he had no real right to touch her hand.	Gatsby pursued Daisy through his deception.
But he had deliberately given Daisy a sense of security; he let her believe that he was a person from much the same stratum as herself—that he was fully able to take care of her.	Gatsby deliberately deceived Daisy into thinking she was from the same "stratum" (or social class) as he.
But he didn't despise himself and it didn't turn out as he had imagined.	Even through his deception, Gatsby was comfortable with himself.
But now he found that he had committed himself to the following of a grail.	Gatsby finally realized that Daisy was an unachievable illusion.

As you can see, we have ample ammunition now with which to create our original story from Gatsby's point of view. The lessons you should have learned here are simple: 1.) Be actively engaged when you first read the excerpt from the Narrative Selection; be sure to comment on the character's PERSONALITY AND MOTIVATIONS, and 2.) Always prewrite. Prewriting is never a waste of time. On the contrary, it actually speeds up the writing process because it helps you create valuable structure.

So, now that we intimately know Gatsby's personality and motivations, let's conduct a bit of narrative prewriting. If you remember, the narrative writing task stated: Write an original story, *from Gatsby's point of view*, to continue where the passage ended. Here is a sample start:

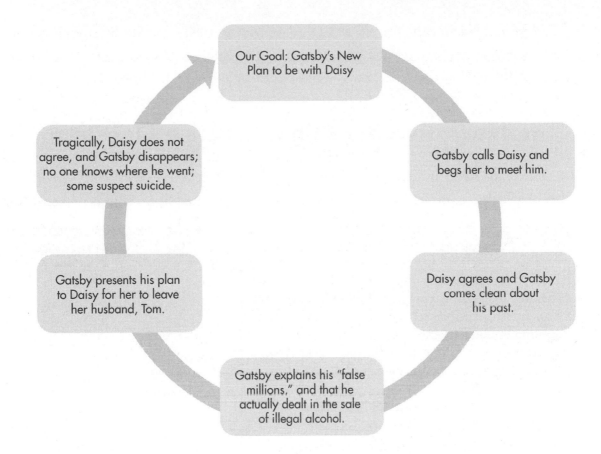

As you can clearly see in the graphic organizer above, we have created a step-by-step plan to write an original story from Gatsby's point of view. The rationale of our tale comes directly from evidence within the text, and we are well on our way to achieving success on the Narrative Selection portion of the PARCC exam.

To summarize: The Narrative Selection will test your abilities in two primary areas: 1.) You will be required to *actively read* a sample narrative selection, paying attention to the character's personality development and motivations, and 2.) You will use the knowledge you gained from your *active reading* in order to write an original/creative story based upon the narrative selection.

We cannot emphasize enough that the single most critical aspect of this section of the PARCC is to test your ability to read narrative text and to understand a character's personality and motivation. All the PARCC's test-question items will stem from your ability to successfully read text in this way. And that's saying something!

Now let's practice the literacy skills that we have learned. You will be given a sample narrative selection and have to complete the reading questions and writing task based upon that passage. Remember the skills that you have learned, and GOOD LUCK!

 # The Narrative Selection: Practice Question

Please read and annotate the excerpt from Anton Chekhov's short story, "The Bet." You will be asked to complete reading and writing activities based upon your active reading.

Excerpt from "The Bet"	My Thought Processes
IT WAS a dark autumn night. The old banker was walking up and down his study and remembering how, fifteen years before, he had given a party one autumn evening. There had been many clever men there, and there had been interesting conversations. Among other things they had talked of capital punishment. The majority of the guests, among whom were many journalists and intellectual men, disapproved of the death penalty. They considered that form of punishment out of date, immoral, and unsuitable for Christian States. In the opinion of some of them the death penalty ought to be replaced everywhere by imprisonment for life.	Remember from 15 years before a get together of severe punishment Didn't believe in death as a punishment anymore
"I don't agree with you," said their host the banker. "I have not tried either the death penalty or imprisonment for life, but if one may judge *a priori*, the death penalty is more moral and more humane than imprisonment for life. Capital punishment kills a man at once, but lifelong imprisonment kills him slowly. Which executioner is the more humane, he who kills you in a few minutes or he who drags the life out of you in the course of many years?"	If severe punishment of prison for life just kill them than cause prison for life kills them slowly torturing them.

(continued)

Excerpt from "The Bet"	My Thought Processes
"Both are equally immoral," observed one of the guests, "for they both have the same object -- to take away life. The State is not God. It has not the right to take away what it cannot restore when it wants to."	Disagree of death penalty
Among the guests was a young lawyer, a young man of five-and-twenty. When he was asked his opinion, he said:	
"The death sentence and the life sentence are equally immoral, but if I had to choose between the death penalty and imprisonment for life, I would certainly choose the second. To live anyhow is better than not at all."	Doesn't want to give up his life.
A lively discussion arose. The banker, who was younger and more nervous in those days, was suddenly carried away by excitement; he struck the table with his fist and shouted at the young man:	
"It's not true! I'll bet you two millions you wouldn't stay in solitary confinement for five years."	
"If you mean that in earnest," said the young man, "I'll take the bet, but I would stay not five but fifteen years."	
"Fifteen? Done!" cried the banker. "Gentlemen, I stake two millions!"	
"Agreed! You stake your millions and I stake my freedom!" said the young man.	Believe life gives freedom.
And this wild, senseless bet was carried out! The banker, spoilt and frivolous, with millions beyond his reckoning, was delighted at the bet. At supper he made fun of the young man, and said:	

(continued)

Excerpt from "The Bet"	My Thought Processes
"Think better of it, young man, while there is still time. To me two millions are a trifle, but you are losing three or four of the best years of your life. I say three or four, because you won't stay longer. Don't forget either, you unhappy man, that voluntary confinement is a great deal harder to bear than compulsory. The thought that you have the right to step out in liberty at any moment will poison your whole existence in prison. I am sorry for you."	Stop wasting your time cause these years are very valuable.
And now the banker, walking to and fro, remembered all this, and asked himself: "What was the object of that bet? What is the good of that man's losing fifteen years of his life and my throwing away two millions? Can it prove that the death penalty is better or worse than imprisonment for life? No, no. It was all nonsensical and meaningless. On my part it was the caprice of a pampered man, and on his part simple greed for money. . . ."	The banker thinks this is childish to bet like this
Then he remembered what followed that evening. It was decided that the young man should spend the years of his captivity under the strictest supervision in one of the lodges in the banker's garden. It was agreed that for fifteen years he should not be free to cross the threshold of the lodge, to see human beings, to hear the human voice, or to receive letters and newspapers. He was allowed to have a musical instrument and books, and was allowed to write letters, to drink wine, and to smoke. By the terms of the agreement, the only relations he could have with the outer world were by a little window made purposely for that object. He might have anything he wanted -- books, music, wine, and so on -- in any quantity he desired by writing an order, but could only receive them through the window. The agreement provided for every detail and every trifle that would make his imprisonment strictly solitary, and bound the young man to stay there exactly fifteen years. . .	Allowed to have a bit of Amenaties but isolated from other humans.

PART A

Based upon the excerpt from "The Bet," what can you infer about the young man?

a. That he is idealistic and does not truly understand the magnitude of the bet	b. That the young man chose to go along with the bet to impress the banker
c. That the young man is destitute and has nothing to lose	d. That the young man will realize his foolishness and cancel the bet

PART B

What excerpt from the passage best supports your answer from Part A?

a. "Capital punishment kills a man at once, but lifelong imprisonment kills him slowly."	b. "The death sentence and the life sentence are equally immoral, but if I had to choose between the death penalty and imprisonment for life, I would certainly choose the second. To live anyhow is better than not at all."
c. "It's not true! I'll bet you two millions you wouldn't stay in solitary confinement for five years." "If you mean that in earnest," said the young man, "I'll take the bet, but I would stay not five but fifteen years."	d. Don't forget either, you unhappy man, that voluntary confinement is a great deal harder to bear than compulsory.

PART C

Choose one word that describes the banker's personality as shown through the excerpt from "The Bet." There is more than one correct choice listed below:

a. aggressive

b. empathetic

c. stern

d. short-sighted

e. reflective

f. peaceful

g. arrogant

h. benevolent

PART D

Find a sentence in the passage with details that support your response to Part C. The computerized test's instructions will tell you to click on that sentence and drag and drop it into the box below.

> What is the good of the man's loosing 15 years of his life and my throwing away two million.

Find another sentence in the passage with details that support your response to Part C. Click on that sentence and drag and drop it into the box below.

> capitul punishment kills a man at once, but lifelong imprisonment kills him slowly.

Narrative Writing Task

In this excerpt from "The Bet," the narrative ends with the young man's entry into confinement for 15 years.

Think about the characters of the young man and the banker as presented in Chekhov's story. Write an original story in which you explore how the tale will progress and end. What will happen to the young man in his confinement?

Be sure to include details in your narrative that are consistent with Chekhov's original story.

Complete the graphic organizer to help you get started on your narrative.

Textual Evidence	The Young Man's Characteristics	The Banker's Characteristics
Not thinking how bad being locked away from the rest of the world will be but only thinking about two million dollars. Thinking how bad life would be for 15 years not hearing anyone voice. Thinking about young mans well being.	Short-sighted	Reflective

Complete the graphic organizer to help you write your original narrative:

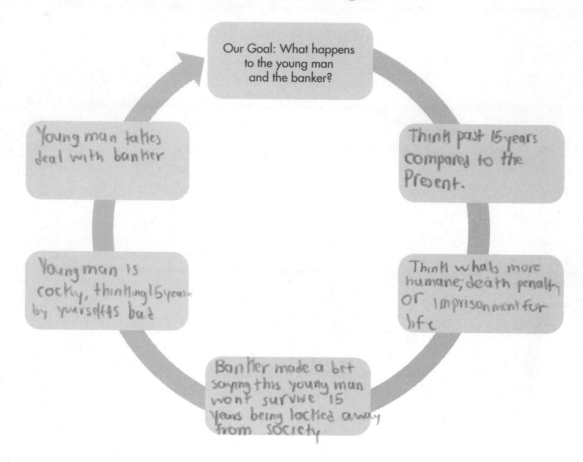

Our Goal: What happens to the young man and the banker?

Think past 15 years compared to the Present.

Think whats more humane; death penalty or imprisonment for life

Banker made a bet saying this young man won't survive 15 years being locked away from society

Young man is cocky, thinking 15 years by yourself is bad

Young man takes deal with banker

ANSWERS:

Part A: Answer choice *a* is best. There is no evidence in the tale to support the other answer choices.

Part B: Choice *c* best illustrates the young man's idealism and naïveté.

Part C: The best answer choices are *a—aggressive*, *c—stern*, and, *e—reflective*. The banker was <u>aggressive</u> in his pursuing of the bet; he was <u>stern</u> in his beliefs about the death penalty and life imprisonment: and he was <u>reflective</u> in that he doubted the logic of the bet.

The Research Simulation Task: Tested Literacy Skills

We've not come to what is probably the most complicated and difficult section of the PARCC test. Known as the Research Simulation Tast, or RST, it will require some of the same literacy skills we've already worked on—such as **inferring, analyzing,** and **critiquing**—but with one more difficult skill added on top: **synthesizing.** This section of Chapter 2 will explain in detail what the hard-acquired skill of synthesizing is, what it will look like on the PARCC, and how you can use this skill to read and write effectively. Lastly, it is with some excitement that in this chapter, we will go beyond traditional print text, as with the literary analysis and narrative tasks, and venture into graphic literacy.

First things first: Let's start with, "What on earth is a research simulation task?" and "How can I do well on it?" As stated previously, the "Research Simulation Task" (aka RST) is a literacy event in which you will

    a.   support a position on a relevant issue

       by

    b.   combining consideration of two out of three sources.

What about the research you ask? By the term *research*, the PARCC does not mean you will "Google" the topic and find sources on your own. Actually, PARCC has done the research for you! You just have to be able to use the three sources with which you are presented to your advantage in order to write a solid, analytic essay.

This sounds like a tall order but you can cut it down to size if you practice the literacy skills outlined in this chapter. Are you ready? Let's look at an example of the RST section of the PARCC and break down, step-by-step, what you will need to do in order to shine! The RST is broken down into three sections. The first two literacy activities are reading and writing exercises that serve as the "warm-up" for the grand finale RST analytic essay.

The theme of our sample RST will be history-related, particularly about the issue of compulsory voting. Let's look closely at the Warm-up Task #1:

Warm-up Task #1: Prose Constructed-Response from Research Simulation Task (Summary)

As stated previously, the RST contains 3 separate sources that pertain to a particular topic. Our topic of interest here is the issue of compulsory (aka mandatory) voting. The first source, an article published in the 1903 *Cleveland Journal*, provides some perspective on the importance of the American vote. The entire text appears below. However, we must remember that when reading text, it is critical to interact with it WHILE YOU READ in a MEANINGFUL manner. When reading expository text such as the article that follows, these are some important questions to ask yourself while reading: "What is the author's intent or motivation in writing the piece?" "Are the data biased or unbiased?" "Is the author trying to prove a point? If so, what is that point?" "What other underlying messages do you notice in the text?"

Since we are equipped with our purpose for reading, we will place the text in a chart similar to the ones that you have already seen in this chapter. In the right column are examples of the kinds of things you should be thinking when you read.

"Something About Voting" Cleveland Journal 3/28/1903	Our Thought Processes
SOMETHING ABOUT VOTING. Not every person looks at the privilege of voting from the same point of view. Some people vote because they are paid. Some vote because their friends vote, and others because they drift with the tide. But the true citizen is he who votes from the standpoint of principle. Pity for the man who votes for any other reason. In the election approaching, every man who is entitled to a vote should cast it. Judicious exercise of suffrage makes a man honorable, wins for him respect, and causes him to feel more like a component part of the great nation of which he is a citizen. Politicians are becoming more careful now, because they realize that people are becoming more thoughtful. Votes are not cast, regardless of consequences purely upon party principles. Those who vote, vote for the men whom they feel will best serve their interests. This is an intelligent exercise of the right of suffrage. Every Afro-American in the city should intelligently exercise his right of suffrage. They should vote for those whom they believe will do the most good for all people, and who will not hesitate to recognize ability and reward merit regardless of color.	• As one can see, the perspective on the importance of the American vote has not changed much since 1903. Voting is now often seen as a privilege. • One must vote independently of anyone else's opinion. • It is imperative that one votes for who the voter thinks will serve our country best.

Are you asking yourself, "Why do I need to make so many annotations while I read?" "Why can't I just read the article?" From a literacy standpoint, the answer is simple: By annotating the text while you read you are more likely to retain information from the text that will help you with the questions on the PARCC that will follow. Let's show you how. Below is the first step of the three-step research simulation task:

Prose Constructed-Response from Research Simulation Task (Summary)

Student Directions

Based on the information in the text, "Something About Voting," write an essay that summarizes and explains the importance of voter turnout.

Remember to use textual evidence to support your ideas.

After reading the above essay task, I am sure that you can see with certainty that the type of reading we are encouraging in this book—the type where you question the author's motives and the data within the text—will help you ace this relatively simple essay. What the PARCC is trying to do with this writing activity is to question and challenge your ability to summarize difficult, expository text. In the sample passage shown above, the difficulty lies in the understanding and balancing of all the data and statistics present. By annotating the text as you go along, the summary essay should be a piece of cake!

Next, let's go to the second step in the RST section of the PARCC:

Warm-up Exercise #2: Making Claims

The second portion of the RST will ask you to consider another piece of text based upon the same theme as text #1, in this case voting. What's exciting and dynamic about the PARCC assessment is that for them, the term *text* means just more than writing. Sometimes on the PARCC they will challenge you with all types of non-traditional text: graphs, charts, videos, artwork, etc. . . . The basic principle, however, of interacting with the text stays the same.

As you read the graph below, you will want to ask yourself some of the following questions: "What do the numbers on the chart imply?" "What patterns in the numbers can you find?" "What do the creators of this graph want me to know?" etc. . . .

OK. So, let's take a shot at this. Below you will find a chart showing poll results published by a local Pennsylvania newspaper during the 2012 presidential campaign. The chart illustrates how the general public felt about President Obama and then-Republican candidate Mitt Romney. Be sure to read the annotations we make carefully:

These results are based on voters' perceptions of Obama vs. Romney on key issues.

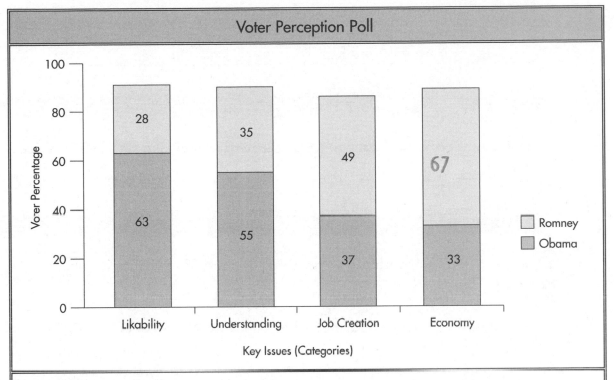

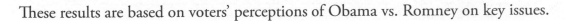

Our Thought Processes:

- These statistics show a clear pattern that the American public tends to trust Obama more than Romney on personal and family issues.

? wins by 12 %

- Neither candidate stands out when it comes to the bigger issues facing the nation: economics, jobs, and taxes.

- Romney is the clear favorite when it comes to the federal budget deficit.

Now that we have successfully dealt with the graph, let's see what the PARCC has in store for you. The next activity in the RST should be familiar to you because we've practiced it already in this chapter:

Below are three claims that one could make based upon the article, "Poll on American trust of current presidential candidate."

	Romney is the more trustworthy candidate.
CLAIMS	Obama is the more trustworthy candidate.
	Neither Romney nor Obama have a clear edge when it comes to being trustworthy.

PART A

Highlight the claim that is supported by the most relevant and sufficient evidence within the article.

PART B

Click on two details within the graph that best provide evidence to support the claim selected in Part A.

OK, so now it's time to consider our three choices and whether or not the data supports these choices. The first selection, "Romney seems the more trustworthy candidate," does not seem to be supported by the data. Looking at the chart, we see Romney as more trustworthy when it comes to the deficit issue, but that is about it. A quick glance at Obama's stats shows he has a double-digit lead and polls well on many more issues important to the voters than Romney. Our next choice, "Obama seems the more trustworthy candidate," is appealing. The data in the top part of the graph shows him significantly more trustworthy than Romney on many more issues. Claim B, therefore, seems like our answer. However, let's just consider Claim C for a moment: "Neither Romney nor Obama have a clear edge when it comes to being trustworthy." The graph, however, indicates that this last claim is not true. Whereas the candidates are tied in trustworthiness on a host of issues, as indicated in the center of the graph, it is Obama who has the clear edge. Our answer, therefore, is unequivocally Claim B.

OK, great. Now, let's consider Part B, "Click on two details within the graph that best provide evidence to support the claim selected in Part A." Because of all the tough inferential work we did for Part A, this activity is pretty much a breeze. Any of the details in the first part of the graph could be used to justify your answer in Part A.

At this point in our exploration of the RST, we moved from an activity that asked you to summarize data-rich text and an activity in which you analyzed a graph. These two activities culminate in the final section of the RST: "The Prose Constructed Response from Research Simulation Task (Analytical Essay)."

RST Task Three: The Prose Constructed-Response from Research Simulation Task (Analytical Essay).

Here's what the question looks like:

You have reviewed three sources regarding the benefits and drawbacks of compulsory voting. These three pieces provide information to begin drafting your own argument.

- Source A: "Survey Answers, Why Don't More Americans Vote?"

- Source B: Poll on American trust of current presidential candidate (local Pennsylvania newspaper)

- Source C: Political cartoon regarding American voting.

Should compulsory voting become a practice in the United States? Write an informative piece that addresses the question and supports your position with evidence from at least two of the three sources. Be sure to acknowledge competing views. Give examples from past and current events or issues to illustrate and clarify your position. You may refer to the sources by their titles (Source A, Source B, Source C).

OK. That question prompt is pretty intense, but let's take it step by step. First, let's start with the issue of Source C, the political cartoon, because we have not yet interacted with that item. Just like *all* of the other texts covered in this chapter, we will employ the same literacy skills to deconstruct the political cartoon. In our chart below, we will place the cartoon in the left column and show you our annotations in the right column. Here are some questions that you should consider while you interact with a political cartoon: "What is exaggerated in the cartoon?" "What type of message is implied in this exaggeration?" "What types of people are presented?" "Do these people represent larger groups within our society?" "What text is in the cartoon" "What is the cartoon mocking or making fun of?" "How do you know?" Are you ready? Let's begin.

Political Cartoon

The Benodellocinch. Illustration shows Benjamin B. Odell with two heads as he acts in the capacity of "Governor" of New York and as "Chairman Rep. State Com." The governor side wields a quill pen labeled "Veto Power" over papers labeled "Legislative favors" and the chairman side holds out a tin cup labeled "Campaign Contributions." illus. Udo Keppler. 1904

Our Thought Processes:

• Even in 1904 we can see that politics was plagued by distrust and dishonesty.

• Why would voters want to be forced to vote for a process that they do not fully trust in the first place?

• While this is not the case with all politics, political parties, and politicians, mandating voters to participate in this process may only contribute to the already imperfect voting process.

Compared to the other two texts in the RST section of this chapter, the political cartoon represents a fresh way to look at the issue of voting in American society. The cartoon clearly does not portray a positive image of the American voter and even suggests that the ordinary individual, particularly the youth, are completely disconnected from the American political process.

After our analysis of the political cartoon we will again ask the RST question: *Should compulsory voting become a practice in the United States?* It is important to consider that we are only required to use two of the three sources. This should be a piece of cake. OK, so let's eliminate one of our choices. Source A was a pretty good text in the sense that the data presented in it explored numerous reasons why Americans do not vote. This information can become potentially useful in answering our RST question. Next, Source B, while showing a lot of good data, does not seem to directly help us in our endeavor to discuss compulsory voting. By default, therefore, we are left with Source C, which, as it turns out, will be very useful when writing about the issue at hand.

The next concern—and it is a critical step—is to decide where we stand on the issue. You should put aside your personal feelings on the matter of compulsory voting and stick with what you believe the texts can support in a possible answer. For instance, while you personally might think that compulsory voting is pretty cool, the data sources might be more beneficial to argue the other side of the issue. In this case, the data seem to better support the notion that compulsory education is unwise. This gives us the grist we need to take a stand on that viewpoint.

As you probably know by now, the most significant step in answering the literacy questions posed on the PARCC is the groundwork involved in making your annotations and doing your prewriting. For the RST, prewriting is absolutely 100% critical. Let's look at the chart below to show how you could effectively prewrite for the RST activity.

Thesis: Compulsory Voting Should Not Become a Practice in the United States.	
Source A "Something About Voting"	**Source C Political Cartoon**
• As one can see, the perspective on the importance of the American vote has not changed much since 1903. Voting is now often seen as a privilege. • One must vote independently of anyone else's opinion. • It is imperative that one votes for who the voter thinks will serve our country best.	• Even from 1904, a similar viewpoint of politics and politicians still exists. Unfortunately (and often,) politics are plagued by distrust and dishonesty. • Why would voters want to be forced to vote for a process that they do not fully trust in the first place? • While this is not the case with all politics, political parties, and politicians, mandating voters to participate in this process may only contribute to the already imperfect voting process.

Common Themes Between the Two Sources:

• Cynicism, disconnect, distrust, and apathy

Now that we have completed our prewriting for the RST, we need to consider some special components within the essay itself that will be critical for you in the composition of your essay.

Synthesis of Sources: Get Them Talking Together!

The RST is not your typical literary analysis or narrative writing task. It requires, as we have discussed, that you synthesize the two sources you are required to use. So, exactly how do you synthesize your sources? In terms of literacy, to synthesize is to take two or more sources and treat them as if they were one. But you can't just smush them together; you have to do some molding. So, in our case here, we have to treat the polling article and the political cartoon as if they were one. How do we do that? Once again, the answer is simpler than you think: 1.) Organize your essay according to thematic topics, and 2.) Get your sources talking to each other.

Now, let's consider the prewriting work we completed above. We provided ourselves with some good ammunition in terms of textual support, but, more importantly, we identified

8/14/2020

common themes between the two sources in the last row of our chart. Therefore, we have the themes by which we will write our essay. The next step is to get the sources talking with each other.

To those students who took Advanced Placement English, the idea of getting texts to talk with each other will be a review. For the rest of you, you may or may not have had to write a synthesis paper, so this may be a first. Either way, we are confident that you can succeed. Let's take some time, since we are learning how to write a synthesis paper, to break down exactly how it is that we will write the essay. Check out the outline below:

I. Introduction
    a. Introductory technique
    b. Thesis statement

II. Body
    a. Theme 1: Apathy
        i. Sources A & C (talking together)
    b. Theme 2: Cynicism
        i. Sources A & C (talking together)

III. Conclusion
    a. Introductory technique revisited
    b. Thesis Statement restated
    c. So what question

Important

So, here we have the skeleton of our RST paper. Let's talk about the introduction first.

As with all good writing, the start of a paper must in some way grab the reader's attention. This can be accomplished in myriad ways such as: a quotation, a startling statement, an anecdote, etc. . . . Our personal favorite is the startling statement. You will see it in action below. In addition to the startling statement, or attention-grabber, we must remember to end our introductory paragraph with a solid, unequivocal thesis statement. To be convincing, you need to end on a convincing note.

Here's our sample introductory paragraph for the RST.

> Imagine living in a world where the uneducated and disaffected youth of the country controlled who holds the highest offices of the government, including the President and members of Congress. In this fictitious world, it is not hard to see figures from pop-culture, such as Simon Cowell of the wildly popular show, *American Idol,* as the man with his finger on the nuclear button. I do not know about you, but this IS NOT the country in which I would want to live. If we as a people make voting compulsory, we put ourselves in the position of destroying this great nation. Mandatory voting is a sure way to drive our country into the ground.

While probably not the best introduction that could have been written, it does illustrate exactly how you can catch your reader's attention with a startling statement and also give your reader a solid thesis statement. Let's look at the body paragraph, the meat of your essay, next. Remember, we decided to organize our paper by themes. In our sample below, we will also illustrate the skill of having your sources talk with each other.

> If enacted in our country, compulsory voting would place those who are apathetic in charge of the most important aspect of our democracy—that is, deciding who will lead us. My fellow citizens, the information found in Source A helps to prove that most Americans are ill-equipped to carry out appropriately this most precious right. According to Source A, the survey found "that 28 percent of infrequent voters and 23 percent of those unregistered said they do not vote or do not register to vote because they are too busy." Too busy to vote? That idea is preposterous. What is even more preposterous is the notion that we, as a country, would ever consider forcing these apathetic inviduals to vote in something as important as choosing our political leaders. Source C, in addition, also supports and illustrates the ludicrous notion that we should force people to vote. As the political cartoon details, political unrest will forever exist. Voter distrust in our political system will only encourage more votes that are haphazardly submitted, without the appropriate care that should be given to such an important political race. Why would we ever want a system where pop culture reigns supreme over our political discourse? The idea itself is overwhelmingly destructive of our most basic principles.

8/14/2020.

Next, if compulsory voting is enacted, we, as a country, will place those who are cynical of the American democratic system in charge of determining its very future. As with the topic of apathy discussed above, there are hard data that show a large portion of citizens are distrustful of government itself. Source A's poll shows that "the perception that politics are controlled by special interests is widely shared among two-thirds of the survey's respondents." This high level of cynicism is shocking, and to be quite frank, a lazy excuse for people to excuse their lack of participation in the political process. The political cartoon in Source C also shows the pervading attitude of cynicism in our country based on citizens' views of the corruption that plagues our political system. The nose rings, the spikes around the neck, and the overall punk rock look of the two-headed monster of the depicted politician illustrates an almost overblown cynicism of politics based on perceptions of greed and distrust in our political machine. Once again, it is not the fact that these types of people are running for office that is the issue at hand, but rather, it is the idea that we should FORCE people (who preconceivably distrust its system in the first place) to vote is absurd. The entire political process would turn Into a joke.

OK. Now that we have presented to you a sample body paragraph, let's look at the salient parts of the essay that you will have to replicate when you take the RST for real. The first point to notice is that these body paragraphs are organized by theme: apathy and cynicism. By choosing these two ideas, we were able in our essay to allow the two sources to talk with each other. For instance, the first source expounded upon the statistics involved in our voting public. These series of sentences set us up perfectly for the political cartoon, which added to the discourse in the essay about the idea of cynicism. Hence, our sources were "talking with each other" in a way that presented a structured and logical response to the RST prompt. This same sequence of events was repeated in the second body paragraph of our essay.

Now, let's consider our sample conclusion:

> My fellow citizens. Our country is one of those special places in the world where the people hold the ultimate choice who runs the country. Politicians, ultimately, are answerable to the people. Our voting system, although flawed, has worked efficiently and correctly for close to 200 hundred years. There are those people who would like to change the voting process by making it mandatory, reminiscent of those communist regimes that force the public to vote for the only political party on the ballot. As a country, we cannot force people to vote any more than we can force people acquiesce to our religious and social views. Compulsory voting, therefore, will not fix our democracy; it will actually hurt it by placing those who are apathetic and cynical in charge. Who would want to live in a place like that? Not I.

True to the outline created, the sample conclusion fulfills all of the requirements. First, we repeated our use of the startling statement as we used in our introduction. Next, we restated our thesis, and finally, we answered that "So What?" question. That "So What" question being, "Why is this essay and my position on the topic important?"

OK, now that we have broken down the RST into its parts and have shown you an example of a RST essay in action, it is time for you to prepare yourself for the PARCC and practice on your own.

Sample RST Essay Practice

For your sample RST essay, you will be given the three texts first and then the actual RST question, with appropriate space to respond. Be sure to follow the steps in the practice piece as they will help you succeed when you actually take the exam. The topic of this RST is art restoration.

8/17/2020

Source A:

The Art of Art Restoration	My Thought Process
Whether it be a masterpiece or a family heirloom, the act of art restoration is great enough to be regarded as an art itself. The many layers of an oil painting must be unveiled in order to re-establish its original beauty. Imagine the awesome task of restoring the characters in Leonardo da Vinci's "The Last Supper," or uncovering the colors Michelangelo had intended for his frescoes that dwell in the Sistine Chapel. This procedure is by no means simple or easy, and the first task is recognizing the signs that a revival is needed.	Restoring Art is Art itself ·How famous artist made art from huge Idew.
Reasons to restore	
Having spent years hanging in the family foyer, it is likely that a painting will eventually show signs of spoil or wear and tear. Discoloration, dullness and yellowing are common indications that you might be missing out on some pizzazz. The causes include light exposure, smoke, extremely dry or moist conditions, atmospheric pollution, and any other contaminants that may linger in the air. The experienced restorer will also look for traces of severe progressive problems such as mold, mildew, or insect damage. Since the shellacs and varnishes used hundreds of years ago were not equipped to survive the test of time, old paintings may become dark and lacking in lustre.	Art doesn't last forever. Our climate wears down art.
Steps to follow	
The first step to restoring an oil painting is making sure the canvas on which it exists is in good condition. Fragile canvases are liable to cracks, punctures and tears, and may require relining or remounting.	
Once the painting is stabilized, the restorer can turn his attention towards the cleaning and refinishing of the piece. The amount and nature of the dirt build-up differs from painting to painting, depending on the environment it has lived in. Cleaning the painting begins by testing different chemical solutions which will be used to first, remove the grime, and second, remove old varnish. A proper mixture will successfully eliminate the discolored varnish, but not the color pigment.	Clean it before restore It.

(continued)

If need be, a third and complicated process comes into play—inpainting. This is done when the restorer must reduce the visibility of damaged areas by making modifications that are aesthetically undetectable. Several methods can be used, but the least complicated is 'diffusion-based inpainting', a procedure by which gas spreads out to fill any given volume. This process allows the colors to diffuse into the missing areas of the image. If the painting is very old and fragile all inpainting is done by hand instead.

Nowadays, an intermediate coat of varnish is applied to the original painting before any inpainting begins. The goal here is to physically separate the new paint from the old to ensure that any future restorations can be done with little or no effect to the original layers. Any paint used thereafter should be non-discoloring synthetic resin paint so that it will not darken faster than the original oil paint. Also, synthetics such as acrylic can be removed with solvents that will not damage the piece.

Finally, the frame must be taken into account to reflect the period in which the painting was created, as it should. Again, a professional restorer will have the ability to replace or mend any broken or missing pieces in the frame, either by re-carving or re-molding the damaged sections using the same material.

To restore, or not to restore

The process of art restoration is a slow one, and understandably so. The restorer must not only be patient, meticulous, and extremely attentive to detail, but also skilled in the art of art restoration. Each painting is unique in its composition, and the necessary chemistry knowledge is needed to customize the mixtures for each treatment. Professional restoration is pricey so the question is, is it worth it?

Make sure every thing makes the painting look it's age.

8/17/2020

Source B:

A series of images shows the damage to the 19th century "Ecce Homo" fresco by artist Elias Garcia Martinez. The picture on the left shows the original work, the one in the middle the pre-renovated fresco and the one on the right the damaged painting. Credit: Centro de Estudios Borjanos

Ecce Homo de Elías García Martínez.

My Thought Process

The one on the right looks like an asian monkey.
Over time when contrast was meant to be in the painting
it blended together over time.

Source C:

Advertisement for Art Restoration Company	My Thought Processes
The Science of Art **How much does restoration cost?** The cost of restoration is determined strictly on the extent of the damage and the work that is necessary to complete the repair. While it is impossible to put a price on sentiment, please be aware that the cost of a professional restoration can far exceed the actual monetary value of the piece. Only you, the client, can justify if the piece warrants the investment. Remember, restoration can save the life of a broken item, thus preserving the legacy, history and memories that go along with it. Of course, having an item restored is a monetary investment but a well-cared-for restoration can last many, many years making a one-time monetary investment worthwhile.	

Research Simulation Task

Art Restoration

As an artist, or as an owner of art, would you want your art restored?

Rationale:

To many, art is meant to be revered and cherished forever. Unfortunately, not all art is kept in its original pristine condition over time. Restoration is a process that attempts to return the work of art to some previous state that the restorer imagines was the "original." This was commonly done in the past. However, in the late 20th century a separate concept of conservation was developed that is more concerned with preserving the work of art for the future, and less with making it look perfect. Restoration is controversial, since it often involves some irreversible change to the original material of the artwork with the goal of making it "look good."

8/19/2020

Task:

You have reviewed three sources regarding art restoration. These three pieces provide information regarding the benefits and risks associated with this process.

- **Source A**: The Art of Art Restoration (article)
- **Source B**: Damage to the "Ecce Homo" (photo)
- **Source C**: The Science of Art (advertisement)

As an artist, or as an owner of art, would you want your art restored? Write an informative piece that addresses the question and supports your position with evidence from **at least two of the three sources**. Be sure to acknowledge competing views. Give examples from past and current events or issues to illustrate and clarify your position. **You may refer to the sources by their titles (Source A, Source B, Source C).**

Source A	Source B
Restoring art is art. Source A explains how art can connect with family heirlooms as memories. Art doesn't last forever because of the climate is always changing. Art might not last forever but if you experienced the fact that, that art was there, then that is art itself.	The art in this source looks like a human posing but it starts to fade away and looks like an asian monkey trying to pose. The art had changed over the years of the change in climate and started to blend and fade.

Write your essay in a notebook or on loose-leaf paper.

A Word about Validity

An article is not just an article. A video is not just a video. There are characters; there are messages; there are purposes. We often take text and, in this case, non-print text for granted, in the sense that we "believe" what they are reading or what they are viewing is a valid, or trustworthy, source of information.

Students need to be cognizant of the fact, however, that all texts are not created equal. Take, for example, the use of the multimedia video on the PARCC assessment. As a test-taker, you need to make yourself acutely aware that the information you are reading is credible, and, if it is not, you should make this observation known in the essays that you write for the research simulation task.

Who is providing this information? What is the background of the author/creator of this information? When is the information from? These sorts of questions should be asked when dealing with all types of information, whether that information is part of a traditional text or otherwise. Images, multimedia videos, and standard articles and passages can all be slanted with some sort of bias. Do not let this distract your argument, however. Concentrate on being conscious of such bias in the delivery of information, and using this information in the most valid way that you can. Couple this given information with your own know-how and real-life experiences.

These practices will inevitably make your argument stronger and persuasive.

CHAPTER 3

8/19/2020

Narrative Writing Task

 Introduction

(Performance-Based Assessment)

As we have discussed in the introduction to the narrative writing task, you must know that organization and style are crucial in meeting with success with this specific exercise. Whether you have to write a short story narrative, draft a rhetorical speech, finish a scientific process, or complete a historical account, your writing must follow a specific formula.

Before we start with the specifics of writing the Narrative Task, we want to stress the following point: When you take the PARCC, you will encounter numerous multiple-choice items before you actually write the Narrative Task. Our purpose in this chapter is not to focus on the multiple-choice (see chapter 2), but instead to concentrate on the skills necessary to successfully complete the Narrative Task. This larger writing task requires intensive reading as well, and is also known as the prose constructed-response.

Let's begin by reviewing some common literary and rhetorical devices. You will need to master these in order to prove that you have the command over language the PARCC expects you to have.

We have separated the common rhetorical and literary devices into two categories: diction devices and syntactical devices. Diction devices use words, and syntactical devices address sentence structure in order to develop a writer's style. Your goal here is to use a combination of both.

Take the time to review the chart below, including the definitions and examples of some devices that we have highlighted. Research these further online or in your English classes!

These are some common rhetorical and literary devices:

8/19/2020

Diction devices:

Rhetorical/literary device	Definition	Example
Apostrophe	An exclamatory passage in a speech or poem addressed to a person or object (typically one who/which is dead or absent)	"Twinkle, twinkle, little star. How I wonder what you are."
Hyperbole	Exaggerated statements or claims not meant to be taken literally	"I'm so hungry I could eat a horse!"
Imagery	Visually descriptive or figurative language	"Her eyes glittered like a starlit night against the ocean's surface."
Metaphor	A figure of speech in which a word or phrase is applied to an object or action to which it is not literally applicable	"He remained *the light of my life*, being my best friend and the only person that I could trust."
Onomatopoeia	A word that is spelled the way that it sounds	"*'Boom!'* The car hit the tree, and all became silent that day."
Paradox	A seemingly absurd or self-contradictory statement or proposition that when investigated or explained may prove to be well founded or true	"At the end of the day, it turns out that *it is cruel to be kind*."
Personification	The attribution of a personal nature or human characteristics to something nonhuman	"The leaves *danced* in the wind that day."
Simile	A figure of speech involving the comparison of one thing with another thing of a different kind, using the words "like," or "as"	"The postal worker moved from house to house, *as busy as a bee*."

(continued)

8/20/2020

Rhetorical/literary device	Definition	Example
Symbol	A thing that represents or stands for something else	"*The American flag* waved proudly that day, representing the freedom that we have come so far to achieve."

Syntactical devices:

Rhetorical/literary device	Definition	Example
Anadiplosis	Repetition of the final words of a sentence or line at the beginning of the next	"Fear leads to *anger. Anger* is just something that we can hide away from."
Anaphora	The repetition of a word or phrase at the beginning of successive clauses	"*Here comes* the wind. *Here comes* the fire. *Here comes* the days we have been waiting for."
Antithesis	A contrast or opposition between two thing	"Colonial Africa and the Western World portrayed a distinct difference in culture."
Asyndeton	Omission of the conjunctions that ordinarily join coordinate words or clauses (as in "I came, I saw, I conquered")	"I went to the *store, park, library, school, church.*"
Epanalepsis	Repetition after intervening words.	"*The thought* of the stars that night brought back so many memories that it was, in the first, worth *the thought.*"
Epistrophe	The repetition of a word at the end of successive clauses or sentences	"I want *the best.* I deserve *the best.* I think what is most important is to have *the best.*"

(continued)

Rhetorical/literary device	Definition	Example
Polysyndeton	Using several conjunctions in close succession, especially where some might be omitted (as in 'he ran and jumped and laughed for joy')	"I went to the *store, and park, and library, and school, and church.*"
Rhetorical Question	A statement that is formulated as a question but that is not supposed to be answered	"*What do I do from here? How do I cope?*"

There are plenty of devices out there, but we wanted to give you those that we found to be the handiest to use with regard to the writing of a narrative. In order to see top-notch results with this section of the PARCC, you will need to purposefully use language. You cannot use language in such a way unless you know specific devices. So, you can memorize the devices, or better yet, you can learn them through practice. We suggest that you use them as you practice, especially with the sample prompts that we have constructed for you. This will help for these stylistic strategies to become routine for you.

Beyond the control and command over language, you should also be able to organize your thoughts in a logical manner. You will have to refer to the PARCC rubric (on the next page) as we continue through the three writing prompts.

Keep in mind that your response should be readable, but it should also be appropriate to the writing topic. For example, you do not write a short story in your English language arts class the way you write a lab report in your biology class.

So, where do we begin? We have come up with a step-by-step guide to help you manage and outline your steps in responding to the question:

What is the question asking of you?		
To write a story?	**To complete a historical account?**	**To complete a scientific procedure?**
• What are the elements of the short story? • Who is the original main character? • What are the character traits of that character? • How can you be true to that character throughout the rest of the story?	• What parts of the historical account have already been revealed? • How do I continue through the historical account? • How does this historical account conclude? • How can I use literary devices to engage the reader?	• What parts of the scientific procedure have already been revealed? • How do I continue through the entire scientific process? • How does this scientific process conclude?

Evaluating the Narrative Writing Task

OK. You might wonder exactly how the PARCC going to grade my narrative writing task. The good news is that we have very precise guidance in this area. You can check out the scoring tables in the back of this book. There you will find 1.) A writing/scoring checklist that you can use to revise and edit your work, and 2.) The rubric the PARCC will use to evaluate your work. As you write your narrative responses, utilize the checklist and rubric to assist you in constructing an excellent essay. If you use these tools after each practice essay, you will start to internalize what the PARCC expects of you. And that will definitely play to your advantage.

English Language Arts Narrative Writing Task—Introduction

As you continue to review the literary devices, along with the thought process associated with this task and its rubric, keep in mind the following structure for your narrative. Be sure to remember where the narrative left off. Continue it from there, and be true to the structure of the short story. We will review this diagram as we look at some sample responses.

This type of organizer, called "Freytag's Pyramid," should help assist you in your brainstorming and pre-writing. Put an identifiable notation next to the part of the short story where you should begin, based on your completed reading of the selection given. Then, make sure to hit all remaining parts of the short story as you move through the narrative writing task.

 ## Freytag's Pyramid

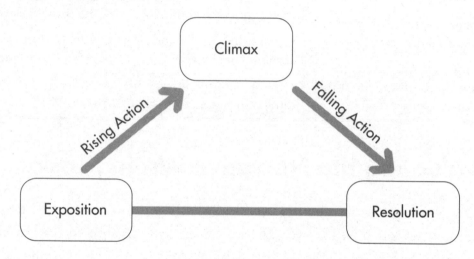

We have put the contents of this pyramid into an easy-to-use graphic organizer on the next page. Thinking about this task in a chronological way will help you organize your ideas in a timely manner. And surely you want to be able to organize your thoughts as quickly as possible.

Think about the point from which you are beginning your story. Is the story currently in the rising action? Has the conflict already occurred? Be true to the story that has already been started for you.

Review the graphic organizer on the next page, as we begin looking at models.

Exposition ↓	
Rising Action ↓	
Climax ↓	
Falling Action ↓	
Resolution	

We are going to start by looking at an authentic text, a short story, and completing it, while also using some of the devices listed in the beginning of this section. Do not worry if you have never read this story before: this task is asking you to take what you have read so far, and use the conventions present in this story to move it forward.

CCSS Alignment	
RL.1	Cite strong and textual evidence.
RL.2	Determine two or more themes.
RL.3	Analyze the impact of the author's choices.
RL.5	Analyze how an author's choices contribute to its overall structure.
L.3	Apply knowledge of language to understand how language functions in different contexts.
L.5	Demonstrate understanding of figurative language, word relationships, and nuances in word meanings.
W.3	Write narratives to develop real or imagined experiences.
W.5	Develop and strengthen writing as needed by planning, revising, editing, and rewriting.
W.6	Use technology to produce, publish, and update individual writing products.

Read read the following introduction to the short story, "The Gift of the Magi," by O. Henry. As you read, pay close attention to characterization, usage of details, and conflict as you prepare to write a narrative story:

ONE dollar and eighty-seven cents. That was all. And sixty cents of it was in pennies. Pennies saved one and two at a time by bulldozing the grocer and the vegetable man and the butcher until one's cheeks burned with the silent imputation of parsimony that such close dealing implied. Three times Della counted it. One dollar and eighty-seven cents. And the next day would be Christmas.

There was clearly nothing to do but flop down on the shabby little couch and howl. So Della did it. Which instigates the moral reflection that life is made up of sobs, sniffles, and smiles, with sniffles predominating.

While the mistress of the home is gradually subsiding from the first stage to the second, take a look at the home. A furnished flat at $8 per week. It did not exactly beggar description, but it certainly had that word on the lookout for the mendicancy squad.

In the vestibule below was a letter-box into which no letter would go, and an electric button from which no mortal finger could coax a ring. Also appertaining thereunto was a card bearing the name "Mr. James Dillingham Young."

The "Dillingham" had been flung to the breeze during a former period of prosperity when its possessor was being paid $30 per week. Now, when the income was shrunk to $20, though, they were thinking seriously of contracting to a modest and unassuming D. But whenever Mr. James Dillingham Young came home and reached his flat above he was called "Jim" and greatly hugged by Mrs. James Dillingham Young, already introduced to you as Della. Which is all very good.

Della finished her cry and attended to her cheeks with the powder rag. She stood by the window and looked out dully at a gray cat walking a gray fence in a gray backyard. Tomorrow would be Christmas Day, and she had only $1.87 with which to buy Jim a present. She had been saving every penny she could for months, with this result. Twenty dollars a week doesn't go far. Expenses had been greater than she had calculated. They always are. Only $1.87 to buy a present for Jim. Her Jim. Many a happy hour she had spent planning for something nice for him. Something fine and rare and sterling—something just a little bit near to being worthy of the honor of being owned by Jim.

There was a pier glass between the windows of the room. Perhaps you have seen a pier glass in an $8 flat. A very thin and very agile person may, by observing his reflection in a rapid sequence of longitudinal strips, obtain a fairly accurate conception of his looks. Della, being slender, had mastered the art.

Suddenly she whirled from the window and stood before the glass. Her eyes were shining brilliantly, but her face had lost its color within twenty seconds. Rapidly she pulled down her hair and let it fall to its full length.

Now, there were two possessions of the James Dillingham Youngs in which they both took a mighty pride. One was Jim's gold watch that had been his father's and his grandfather's. The other was Della's hair. Had the queen of Sheba lived in the flat across the airshaft, Della would have let her hair hang out the window some day to dry just to depreciate Her Majesty's jewels and gifts. Had King Solomon been the janitor, with all his treasures piled up in the basement, Jim would have pulled out his watch every time he passed, just to see him pluck at his beard from envy.

So now Della's beautiful hair fell about her rippling and shining like a cascade of brown waters. It reached below her knee and made itself almost a garment for her. And then she did it up again nervously and quickly. Once she faltered for a minute and stood still while a tear or two splashed on the worn red carpet.

On went her old brown jacket; on went her old brown hat. With a whirl of skirts and with the brilliant sparkle still in her eyes, she fluttered out the door and down the stairs to the street.

Where she stopped the sign read: "Mme. Sofronie. Hair Goods of All Kinds." One flight up Della ran, and collected herself, panting. Madame, large, too white, chilly, hardly looked the "Sofronie."

"Will you buy my hair?" asked Della.

"I buy hair," said Madame. "Take yer hat off and let's have a sight at the looks of it."

Down rippled the brown cascade.

"Twenty dollars," said Madame, lifting the mass with a practised hand.

"Give it to me quick," said Della.

Oh, and the next two hours tripped by on rosy wings. Forget the hashed metaphor. She was ransacking the stores for Jim's present.

She found it at last. It surely had been made for Jim and no one else. There was no other like it in any of the stores, and she had turned all of them inside out. It was a platinum fob chain simple and chaste in design, properly proclaiming its value by substance alone and not by meretricious ornamentation—as all good things should do. It was even worthy of The Watch. As soon as she saw it she knew that it must be Jim's. It was like him. Quietness and value—the description applied to both. Twenty-one dollars they took from her for it, and she hurried home with the 87 cents. With that chain on his watch Jim might be properly anxious about the time in any company. Grand as the watch was, he sometimes looked at it on the sly on account of the old leather strap that he used in place of a chain.

Narrative Essay (Performance-Based Task)

50 Minutes

In the above passage, the author develops an interesting husband/wife relationship between Jim and Della. Think about this relationship and the details the author uses to create the situation of gift-purchasing. The passage ends with Della purchasing a chain to match her husband's beautiful gold watch.

Write an original story to continue where the passage ends. In your story, be sure to use what you have learned about the husband and wife characters as you tell what happens next.

Model essay:

Swish, swish, swish. The chain rubbed against itself in Della's pocket. Every now and then, she would place her hand in that same pocket to make sure the chain was properly in place.

Then, Della looked at herself in the mirror in her small bedroom. Her hair was short. Strands of hair lay on her dresser below the mirror. She looked at those strands for what seemed to be like hours.

Her cry crackled among the silence of the empty house. She placed the 0.87 cents onto the surface of her dresser and waited for Jim to get home. He entered shortly after.

Jim came in, "Della! I've missed you all day!"

Della shared, "You too, my love."

He stopped short, as he looked at Della's hair. He stopped short, as he stared at the strands of hair on Della's dresser.

Della handed Jim the golden chain. He interwove the chain between his fingers, as both of them stood in solemn silence. Its links gladly glimmered under the table's bright light. Could this gift be any more perfect for the man Della loved most of all?

With joy, Jim reached into his pocket to pull out the watch. All of a sudden in a panic, he searched and searched. He ransacked the bedroom, much like Della ransacked the stores during her shopping spree.

He could find nothing. His empty pocket remained, as he still placed the chain around his neck. Della appreciated this gesture.

Della's hair, though, still remained scant. Jim ran his hand through her much shortened locks, then using the chain from his neck to adorn Della's abrupt curls. She looked at Jim longingly, as she looked into the mirror once again — this time, with a slight smile. Jim stood behind her, with a similar grin.

Read through this model narrative writing response. We have filled out the graphic organizer, linking our story to its corresponding elements. Fill in any other details that you think may link appropriately.

Exposition ↓	• Characters: Husband (Jim), wife (Della) • Setting: The characters speak in their shabby home. Della goes to a nearby hair goods store.
Rising Action ↓	• It is the holiday, and Della only has $1.87 to buy her husband, Jim, a gift. • We learn that the couple possess two items of pride: Jim's gold watch, and Della's beautifully long hair.
Climax ↓	• Della, for $20.00, decides to sell her hair in order to purchase her husband a chain for his gold watch.

(continued)

Falling Action ↓	• Della reminisces about her hair as the strands of hair lay on her dresser.
Resolution	• Jim receives the chain from Della. • His watch, however, goes missing!

Here's what you were looking for:

Onomatopoeia: Swish, swish, swish

Alliteration: cry crackled

Symbol: strands of hair

Dialogue: "Della! I've missed you all day!"

Rhetorical question: Could this gift be any more perfect for the man Della loved most of all?

Anaphora: He stopped short… He stopped short.

Alliteration: gladly glimmered

Details used from original story: He ransacked the bedroom, much like Della ransacked the stores during her shopping spree.

Metaphor/imagery: the chain

After reviewing the model essay, along with the devices used throughout, take the time to jot down notes about the impact these devices have on the overall effect of the story. Use the note-taking chart on the next page.

8/25/2020

Device	Impact on story
onomatopoeia	
alliteration	
symbol	
dialogue	
rhetorical questions	
anaphora	
alliteration	
details	
metaphor	

The narrative writing task is one where you need to keep a few things in mind at all times:

- The elements of the short story.
- The need to stay true to the original story.
- The usage of literary devices to contribute to the impact of the story.

8/26/2020

Writing Tasks

Practice Narrative Writing Task #1

CCSS Alignment	
RL.1	Cite strong and textual evidence.
RL.2	Determine two or more themes.
RL.3	Analyze the impact of the author's choices.
RL.5	Analyze how an author's choices contribute to its overall structure.
RI.10	Read and comprehend complex texts.
L.3	Apply knowledge of language to understand how language functions in different contexts.
L.5	Demonstrate understanding of figurative language, word relationships, and nuances in word meanings.
W.3	Write narratives to develop real or imagined experiences.
W.5	Develop and strengthen writing as needed by planning, revising, editing, and rewriting.
W.6	Use technology to produce, publish, and update individual writing products.

Read the following introduction to the short story, "Young Goodman Brown," by Nathaniel Hawthorne. As you read, pay close attention to characterization, usage of details, and conflict as you prepare to write a narrative story:

Young Goodman Brown came forth at sunset into the street at Salem village; but put his head back, after crossing the threshold, to exchange a parting kiss with his young wife. And Faith, as the wife was aptly named, thrust her own pretty head into the street, letting the wind play with the pink ribbons of her cap while she called to Goodman Brown.

"Dearest heart," whispered she, softly and rather sadly, when her lips were close to his ear, "prithee put off your journey until sunrise and sleep in your own bed to-night. A lone woman is troubled with such dreams and such thoughts that she's afeard of herself sometimes. Pray tarry with me this night, dear husband, of all nights in the year."

"My love and my Faith," replied young Goodman Brown, "of all nights in the year, this one night must I tarry away from thee. My journey, as thou callest it, forth and back again, must needs be done 'twixt now and sunrise. What, my sweet, pretty wife, dost thou doubt me already, and we but three months married?"

"Then God bless you!" said Faith, with the pink ribbons; "and may you find all well when you come back."

"Amen!" cried Goodman Brown. "Say thy prayers, dear Faith, and go to bed at dusk, and no harm will come to thee."

So they parted; and the young man pursued his way until, being about to turn the corner by the meeting-house, he looked back and saw the head of Faith still peeping after him with a melancholy air, in spite of her pink ribbons.

"Poor little Faith!" thought he, for his heart smote him. "What a wretch am I to leave her on such an errand! She talks of dreams, too. Methought as she spoke there was trouble in her face, as if a dream had warned her what work is to be done tonight. But no, no; 't would kill her to think it. Well, she's a blessed angel on earth; and after this one night I'll cling to her skirts and follow her to heaven."

With this excellent resolve for the future, Goodman Brown felt himself justified in making more haste on his present evil purpose. He had taken a dreary road, darkened by all the gloomiest trees of the forest, which barely stood aside to let the narrow path creep through, and closed immediately behind. It was all as lonely as could be; and there is this peculiarity in such a solitude, that the traveller knows not who may be concealed by the innumerable trunks and the thick boughs overhead; so that with lonely footsteps he may yet be passing through an unseen multitude.

"There may be a devilish Indian behind every tree," said Goodman Brown to himself; and he glanced fearfully behind him as he added, "What if the devil himself should be at my very elbow!"

His head being turned back, he passed a crook of the road, and, looking forward again, beheld the figure of a man, in grave and decent attire, seated at the foot of an old tree. He arose at Goodman Brown's approach and walked onward side by side with him.

"You are late, Goodman Brown," said he. "The clock of the Old South was striking as I came through Boston, and that is full fifteen minutes agone."

"Faith kept me back a while," replied the young man, with a tremor in his voice, caused by the sudden appearance of his companion, though not wholly unexpected.

It was now deep dusk in the forest, and deepest in that part of it where these two were journeying. As nearly as could be discerned, the second traveller was about fifty years old, apparently in the same rank of life as Goodman Brown, and bearing a considerable resemblance to him, though perhaps more in expression than features. Still they might have been taken for father and son. And yet, though the elder person was as simply clad as the younger, and as simple in manner too, he had an indescribable air of one who knew the world, and who would not have felt abashed at the governor's dinner table or in King William's court, were it possible that his affairs should call him thither. But the only thing about him that could be fixed upon as remarkable was his staff, which bore the likeness of a great black snake, so curiously wrought that it might almost be seen to twist and wriggle itself like a living serpent. This, of course, must have been an ocular deception, assisted by the uncertain light.

"Come, Goodman Brown," cried his fellow-traveller, "this is a dull pace for the beginning of a journey. Take my staff, if you are so soon weary."

"Friend," said the other, exchanging his slow pace for a full stop, "having kept covenant by meeting thee here, it is my purpose now to return whence I came. I have scruples touching the matter thou wot'st of."

"Sayest thou so?" replied he of the serpent, smiling apart. "Let us walk on, nevertheless, reasoning as we go; and if I convince thee not thou shalt turn back. We are but a little way in the forest yet."

"Too far! too far!" exclaimed the goodman, unconsciously resuming his walk. "My father never went into the woods on such an errand, nor his father before him. We have been a race of honest men and good Christians since the days of the martyrs; and shall I be the first of the name of Brown that ever took this path and kept—"

Practice Narrative Writing Task #1

50 minutes

In the above passage, the author developed an interesting journey for the character of Young Goodman Brown, as he meets a stranger in the course of his one-night quest. Think about this encounter, along with the details the author used to create this experience.

Write an original story to continue where the passage ended. In your story, be sure to use what you have learned about Young Goodman Brown, his impending journey, and the concept of faith as you tell what happens next.

8/27/2020

Exposition ↓	
Rising Action ↓	
Climax ↓	
Falling Action ↓	
Resolution	

Write your original story in a notebook or on loose-leaf paper.

When you finish, take a look at your Scoring Checklist at the back of the book.
Then ask a friend to go through it using the Scoring Rubric
for Analytic Writing that follows the Checklist.

Practice Narrative Writing Task #2

CCSS Alignment	
RL.1	Cite strong and textual evidence.
RL.2	Determine two or more themes.
RL.3	Analyze the impact of the author's choices.
RL.5	Analyze how an author's choices contribute to its overall structure.
RL.10	Read and comprehend complex texts.
L.3	Apply knowledge of language to understand how language functions in different contexts.
L.4	Determine or clarify the meaning of unknown and multiple-meaning words and phrases.
L.5	Demonstrate understanding of figurative language, word relationships, and nuances in word meanings.
W.3	Write narratives to develop real or imagined experiences.
W.5	Develop and strengthen writing as needed by planning, revising, editing, and rewriting.
W.6	Use technology to produce, publish, and update individual writing products.

Next you will read the following introduction to the novel, *Metamorphosis*, by Franz Kafka. As you read, pay close attention to characterization, usage of details, and conflict as you prepare to write a narrative story.

8/27/2020

As Gregor Samsa awoke one morning from uneasy dreams he found himself transformed in his bed into a gigantic insect. He was lying on his hard, as it were armor-plated, back and when he lifted his head a little he could see his dome-like brown belly divided into stiff arched segments on top of which the bed quilt could hardly keep in position and was about to slide off completely. His numerous legs, which were pitifully thin compared to the rest of his bulk, waved helplessly before his eyes.

What has happened to me? he thought. It was no dream. His room, a regular human bedroom, only rather too small, lay quiet between the four familiar walls. Above the table on which a collection of cloth samples was unpacked and spread out—Samsa was a commercial traveler—hung the picture which he had recently cut out of an illustrated magazine and put into a pretty gilt frame. It showed a lady, with a fur cap on and a fur stole, sitting upright and holding out to the spectator a huge fur muff into which the whole of her forearm had vanished! Gregor's eyes turned next to the window, and the overcast sky—one could hear rain drops beating on the window gutter—made him quite melancholy. What about sleeping a little longer and forgetting all this nonsense, he thought, but it could not be done, for he was accustomed to sleep on his right side and in his present condition he could not turn himself over. However violently he forced himself towards his right side he always rolled on to his back again. He tried it at least a hundred times, shutting his eyes to keep from seeing his struggling legs, and only desisted when he began to feel in his side a faint dull ache he had never experienced before.

Oh God, he thought, what an exhausting job I've picked on! Traveling about day in, day out. It's much more irritating work than doing the actual business in the office, and on top of that there's the trouble of constant traveling, of worrying about train connections, the bed and irregular meals, casual acquaintances that are always new and never become intimate friends. The devil take it all! He felt a slight itching up on his belly; slowly pushed himself on his back nearer to the top of the bed so that he could lift his head more easily; identified the itching place which was surrounded by many small white spots the nature of which he could not understand and made to touch it with a leg, but drew the leg back immediately, for the contact made a cold shiver run through him.

He slid down again into his former position. This getting up early, he thought, makes one quite stupid. A man needs his sleep. Other commercials live like harem women. For instance, when I come back to the hotel of a morning to write up the orders I've got, these others are only sitting down to breakfast. Let me just try that with my chief; I'd be sacked on the spot. Anyhow, that might be quite a good thing for me, who can tell? If I didn't have to hold my hand because of my parents I'd have given notice long ago, I'd have gone to the chief and told him exactly what I think of him. That would knock him endways from his desk! It's a queer way of doing, too, this sitting on high at a desk and talking down to employees, especially when they have to come quite near because the chief is hard of hearing. Well, there's still hope; once I've saved enough money to pay back my parents' debts to him—that should take another five or six years—I'll do it without fail. I'll cut myself completely loose then. For the moment, though, I'd better get up, since my train goes at five.

Practice Narrative Writing Task #2

50 Minutes

In the above excerpt, the author developed an interesting situation for Gregor Samsa. Think about this shocking revelation, the main character's sudden confusion, along with the implications Kafka created that may be associated with Gregor's situation.

Write an original story to continue where the passage ended. In your story, be sure to use what you have learned about the character of Gregor as you tell what happens next.

Exposition ↓	
Rising Action ↓	
Climax ↓	
Falling Action ↓	
Resolution	

Write your continuation to the story in a notebook or on loose-leaf paper. Then consult the Scoring Checklist and the Scoring Rubric at the back of the book.

Narrative Writing Task: Historical Account—Introduction

Now that you have read through the narrative writing task basics, and worked through a few practice questions, let's review the steps in taking these same skills and applying them to a similar task, only this time related to social studies.

As we have mentioned before, the following questions should be considered when working through this type of task:

- What parts of the historical account have already been revealed?
- How do I continue through the historical account?
- How does this historical account conclude?
- How can I use literary devices to engage the reader?

The PARCC will ask you to refer to your knowledge of history in order to complete a historical account. Keep in mind, though, that you must not forget the skills from the previous pages, while also referencing your knowledge of history with accuracy.

Think of this more as a "narrative description," rather than a narrative story. You are still using diction and syntactical devices, but you will not be following the same exact structure of the short story.

You should, however, work through this prompt, chronologically, moving from the beginning to the end of this historical account, using vivid language to paint a picture in the reader's mind, just as you would with any narrative.

Read the beginning of a historical account, related to the Trail of Tears. As you read, pay close attention to historical details and conflict as you prepare to complete a historical account.

CCSS Alignment	
RI.3	Analyze a complex set of ideas or sequence of events and explain how specific individuals, ideas, or events interact and develop over the course of the text.
RI.10	Read and comprehend literary nonfiction at the high end of the grades text complexity.
WHST.1	Introduce precise, knowledgeable claims, and create an organization that logically sequences the claims.
WHST.2	Write informative texts, including the narration of historical events, scientific procedures, or technical processes.
L.3	Apply knowledge of language to understand how language functions in different contexts.
L.4	Determine or clarify the meaning of unknown and multiple-meaning words and phrases.
L.5	Demonstrate understanding of figurative language, word relationships, and nuances in word meanings.
W.3	Write narratives to develop real or imagined experiences.
W.5	Develop and strengthen writing as needed by planning, revising, editing, and rewriting.
W.6	Use technology to produce, publish, and update individual writing products.

At the beginning of the 1830s, nearly 125,000 Native Americans were removed from the land that they had occupied for generations and generations. This is the area that we now refer to as Alabama, Florida, Georgia, North Carolina, and Tennessee, made up of millions of acres of land. Wanting to use this land to grow cotton crops, the federal government forced the Native Americans to walk thousands of miles to a designated "Indian territory" across the Mississippi River.

Narrative Writing Task: Historical Account — Introduction

50 Minutes

In the above passage, a historical account of the Trail of Tears has been introduced. Think about the sequence of events that occurred after the U.S. government took control and share these events in a well-written narrative description.

Complete this historical account, and discuss the Native Americans journey known as the Trail of Tears. In your narrative, be sure to use accurate details from what you have learned about these events as you explain what happens next.

Look to see how we modeled our response using the following graphic organizer to begin structuring our thoughts.

Introduction of Historical Account
• White settlers resented Native Americans
• Yearn for money (greed) presented intolerance
• Land in these states was soon learned to be extremely valuable
• State governments joined in federal government's efforts

Sequence of Main Events		
Event 1	**Event 2**	**Event 3**
• Andrew Jackson signs the Indian Removal Act • "Indian territory" = part of the land of Louisiana Purchase	• Native Americans started on their trip, known as the Trail of Tears. • Refusal of Cherokee petition • Different perspectives and reactions from Cherokee tribe	• Government resorted to force after Van Buren took office. • situation became violent.

Completion of Historical Account
• Thousands of Native Americans killed, starved, and exterminated.
• Oklahoma became a state, rendering Indian territory lost forever.
• Generations of history now lost.

After we have worked through our graphic organizer, and structured our thoughts, it is now time to write. As we do, we must remember that we do not write in social studies the same way that we write for English language arts. While we are using figurative language to help the reader envision the historical account, we are also keeping to the facts, and avoiding exaggerations. So, let's get started!

Model essay:

The federal government entered the millions of peaceful acres of the Cherokees. The Cherokees fought, but the government trudged through. The Cherokees verbally protested, but the government trudged through. The Cherokees tried to use reason, but the government trudged through. The 1830s would change everything for the Native Americans who settled here far before the white settlers arrived.

With these white settlers came large dreams. These large dreams included the removal of an entire group of people that were simply dismissed to usurp their land to grow cash crops. Shoveling, drilling, disrupting, disturbing the land. While these settlers knew the value in this land, the land was certainly not valued at all, as state governments joined the federal government in their efforts to rip this land from their original inhabitants.

The serene, lush evergreen of the land and the deep, rich brown of the earth were soon colored by the gray of greed, after the "Indian territory" was new established after the Louisiana Purchase and President Andrew Jackson signed the Indian Removal Act.

Ousted from their homes, these Native Americans were sent out with little notice. Many left willingly, simply because they knew that there was very little fight in them, or because they knew that no fight would be enough. This Trail of Tears was filled with much more than tears: starvation, sadness, shame, blood, and anguish. Many Cherokees tried to remain, creating a peaceful petition that was eventually ignored by the federal government.

After Van Buren became president, the federal government no longer gave the Native Americans the time to pack up their things. They entered with force, using violence to rid this peacefully cultivated land of those who respected it so dearly. Ransacking the small homes with bayonets, soldiers infiltrated, exterminating mothers, fathers, and children. They cried on those days, shedding tears even if they didn't move onward on this treacherous trail.

Others fled, embarking on this trail, and dying often along the way. This trail was no easy path. It was filled with roadblocks — distrust, violence, and extreme sadness. Thousands died along the way, and once those who made it to their "Indian territory," life was still very much teary-eyed for this downtrodden group of people. Little by little, bodies were left along the way, as they fought (and often lost) for survival.

With the establishment of the state of Oklahoma, all of this once peaceful land of generations and generations has been lost. The gusty winds and picturesque landscapes of the Midwest currently exist today, but the history of this land remains to be a sad, awful, and sickening one, blurred by greed and supposed opportunity.

Now, take the time to identify some **literary devices** that you can notice, and try to recognize how the usage of these literary devices impacts the overall effect of the historical account as a whole.

Model essay:

The federal government entered the millions of peaceful acres of the Cherokees. The Cherokees fought, but the government trudged through. The Cherokees verbally protested, but the government trudged through. The Cherokees tried to use reason, but the government trudged through. The 1830s would change everything for the Native Americans who settled here far before the white settlers arrived.

With these white settlers came large dreams. These large dreams included the removal of an entire group of people that were simply dismissed to usurp their land to grow cash crops. Shoveling, drilling, disrupting, disturbing the land. While these settlers knew the value in this land, the land was certainly not valued at all, as state governments joined the federal government in their efforts to rip this land from their original inhabitants.

The serene, lush evergreen of the land and the deep, rich brown of the earth were soon colored by the gray of greed, after the "Indian territory" was new established after the Louisiana Purchase and President Andrew Jackson signed the Indian Removal Act.

Ousted from their homes, these Native Americans were sent out with little notice. Many left willingly, simply because they knew that there was very little fight in them, or because they knew that no fight would be enough. This Trail of Tears was filled with much more than tears: starvation, sadness, shame, blood, anguish. Many Cherokees tried to remain, creating a peaceful petition that was eventually ignored by the federal government.

After Van Buren became president, the federal government no longer gave the Native Americans the time to pack up their things. They entered with force, using violence to rid this peacefully cultivated land of those who respected it so dearly. Ransacking the small homes with bayonets, soldiers infiltrated, exterminating mothers, fathers, and children. They cried on those days, shedding tears even if they didn't move onward on this treacherous trail.

Others fled, embarking on this trail, and dying often along the way. This trail was no easy path. It was filled with roadblocks — distrust, violence, and extreme sadness. Thousands died along the way, and once those who made it to their "Indian territory," life was still very much teary-eyed for this downtrodden group of people. Little by little, bodies were left along the way, as they fought (and often lost) for survival. What were they to do now? Simply, they had no answers.

With the establishment of the state of Oklahoma, all of this once peaceful land of generations and generations has been lost. The gusty winds and picturesque landscapes of the Midwest currently exist today, but the history of this land remains to be a sad, awful, and sickening one, blurred by greed and supposed opportunity.

What you may have seen:

Epistrophe: The Cherokees fought, but the government trudged through. The Cherokees verbally protested, but the government trudged through.

Asyndeton: Shoveling, drilling, disrupting, disturbing

Paradox: While these settlers knew the value in this land, the land was certainly not valued at all,

Imagery: The serene, lush evergreen of the land and the deep, rich brown of the earth were soon colored by the gray of greed,

Asyndeton: starvation, sadness, shame, blood, anguish

Alliteration: peaceful: petition

Imagery: Ransacking the small homes with bayonets, soldiers infiltrated, exterminating mothers, fathers, and children. They cried on those days, shedding tears even if they didn't move onward on this treacherous trail.

Rhetorical question: What were they to do now?

Now that you have reviewed the model essay, along with the devices used throughout, take the time to jot down notes about the impact these devices have on the overall effect of the story. Use the note-taking chart below:

Device	Impact on story
epistrophe	
asyndeton	
paradox	
imagery	
alliteration	
imagery	
rhetorical question	

Historical Account—Practice Narrative Description Task #1

CCSS Alignment	
RI.3	Analyze a complex set of ideas or sequence of events and explain how specific individuals, ideas, or events interact and develop over the course of the text.
RI.10	Read and comprehend literary nonfiction at the high end of the grades text complexity.
WHST.1	Introduce precise, knowledgeable claims, and create an organization that logically sequences the claims.
WHST.2	Write informative texts, including the narration of historical events, scientific procedures, or technical processes.
L.3	Apply knowledge of language to understand how language functions in different contexts.
L.4	Determine or clarify the meaning of unknown and multiple-meaning words and phrases.
L.5	Demonstrate understanding of figurative language, word relationships, and nuances in word meanings.
W.3	Write narratives to develop real or imagined experiences.
W.5	Develop and strengthen writing as needed by planning, revising, editing, and rewriting.
W.6	Use technology to produce, publish, and update individual writing products.

Today you will read the beginning of a historical account, related to the Dust Bowl. As you read, pay close attention to historical details and conflict as you prepare to complete a historical account.

> The droughts of the 1930s devastated the Great Plains region of the United States. With the impact on this 150,000-square-mile area, life in the Midwest would be changed for quite some time. From 1934 to 1937, the land of Oklahoma, Texas, and sections of Kansas, New Mexico, and Colorado, would be changed drastically.

Historical Account — Practice Narrative Description Task #1

In the above passage, a historical account of the Dust Bowl has been introduced. Think about the sequence of events that occurred after these droughts and share these events in a well-written narrative description.

Complete this historical account, and discuss the Dust Bowl experience. In your narrative, be sure to use accurate details from what you have learned about these events as you explain what happens next.

Introduction of Historical Account		
Sequence of Main Events		
Event 1	Event 2	Event 3

Completion of Historical Account

Complete the account in a notebook or on loose-leaf paper. Be sure to check the Scoring Checklist and the Rubrics.

Historical Account—Practice Narrative Description Task #2

CCSS Alignment	
RI.3	Analyze a complex set of ideas or sequence of events and explain how specific individuals, ideas, or events interact and develop over the course of the text.
RI.10	Read and comprehend literary nonfiction at the high end of the grades text complexity.
WHST.1	Introduce precise, knowledgeable claims, and create an organization that logically sequences the claims.
WHST.2	Write informative texts, including the narration of historical events, scientific procedures, or technical processes.
L.3	Apply knowledge of language to understand how language functions in different contexts.
L.4	Determine or clarify the meaning of unknown and multiple-meaning words and phrases.
L.5	Demonstrate understanding of figurative language, word relationships, and nuances in word meanings.
W.3	Write narratives to develop real or imagined experiences.
W.5	Develop and strengthen writing as needed by planning, revising, editing, and rewriting.
W.6	Use technology to produce, publish, and update individual writing products.

Read the beginning of a historical account, related to the Civil War. As you read, pay close attention to historical details and conflict as you prepare to complete a historical account.

> From 1861–1865, western expansion became a prevalent topic in the United States, as slavery and northern vs. southern states became the norm. With the election of an anti-slavery president, Abraham Lincoln, a shift occurred, starting the Civil War.

Historical Account — Practice Narrative Description Task #2

50 Minutes

In the above passage, a historical account of the Civil War has been introduced. Think about the sequence of events that occurred after the northern United States began to feud with the southern United States, and discuss these events in a well-written narrative description.

Complete this historical account, and discuss the Civil War experience. In your narrative, be sure to use accurate details from what you have learned about these events as you explain what happens next.

Introduction of Historical Account

(continued)

Sequence of Main Events		
Event 1	Event 2	Event 3
Completion of Historical Account		

Complete your version of the historical event in a notebook or on loose-leaf paper. Be sure to check the Scoring Checklist and take advantage of the Scoring Rubric at the back of the book.

Historical Account—Practice Narrative Description Task #3

CCSS Alignment	
RI.3	Analyze a complex set of ideas or sequence of events and explain how specific individuals, ideas, or events interact and develop over the course of the text.
RI.10	Read and comprehend literary nonfiction at the high end of the grades text complexity.
WHST.1	Introduce precise, knowledgeable claims, and create an organization that logically sequences the claims.

(continued)

CCSS Alignment	
WHST.2	Write informative texts, including the narration of historical events, scientific procedures, or technical processes.
L.3	Apply knowledge of language to understand how language functions in different contexts.
L.4	Determine or clarify the meaning of unknown and multiple-meaning words and phrases.
L.5	Demonstrate understanding of figurative language, word relationships, and nuances in word meanings.
W.3	Write narratives to develop real or imagined experiences.
W.5	Develop and strengthen writing as needed by planning, revising, editing, and rewriting.
W.6	Use technology to produce, publish, and update individual writing products.

For this exercise you will read the beginning of a historical account related to the Great Depression. As you read, pay close attention to historical details and conflict as you prepare to complete a historical account.

In the United States, the Great Depression began on October 29, 1929, known as "Black Tuesday," which sent the country into a tailspin. The nation's money supply diminished and this had a rippling effect in all parts of the country. President Herbert Hoover, however, attempted to urge the country's citizens to remain encouraged and self-reliant. When things got worse, President Franklin Roosevelt took office in 1933, eventually impacting the United States government's relationship with its citizens throughout what we know as the New Deal.

Historical Account — Practice Narrative Description Task #3

50 Minutes

In the above passage, a historical account of the New Deal has been introduced. Think about the sequence of events that occurred after the implementation of the New Deal and share these events in a well-written narrative description.

Complete this historical account, and discuss the New Deal experience. In your narrative, be sure to use accurate details from what you have learned about these events as you explain what happens next.

Introduction of Historical Account

Sequence of Main Events		
Event 1	Event 2	Event 3

Completion of Historical Account

Complete the historical event of the Great Depression in a notebook or on loose-leaf paper. Use the Scoring Checklist and the Scoring Rubric found at the back of this book to assess your progress with this type of question.

Narrative Writing Task: Scientific Process— Introduction

You have already read through the narrative writing task basics, and worked through a series of practice questions for English language arts and history. We will now review the steps in taking these same skills and applying them to a similar task, only related to science.

As we have mentioned in the introduction, the following questions should be considered when working through this type of task:

- What parts of the scientific procedure have already been revealed?

- How do I continue through the entire scientific process?

- How does this scientific process conclude?

The PARCC will ask you to refer to your knowledge of scientific procedures in order to complete a scientific process. Keep in mind, though, that you must not forget the skills from the previous pages, while also referencing your knowledge of science with accuracy.

Think of this more as a "narrative description," rather than a narrative story (just as you did with your historical account). You are still using diction and syntactical devices, but you will not be following the same structure of the short story. Rather, your focus with the scientific process task is on the usage of details and organizing the procedural steps with precision.

You should, however, work through this prompt chronologically, moving from the beginning to the end of this scientific process using vivid language to paint a picture in the reader's mind, just as you would with any narrative.

Read the beginning of a scientific process, related to cellular division. As you read, pay close attention to scientific details as you prepare to complete the scientific process.

CCSS Alignment	
RI.3	Analyze a complex set of ideas or sequence of events and explain how specific individuals, ideas, or events interact and develop over the course of the text.
RI.10	Read and comprehend literary nonfiction at the high end of the grades text complexity.
WHST.1	Introduce precise, knowledgeable claims, and create an organization that logically sequences the claims.
WHST.2	Write informative texts, including the narration of historical events, scientific procedures, or technical processes.
L.3	Apply knowledge of language to understand how language functions in different contexts.
L.4	Determine or clarify the meaning of unknown and multiple-meaning words and phrases.
L.5	Demonstrate understanding of figurative language, word relationships, and nuances in word meanings.
W.3	Write narratives to develop real or imagined experiences.
W.5	Develop and strengthen writing as needed by planning, revising, editing, and rewriting.
W.6	Use technology to produce, publish, and update individual writing products.

Mitosis, the division of a cell's nucleus, begins with interphase, in which a cell's chromosomes are doubled but still remain as threadlike coils. This phase serves as the period between cell divisions. A human cell contains 46 chromosomes. By the end of this phase, each chromosome and its sister chromosome changes to chromatids.

Narrative Writing Task: Scientific Process

50 Minutes

In the above passage, a scientific process of cellular division has been introduced. Think about the sequence of events that occurred after interphase and share the following stages in a well-written, logically organized narrative description.

Complete this scientific process, and discuss the important stages that occur during mitosis. In your narrative, be sure to use accurate facts from what you have learned about these stages as you explain what happens next.

See how we modeled our response using the graphic organizer on the next page to begin structuring our thoughts.

Introduction to Scientific Process
• Interphase has already occurred
• Acts as the period between cell divisions
• Chromosomes have doubled
• Each DNA strand unzips into two strands. Floating bases attach to the unzipped strands.
• Two pairs of centrioles (cylindrical structures), made of fibers, exist outside the nucleus.

Sequence of Scientific Process		
First Steps	**Second Steps**	**Third Steps**
• Prophase: Chromosomes begin to condense, and develop as two identical copies. A spindle begins to form from the centrioles. • Centrioles begin to separate. • Membrane of the nucleus begins to fragment.	• Metaphase: Chromosomes line up on the metaphase plate. • Fibers tug chromosomes toward opposite ends of the cell. • Anaphase: Chromosomes are fully pulled toward opposite ends of the cell.	• Telophase: After chromatids (now chromosomes) settle at the opposite ends of the cells, new nuclear membranes form. • Mitosis ends.

(continued)

Completion of Scientific Process
• Cytokinesis: Cell membrane moves inward.
• Two daughter cells are created, each with its own nucleus and identical chromosomes.

After we have worked through our graphic organizer, and structured our thoughts, it is now time to write. As we do, we must remember that we do not write in science the same way that we write for English language arts or social studies. While we are describing the process of mitosis to help the reader envision its stages, we are paying particular attention to what is important in science—the facts! So, let's get started!

When writing for science, it is important to focus our efforts on the logical, sequential steps of the scientific process, and not necessarily the literary devices used. You must move through the scientific process in an easy-to-follow, logical manner.

Model essay:

Since interphase has already occurred, the chromosomes have now doubled. With each strand of DNA unzipping into two strands, floating bases attach to each of the strands. As a result, two pairs of centrioles, which are cylindrical structures made of fibers, exist outside the cell's nucleus.

Chromosomes begin to condense during prophase, the second stage of mitosis. Here, chromosomes develop as two identical copies. A spindle begins to form from the centrioles, and as a result, centrioles begin to separate. As this is going on, the membrane of the nucleus begins to fragment. After prophase, metaphase moves the chromosomes to line up on the metaphase plate, an imaginary line in the center of the cell. During this stage, fibers begin to tug chromosomes toward opposite ends of the cell.

As fibers continue to tug chromosomes, anaphase pulls chomosomes fully toward opposite ends of the cell. At this point, chromosomes are located on completely opposite sides of the cell. During telophase, chromosomes settle at opposite ends of the cells, and new nuclear members form. This ends mitosis.

With the nuclear membranes now formed, cytokinesis moves each of the two cell membranes inward. Two daughter cells have now been created, each with its own nucleus and identical chromosomes.

You will notice a difference in this response over our narratives regarding English language arts topics and historical accounts. The narrative description of the scientific process is straightforward and delineates and sequentially organizes the necessary steps that move this scientific process forward to completion.

Try out similar responses with our practice questions!

Scientific Process—Practice Narrative Description Task #1

CCSS Alignment	
RI.3	Analyze a complex set of ideas or sequence of events and explain how specific individuals, ideas, or events interact and develop over the course of the text.
RI.10	Read and comprehend literary nonfiction at the high end of the grades text complexity.
WHST.1	Introduce precise, knowledgeable claims, and create an organization that logically sequences the claims.
WHST.2	Write informative texts, including the narration of historical events, scientific procedures, or technical processes.
L.3	Apply knowledge of language to understand how language functions in different contexts.
L.4	Determine or clarify the meaning of unknown and multiple-meaning words and phrases.
L.5	Demonstrate understanding of figurative language, word relationships, and nuances in word meanings.
W.3	Write narratives to develop real or imagined experiences.
W.5	Develop and strengthen writing as needed by planning, revising, editing, and rewriting.
W.6	Use technology to produce, publish, and update individual writing products.

Read the beginning of a scientific process, related to cellular respiration. As you read, pay close attention to scientific details as you prepare to complete the scientific process.

> Cellular respiration involves four phases, starting with glycolysis, which takes place outside the mitochondria and does not require the presence of oxygen. All other cellular respiration phases take place inside the mitochondria, where oxygen is the final acceptor of electrons. Glycolysis breaks down glucose to two molecules of pyruvate.

Scientific Process — Practice Narrative Description Task #1

50 Minutes

In the above passage, a scientific process of cellular respiration has been introduced. Think about the sequence of events that occur after the glycolysis phase and share the following phases in a well-written, logically organized narrative description.

Complete this scientific process, and discuss the consecutive phases, using examples to illustrate your point. In your narrative, be sure to use accurate facts from what you have learned about these phases, noting the role of CO_2 and H_2O as you explain what happens next.

Introduction of Scientific Process

Sequence of Scientific Process		
First Steps	Second Steps	Third Steps

(continued)

Completion of Scientific Process

Write your essay in a notebook or on loose-leaf paper. With a friend, check each others papers using the Scoring Checklist and Scoring Rubrics at the back of the book.

Scientific Process—Practice Narrative Description Task #2

CCSS Alignment	
RI.3	Analyze a complex set of ideas or sequence of events and explain how specific individuals, ideas, or events interact and develop over the course of the text.
RI.10	Read and comprehend literary nonfiction at the high end of the grades text complexity.
WHST.1	Introduce precise, knowledgeable claims, and create an organization that logically sequences the claims.
WHST.2	Write informative texts, including the narration of historical events, scientific procedures, or technical processes.
L.3	Apply knowledge of language to understand how language functions in different contexts.
L.4	Determine or clarify the meaning of unknown and multiple-meaning words and phrases.
L.5	Demonstrate understanding of figurative language, word relationships, and nuances in word meanings.
W.3	Write narratives to develop real or imagined experiences.

(continued)

CCSS Alignment	
W.5	Develop and strengthen writing as needed by planning, revising, editing, and rewriting.
W.6	Use technology to produce, publish, and update individual writing products.

Read the beginning of a scientific process, which is related to Newton's laws of motion. As you read, pay close attention to scientific details as you prepare to complete the scientific process.

Newton's physical laws of motion describe the relationship between forces acting on the body and its effected motion as a result of these forces. The first law of motion states that every object in a state of uniform motion tends to remain in that state of motion unless an external force is applied to it.

Scientific Process — Practice Narrative Description Task #2

50 Minutes

In the above passage, a scientific process of Newton's laws of motion has been introduced. Think about the sequence of events that occur after Newton's first law of motion and share the following laws in a well-written, logically organized narrative description.

Complete this scientific process, and discuss the consecutive laws of motion, using examples to illustrate your point. In your narrative, be sure to use accurate facts from what you have learned about these laws as you explain what happens next.

Introduction of Scientific Process

(continued)

Sequence of Scientific Process		
First Steps	Second Steps	Third Steps

Completion of Scientific Process

Write your finding in a notebook or on loose-leaf paper. Check your writing by using the Scoring Checklist and Scoring Rubrics.

Scientific Process—Practice Narrative Description Task #3

CCSS Alignment	
RI.3	Analyze a complex set of ideas or sequence of events and explain how specific individuals, ideas, or events interact and develop over the course of the text.
RI.10	Read and comprehend literary nonfiction at the high end of the grades text complexity.
WHST.1	Introduce precise, knowledgeable claims, and create an organization that logically sequences the claims.
WHST.2	Write informative texts, including the narration of historical events, scientific procedures, or technical processes.

(continued)

CCSS Alignment	
L.3	Apply knowledge of language to understand how language functions in different contexts.
L.4	Determine or clarify the meaning of unknown and multiple-meaning words and phrases.
L.5	Demonstrate understanding of figurative language, word relationships, and nuances in word meanings.
W.3	Write narratives to develop real or imagined experiences.
W.5	Develop and strengthen writing as needed by planning, revising, editing, and rewriting.
W.6	Use technology to produce, publish, and update individual writing products.

Osmosis is a process in which a fluid (often water) passes through a semi-permeable membrane. This fluid, often water, moves from an area in which a solute (such as salt) is present in low concentrations, to an area in which the solute is present in high concentrations. This process begins with osmotic pressure, which is created due to the presence of two different concentrated solutions alongside one another.

Scientific Process — Practice Narrative Description Task #3

50 Minutes

In the above passage, scientific process of osmosis has been introduced. Think about the sequence of events that occur after the two different concentrations of solutions are side by side and share the following steps in a well-written, logically organized narrative description.

Complete this scientific process, and discuss the consecutive steps of this process, using examples to illustrate your point. In your narrative, be sure to use accurate facts from what you have learned about these steps, noting relevant terms (osmotic pressure, solvent, solute, solution, hypotonic, hypertonic) as you explain what happens next.

Introduction of Scientific Process

Sequence of Scientific Process		
First Steps	Second Steps	Third Steps

Completion of Scientific Process

Write your completion of the process in a notebook or on loose-leaf paper. Then make use of the Scoring Checklist and Scoring Rubrics found at the back of this book.

CHAPTER 4

Literary Analysis Task

Introduction
(Performance-Based Assessment)

As we have emphasized repeatedly, the makers of the PARCC view reading and writing as connected activities. One feeds off of the other. This holds true for the literary analysis section of the exam, which is the subject of this chapter. So here again, once you get the reading down, half the battle is won. The writing, then, just becomes an extension of the hard work you did with the reading.

In this chapter we will show you exactly how you should interact with (or analyze) the texts present on the PARCC literary analysis task so that you can write an exemplary essay. Moreover, we will provide you with ample practice to put these principles of analysis into action.

Before we start with the specifics of writing the Literary Analysis Task, we want to remind you that you will encounter numerous multiple-choice items before you actually write the Literary Analysis Task. Our purpose in this chapter is *not* to focus on the multiple-choice but instead to concentrate on the skills necessary to successfully complete the Literary Analysis Task. Please refer to Chapter 2 for a treatment of the multiple-choice items you will encounter on the PARCC. As we have discussed in our introductory chapter, each PBA will focus on a larger "anchor text" that will require students to answer related multiple-choice questions. For the purposes of this chapter, we are focusing on the larger writing task (which requires intensive reading as well), also known as the prose constructed-response.

First, you should know that the literary analysis task requires that you read and interact with two texts of high literary value. By "high literary value," we mean that the texts are found in most high school English departments around the country and that these texts contain writing that is rich with theme, symbolism, and literary devices.

For our purposes though, we will be keenly focused on the author's choice of words (i.e. the author's diction) and how these words give rise to a thematic message of the text. Put another way, our focus is to see how the author's choice of words is a deliberate action to create a message within the text. Sound difficult? Don't worry at all. Like much else, analysis of text gets easier the more you do it. Here are some questions that you could ask yourself *while you read*:

- Are there any words or terms that are symbolic in nature?

- Are any words or terms repeated?

- Is any irony present (i.e. the opposite of what's being said)?

- What type of imagery is used? Why?

- What is the tone (attitude) of the passage? How do you know?

- Do you see any patterns in the language the author uses?

- Does the author use a special dialect? If so, why?

- Are there any literary devices used? (i.e. simile, metaphor, rhetorical questions, etc. . . .)

- What might be the theme or the message of the text? How do you know?

It will not be necessary for you to memorize the above questions, although they are very helpful. The more important thing is to understand that authors carefully and deliberately choose specific words (diction) to create a theme, or a message. Your job is to find these terms in order to find the message.

Our first piece of literature is an excerpt from Paul Laurence Dunbar's "We Wear the Mask," and there is a very heavy emphasis on race relations in the piece between whites and African Americans. On the right side of the column are our thoughts about the text as we read. This process of interacting with (i.e. analyzing) the text is essential to enhance your ability to complete successfully the literary analysis essay. As you read the excerpt and our thoughts, pay attention to the ways in which we commented on the text. Ask yourself, "Why was this comment written?" and "What does the comment have to do with the thematic message of Dunbar's poem?"

"We Wear the Mask"	Our Thought Processes
We wear the mask that grins and lies, It hides our cheeks and shades our eyes,— This debt we pay to human guile; With torn and bleeding hearts we smile, And mouth with myriad subtleties. Why should the world be over-wise, In counting all our tears and sighs? Nay, let them only see us, while We wear the mask. We smile, but, O great Christ, our cries To thee from tortured souls arise. We sing, but oh the clay is vile Beneath our feet, and long the mile; But let the world dream otherwise, We wear the mask!	• Dunbar likens being a target of racism as an experience to endure. • Despite the horrific words, and the violence, it is important to paint a smile on our faces. • Don't let those who hurt us see how much we've been hurt. • Even though the narrator has to endure the impact of racism, he encourages the reader to continue trotting along their path. • The repetition of "We wear the mask," but with exclamation, helps to emphasize the necessity to move onward accordingly.

Thematic Messages Found in Text

• Strong element of segregation: Dunbar's poem shows a quiet type of racisms in that it is subtle and commonplace.

• Façade of goodness and cooperation: Through Dunbar's suggestion to wear a mask, he encourages those being impacted by racism to not show any signs of such effects.

Let's break down what just happened with our analysis of Dunbar's poem. 1.) As we read, we asked ourselves the importance of the words the author chose, and 2.) We thought about how these words create meaning within the text, and lastly, 3.) We identified major themes we found in Dunbar's text and recorded these themes at the bottom of our chart with a brief explanation. These are the three steps you need to follow each time you are presented with literature on the literary analysis section.

At this point, you might be saying, "Well, that's not that bad! How hard could the literary analysis be?" The answer: It's doubly hard! On the PARCC, when you finally write your literary analysis essay, you will have to compare a second text to the first. This skill, that of comparison, is the next topic of this chapter.

The Second Text

In keeping in line with the theme of racism, here is another text, this time an excerpt from *The Articles of Frederick Douglass*. This second text presents some formidable challenges to us because it is a different genre than Dunbar's work. However, you can be assured that both works—that of Dunbar's and that of Douglass's—will be connected thematically. As we have done throughout this book, we present a chart in which Frederick Douglass's text appears in the left column and our thought processes appear on the right. As with Dunbar's work, we can use the following questions to guide us in our analysis:

- Are there any words or terms that are symbolic in nature?

- Are any words or terms repeated?

- Is any irony present (i.e. the opposite of what's being said)?

- What type of imagery is used? Why?

- What is the tone (attitude) of the passage? How do you know?

- Do you see any patterns in the language the author uses?

- Does the author use a special dialect? If so, why?

- Are there any literary devices used? (i.e. simile, metaphor, rhetorical questions, etc. . .)

- What might be the theme or the message of the text? How do you know?

Excerpt from: Collected Articles of Frederick Douglass	Our Thought Processes
My free life began on the third of September, 1838. On the morning of the fourth of that month, after an anxious and most perilous but safe journey, I found myself in the big city of New York, a FREE MAN— one more added to the mighty throng which, like the confused waves of the troubled sea, surged to and fro between the lofty walls of Broadway. Though dazzled with the wonders which met me on every hand, my thoughts could not be much withdrawn from my strange situation. For the moment, the dreams of my youth and the hopes of my manhood were completely fulfilled. The bonds that had held me to "old master" were broken. No man now had a right to call me his slave or assert mastery over me. I was in the rough and tumble of an outdoor world, to take my chance with the rest of its busy number. I have often been asked how I felt when first I found myself on free soil. There is scarcely anything in my experience about which I could not give a more satisfactory answer. A new world had opened upon me. If life is more than breath and the "quick round of blood," I lived more in that one day than in a year of my slave life. It was a time of joyous excitement which words can but tamely describe. In a letter written to a friend soon after reaching New York, I said: "I felt as one might feel upon escape from a den of hungry lions." Anguish and grief, like darkness and rain, may be depicted; but gladness and joy, like the rainbow, defy the skill of pen or pencil. During ten or fifteen years I had been, as it were, dragging a heavy chain which no strength of mine could break; I was not only a slave, but a slave for life. I might become a husband, a father, an aged man, but through all, from birth to death, from the cradle to the grave, I had felt myself doomed. All efforts I had previously made to secure my freedom had not only failed, but had seemed only to rivet my fetters the more firmly, and to render my escape more difficult. Baffled, entangled, and discouraged, I had at times asked myself the question, May	• Douglass discusses the paradox of his newfound freedom from slavery, mentioning his journey as "perilous but safe." • This journey is further explained as "strange." • The exultation of finally being free—feeling alive for the first time in his life. This one day had more significance over the rest of the days of his life.

(continued)

Excerpt from: Collected Articles of Frederick Douglass	Our Thought Processes
not my condition after all be God's work, and ordered for a wise purpose, and if so, Is not submission my duty? A contest had in fact been going on in my mind for a long time, between the clear consciousness of right and the plausible make-shifts of theology and superstition. The one held me an abject slave—a prisoner for life, punished for some transgression in which I had no lot nor part; and the other counseled me to manly endeavor to secure my freedom. This contest was now ended; my chains were broken, and the victory brought me unspeakable joy. But my gladness was short-lived, for I was not yet out of the reach and power of the slave-holders. I soon found that New York was not quite so free or so safe a refuge as I had supposed, and a sense of loneliness and insecurity again oppressed me most sadly. I chanced to meet on the street, a few hours after my landing, a fugitive slave whom I had once known well in slavery. The information received from him alarmed me. The fugitive in question was known in Baltimore as "Allender's Jake," but in New York he wore the more respectable name of "William Dixon." Jake, in law, was the property of Doctor Allender, and Tolly Allender, the son of the doctor, had once made an effort to recapture MR. DIXON, but had failed for want of evidence to support his claim. Jake told me the circumstances of this attempt, and how narrowly he escaped being sent back to slavery and torture. He told me that New York was then full of Southerners returning from the Northern watering-places; that the colored people of New York were not to be trusted; that there were hired men of my own color who would betray me for a few dollars; that there were hired men ever on the lookout for fugitives; that I must trust no man with my secret; that I must not think of going either upon the wharves or into any colored boarding-house, for all such places were closely watched; that he was himself unable to help	• This type of journey has many mixed feelings. • Although Douglass was indeed considered "free" from the power of his slave-holders, this notion was not absolute.

(continued)

Excerpt from: Collected Articles of Frederick Douglass	Our Thought Processes
me; and, in fact, he seemed while speaking to me to fear lest I myself might be a spy and a betrayer. Under this apprehension, as I suppose, he showed signs of wishing to be rid of me, and with whitewash brush in hand, in search of work, he soon disappeared. This picture, given by poor "Jake," of New York, was a damper to my enthusiasm. My little store of money would soon be exhausted, and since it would be unsafe for me to go on the wharves for work, and I had no introductions elsewhere, the prospect for me was far from cheerful. I saw the wisdom of keeping away from the ship-yards, for, if pursued, as I felt certain I should be, Mr. Auld, my "master," would naturally seek me there among the calkers. Every door seemed closed against me. I was in the midst of an ocean of my fellow-men, and yet a perfect stranger to every one. I was without home, without acquaintance, without money, without credit, without work, and without any definite knowledge as to what course to take, or where to look for succor. In such an extremity, a man had something besides his new-born freedom to think of. While wandering about the streets of New York, and lodging at least one night among the barrels on one of the wharves, I was indeed free—from slavery, but free from food and shelter as well. I kept my secret to myself as long as I could, but I was compelled at last to seek some one who would befriend me without taking advantage of my destitution to betray me. Such a person I found in a sailor named Stuart, a warm-hearted and generous fellow, who, from his humble home on Centre street, saw me standing on the opposite sidewalk, near the Tombs prison. As he approached me, I ventured a remark to him which at once enlisted his interest in me. He took me to his home to spend the night, and in the morning went with me to Mr. David Ruggles, the secretary of the New York Vigilance Committee, a co-worker with Isaac T. Hopper, Lewis and Arthur Tappan, Theodore S. Wright, Samuel Cornish,	• Douglass learns of information from a fugitive slave. • Douglass needed to watch his back, even as a "free man." • It seems as though, through Douglass's description, that even though he is free, Douglass still is very much alone in the free world.

(continued)

Excerpt from: Collected Articles of Frederick Douglass	Our Thought Processes
Thomas Downing, Philip A. Bell, and other true men of their time. All these (save Mr. Bell, who still lives, and is editor and publisher of a paper called the "Elevator," in San Francisco) have finished their work on earth. Once in the hands of these brave and wise men, I felt comparatively safe. With Mr. Ruggles, on the corner of Lispenard and Church streets, I was hidden several days, during which time my intended wife came on from Baltimore at my call, to share the burdens of life with me. She was a free woman, and came at once on getting the good news of my safety. We were married by Rev. J. W. C. Pennington, then a well-known and respected Presbyterian minister. I had no money with which to pay the marriage fee, but he seemed well pleased with our thanks.	• According to Douglass, he is safer now, all things considered, than during his time as a slave. • Douglass married a free woman.

Thematic Messages

• Not satisfied with the status quo: Douglass feels the time for action is needed. He is not apologetic for this need for change.

• The time for acceptance of the slave experience is at an end: Douglass, through action, is moving towards creating a new life for himself as a more "free man."

As you undoubtedly know, Douglass's text is quite different from Dunbar's, yet both directly deal with the theme of white racism over blacks. Having read both texts carefully and having completed our textual analyses, we are ready to turn our attention to the literary analysis writing prompt:

CCSS Alignment	
RL.1	Cite strong and textual evidence.
RL.2	Determine two or more themes.
RL.3	Analyze the impact of the author's choices.
RL.5	Analyze how an author's choices contribute to its overall structure.

(continued)

CCSS Alignment	
RL.9	Demonstrate knowledge of foundational works of American literature, including how two or more texts from the same period treat similar themes and topics.
L.1	Demonstrate command of the conventions of standard English grammar and usage when writing.
L.3	Apply knowledge of language to understand how language functions in different contexts.
L.5	Demonstrate understanding of figurative language, word relationships, and nuances in word meanings.
W.3	Write narratives to develop real or imagined experiences.
W.5	Develop and strengthen writing as needed by planning, revising, editing, and rewriting.
W.6	Use technology to produce, publish, and update individual writing products.

Literary Analysis Writing Prompt

Student Directions (80 minutes)

Use what you have learned by reading Paul Laurence Dunbar's "We Wear the Mask" and Frederick Douglass's excerpt from his Collected Articles to write an essay that analyzes how both texts treat the issue of racism.

Develop your essay by providing textual evidence from both sources. Be sure to follow the conventions of Standard English.

Well, at this point in our preparation, you should be 100% convinced that reading carefully—that is, paying attention to the author's word choices and understanding the connection of these choices to the meaning of the text—is a sure way to succeed on the written portion of the literary analysis. Our hard work has paid off and we are two steps ahead in the planning and writing of our essay.

So, let's now turn our attention to the actual planning of the literary analysis essay, and, make no mistakes about it, planning is also 100% necessary. Don't skip it. Even under timed conditions, brief and basic prewriting will pay off dividends. Look at the graphic organizer below to see exactly how you could prewrite for an essay such as the one presented here.

Issue of Racism	
"We Wear the Mask"	Excerpt from: Collected Articles of Frederick Douglass
Subtle "It hides our cheeks and shades our eyes,— This debt we pay to human guile;"	Overt "My free life began on the third of September, 1838. On the morning of the fourth of that month, after an anxious and most perilous but safe journey, I found myself in the big city of New York."
Status Quo "But let the world dream otherwise, We wear the mask!"	Create Change "My little store of money would soon be exhausted, and since it would be unsafe for me to go on the wharves for work, and I had no introductions elsewhere, the prospect for me was far from cheerful."
Thesis Statement: Paul Laurence Dunbar's "We Wear the Mask" and Frederick Douglass's collected articles present two viewpoints on racism in the United States: One from the perspective that advocates the status quo and one from the perspective that advocates action.	

We are quite sure that if you read and examined the table above, you would see the value in prewriting. The four minor themes—subtle, status quo, overt, and revolutionary or create change—come directly from our analytic reading of the texts. In addition, not only do we have a solid thesis statement based upon evidence in the texts, we have supporting quotations to incorporate into our essay. As you prepare for the literary analysis section of the PARCC, you should begin to internalize the process of prewriting and analyzing text so that doing so becomes second nature for you.

Writing the Literary Analysis Essay

As with all essay writing, the literary analysis requires that you utilize a writing technique to grab the reader's attention. These techniques include, but are not limited to, a rhetorical question, an anecdote, a quotation, a startling statement, a compelling fact, etc. In addition to the opening technique, your first paragraph must contain your original thesis statement. Below is an example of an introduction.

Sample Introduction

Each day, boys and girls across the United States, dutifully recite the words from our Pledge of Allegiance, "with liberty and justice for all." How many children, however, understand the true meaning of these words, and if these words are historically accurate? Unfortunately, a student of history, especially of historical literature, knows that liberty and justice for all was more of an illusion than a reality. One need only look to the work of Paul Laurence Dunbar and Frederick Douglass for proof. Paul Laurence Dunbar's "We Wear the Mask" and Frederick Douglass's excerpt from *Collected Articles* present two viewpoints on racism in the United States: One from the perspective that advocates the status quo and one from the perspective that advocates action.

As you can see, our introduction satisfies all of the requirements of a quality introduction that we noted above. There is an attention grabber, background on the essay topic, and a very strong thesis statement. Thanks to all the hard work we did with reading and prewriting, we were able to breeze through this part of the literary analysis task. Now, let's turn our attention to the body of the essay.

Sample Body

As you write the body paragraphs of your essay, it is imperative that you keep three things in mind:

a. You must have a clearly written topic sentence for each paragraph,

b. You must use appropriate quotations from the texts, and

c. You must use transitional words, phrases, and sentences in order to organize and structure the body portion of your essay.

OK, let's first address the issue of topic sentences. We find that most students struggle in this area. It's not that students do not "know" what a topic sentence is; it's more of a problem of appropriately using it in actual essay writing.

Let's look at the body of our essay on racism in "We Wear the Mask" and the excerpt from Frederick Douglass's *Collected Articles*. A topic sentence is just what it says: It's a sentence that tells what the paragraph is about. That's simple enough, and, we are actually one step ahead of the game. Remember our prewriting chart? Well, take another look. Our topic sentences are simply the mini-themes in the boxes of our graphic organizer. So, look at the chart below. Here are the topic sentences through the entire body of our literary analysis task:

Mini-themes	Topic Sentences
Subtle vs. Overt Racism	"We Wear the Mask" and *Collected Articles* present two sides of the same coin: one type of racism that is subtle; the other that is overt. First, this essay will explore the subtle, but no less dangerous, racism in "We Wear the Mask."
Status Quo vs. Revolutionary	"We Wear the Mask" and *Collected Articles* present another conflicting dichotomy of racism: One that advocates the status quo and one that seeks action. First, this section of the essay will explore the type of racism that pushes the status quo.

As you can clearly see in the examples above, the topic sentences are clear and very direct. There is no uncertainty or ambiguity about the purpose of the paragraph. The second sentence in each of the samples above even goes so far as to show you how you can transition to "We Wear the Mask." Another similar sentence could serve as a transition to a discussion of Frederick Douglass's excerpt from *Collected Articles*. Let's now take a look at working with quotations.

There is absolutely no getting out of any English class in our country without hearing your teacher say over and over, "You must use quotations from the text to support your work." Well, the PARCC is no different. Let us show you exactly how to incorporate quotations into your body paragraphs by building upon our sample topic sentences:

> "We Wear the Mask" and the excerpt from Douglass's *Collected Articles* present two sides of the same coin: one type of reaction to racism that is subtle; the other that is more overt. First, this essay will explore the subtle, but no less dangerous, racism and reaction in "We Wear the Mask." In Dunbar's poem, it is the concerned narrator who urges his reader to remain steadfast in their wearing of their masks. A close look at Dunbar's language reveals that the narrator here is particularly controlled in his tone, as his advice also suggests. We must not react to those that commit acts of racism upon us because, as detailed in the poem, "Why should the world be over-wise, / In counting all our tears and sighs?" it provides those racists with more power if we let them see our emotions. Dunbar chooses to be silent, and to keep the hurtful feelings within himself. Whereas Dunbar's type of reaction to racism is more covert and subtle in nature, Frederick Douglass responds to the racist threat from whites through more overt action.

Our hope is that by now you can see how successful you can be on the literary analysis task of the PARCC if you are willing to invest the time into interacting with the text and by prewriting (see flow chart in the appendix). The benefits of both will be shown in your actual essay writing.

Transitions

One of the undeniable aspects of quality essay writing—for the PARCC and for *all* other situations—is a writer's ability to successfully use transitional words, phrases and sentences. The body paragraph we wrote appears below. However, this time we only show those words and phrases and sentences that are the transitions:

- "We Wear the Mask" and the excerpt from Douglass's Collected Articles present two sides of the same coin: **one type** of reaction to racism that is subtle; the **other** that is more overt. First, this essay will explore the subtle, but no less damaging, racism and reaction in "We Wear the Mask."

- **Whereas** Dunbar's type of reaction to racism is more covert and subtle in nature, Frederick Douglass responds to the racist threat from whites through more overt action.

Transitions can be thought of as the "glue" that binds the paragraph together. These words and phrases allow the reader to easily and fluidly follow the writer's train of thought. Without these transitions, a paragraph would seem disjointed, thrown together, and even sloppy.

To help you in your literary analysis writing, we include a list of transitions that you might wish to consider using in your writing. The idea here is not to overload your essay with a transition for every sentence, but to use these terms only when it is wise and appropriate to do so.

Types of Transitions	Transitional Words/Phrases
Similarity	also, in the same way, just as . . . so too, likewise, similarly
Exception/Contrast	but, however, in spite of, on the one hand . . . on the other hand, nevertheless, nonetheless, notwithstanding, in contrast, on the contrary, still, yet
Sequence/Order	first, second, third, . . . next, then, finally
Time	after, afterward, at last, before, currently, during, earlier, immediately, later, meanwhile, now, recently, simultaneously, subsequently, then
Example	for example, for instance, namely, specifically, to illustrate

(continued)

Types of Transitions	Transitional Words/Phrases
Emphasis	even, indeed, in fact, of course, truly
Place/Position	above, adjacent, below, beyond, here, in front, in back, nearby, there
Cause and Effect	accordingly, consequently, hence, so, therefore, thus
Additional Support or Evidence	additionally, again, also, and, as well, besides, equally important, further, furthermore, in addition, moreover, then
Conclusion/Summary	finally, in a word, in brief, briefly, in conclusion, in the end, in the final analysis, on the whole, thus, to conclude, to summarize, in sum, to sum up, in summary

Writing Conclusions

So, what makes a good conclusion? The overwhelming answer from students is, "Restate your thesis." Well, we take slight issue with this approach. For one, simply restating your thesis is a pretty boring way to end. Second, restating the thesis does not address the "So What?" questions. While we believe that restating the thesis statement in some way is appropriate for a conclusion, simply doing so will not ensure that your reader feels satisfied about the essay you wrote. Instead of just restating the thesis, we recommend that you answer the "So What?" question. What is the "So What?" question? It addresses these issues:

- What is it about this essay that I have written that is really important?

- What should a reader of my essay learn about human nature?

- Why is my essay, that I spent all this time and energy writing, important?

- What is my call to action?

So, let's practice what we preach by writing a sample conclusion for our essay about "We Wear the Mask" and Frederick Douglass's excerpt from his *Collected Articles*. Remember, our thesis statement was: *Paul Laurence Dunbar's "We Wear the Mask" and Frederick Douglass's collected articles present two viewpoints on racism in the United States: One from the perspective that advocates the status quo and one from the perspective that advocates action.*

Sample Conclusion

Equality and the pursuit of liberty are woven into the fabric of the American psyche. These two principles are promised to us in the constitution and are part of what makes America great. However, one would be naïve, or even worse, ignorant, to believe that America is populated with citizens who are equal in their pursuit of liberty. Dunbar's and Douglass's texts are proof of America's dark past and are reminders that we cannot rest in the equal application of America's ideals. There-fore, the next time that you recite "The Pledge of Allegiance," please remember that equality and liberty are not universally enjoyed and are always worthy for which to be fought.

As you read our sample conclusions, a few properties of the writing should be clear to you.

1. The thesis statement of the essay is "recited" but it is definitely not "repeated" word-for-word.

2. The author clearly and directly answers the "So What?" question, stating that inequality still remains in our country, and

3. There is a clear call to action.

All of these elements make this conclusion well written and solid.

Final Thoughts on the Literary Analysis Task

Before you practice with your own literary analysis tasks, we want to emphasize the major points learned in this chapter.

1. The better and harder that you read the better and easier your essay will be.

2. Prewriting in NOT an option; it is critical.

3. The use of graphic organizers, like the ones in this chapter, will help you write a very successful literary analysis essay.

4. The literary analysis essay can be mastered with enough practice.

Please. It is critical that you keep these points in mind. As you practice below on your own, we will replicate the graphic organizers used. Fill them in as you progress through each stage of the reading and writing process.

Grading the Literary Analysis Essay

As discussed in the previous chapter, we encourage you to use the writing checklist and PARCC rubric to evaluate your work. Doing so after **each** essay will help you to internalize the criteria by which the PARCC will evaluate (and score) your work. In this chapter, we present the checklist and rubric after each practice essay.

Practice Literary Analysis Task #1

CCSS Alignment	
RL.1	Cite strong and textual evidence.
RL.2	Determine two or more themes.
RL.3	Analyze the impact of the author's choices.
RL.5	Analyze how an author's choices contribute to its overall structure.
RL.9	Demonstrate knowledge of foundational works of American literature, including how two or more texts from the same period treat similar themes and topics.
L.1	Demonstrate command of the conventions of standard English grammar and usage when writing.
L.3	Apply knowledge of language to understand how language functions in different contexts.
L.5	Demonstrate understanding of figurative language, word relationships, and nuances in word meanings.
W.3	Write narratives to develop real or imagined experiences.
W.5	Develop and strengthen writing as needed by planning, revising, editing, and rewriting.
W.6	Use technology to produce, publish, and update individual writing products.

For your first literary analysis task, you'll need to read two poems, both written by the famous American poet Emily Dickinson. As you read and interact with each text, the themes that are similar between them should become vividly clear to you.

Text #1: "Because I could not stop for Death"

"Because I could not stop for Death"	My Thought Processes
Because I could not stop for Death— He kindly stopped for me— The Carriage held but just Ourselves— And Immortality. We slowly drove—He knew no haste And I had put away My labor and my leisure too, For His Civility— We passed the School, where Children strove At Recess—in the Ring— We passed the Fields of Gazing Grain— We passed the Setting Sun— Or rather—He passed us— The Dews drew quivering and chill— For only Gossamer, my Gown— My Tippet—only Tulle— We paused before a House that seemed A Swelling of the Ground— The Roof was scarcely visible— The Cornice—in the Ground— Since then—'tis Centuries—and yet Feels shorter than the Day I first surmised the Horses' Heads Were toward Eternity—	

Thematic Messages

Text #2: "I Felt a Funeral, in my Brain"

"I Felt a Funeral, in my Brain"	My Thought Processes
I felt a Funeral, in my Brain, And Mourners to and fro Kept treading—treading—till it seemed That Sense was breaking through— And when they all were seated, A Service, like a Drum— Kept beating—beating—till I thought My Mind was going numb— And then I heard them lift a Box And creak across my Soul With those same Boots of Lead, again, Then Space—began to toll, As all the Heavens were a Bell, And Being, but an Ear, And I, and Silence, some strange Race Wrecked, solitary, here— And then a Plank in Reason, broke, And I dropped down, and down— And hit a World, at every plunge, And Finished knowing—then—	

Thematic Messages

Literary Analysis #1 Writing Prompt

Student Directions (80 minutes)

Use what you have learned by reading Emily Dickinson's "Because I could not stop for Death" and "I Felt a Funeral, in my Brain" to write an essay that analyzes how both texts treat the issue of Death.

Develop your essay by providing textual evidence from both sources. Be sure to follow the conventions of Standard English.

Prewriting

Issue of Death	
"Because I could not stop for Death"	**"I Felt a Funeral, in my Brain"**
Mini-theme #1 (fill in): Quotations (fill in):	Mini-theme #1 (fill in): Quotations (fill in):
Mini-theme #2 (fill in): Quotations (fill in)	Mini-theme #2 (fill in): Quotations (fill in)
Thesis Statement:	

(continued)

Mini-themes	Topic Sentences

> Write your essay in a notebook or on loose-leaf paper. Then consult the Scoring Checklist and the Scoring Rubric found at the back of the book.

Practice Literary Analysis Task #2

CCSS Alignment	
RL.1	Cite strong and textual evidence.
RL.2	Determine two or more themes.
RL.3	Analyze the impact of the author's choices.
RL.5	Analyze how an author's choices contribute to its overall structure.
RL.9	Demonstrate knowledge of foundational works of American literature, including how two or more texts from the same period treat similar themes and topics.
L.1	Demonstrate command of the conventions of standard English grammar and usage when writing.
L.3	Apply knowledge of language to understand how language functions in different contexts.
L.5	Demonstrate understanding of figurative language, word relationships, and nuances in word meanings.
W.3	Write narratives to develop real or imagined experiences.
W.5	Develop and strengthen writing as needed by planning, revising, editing, and rewriting.
W.6	Use technology to produce, publish, and update individual writing products.

For this first literary analysis task, you will analyze an excerpt from an essay written by George Orwell, entitled, "Politics and the English Language" and a poem written by Susan Stewart, entitled "A Language." As you read and interact with each text, the themes that are similar between each text should become vividly clear to you.

Text #1: Excerpt from "Politics and the English Language"

"Politics and the English Language"	My Thought Processes
To begin with it [the defense of the English language] has nothing to do with archaism, with the salvaging of obsolete words and turns of speech, or with the setting up of a "standard English" which must never be departed from. On the contrary, it is especially concerned with the scrapping of every word or idiom which has outworn its usefulness. It has nothing to do with correct grammar and syntax, which are of no importance so long as one makes one's meaning clear, or with the avoidance of Americanisms, or with having what is called a "good prose style." On the other hand, it is not concerned with fake simplicity and the attempt to make written English colloquial. Nor does it even imply in every case preferring the Saxon word to the Latin one, though it does imply using the fewest and shortest words that will cover one's meaning. What is above all needed is to let the meaning choose the word, and not the other way around. In prose, the worst thing one can do with words is surrender to them. When you think of a concrete object, you think wordlessly, and then, if you want to describe the thing you have been visualizing you probably hunt about until you find the exact words that seem to fit it. When you think of something abstract you are more inclined to use words from the start, and unless you make a conscious effort to prevent it, the existing dialect will come rushing in and do the job for you, at the expense of blurring or even changing your meaning. Probably it is better to put off using words as long as possible and get one's meaning as clear as one can through pictures and sensations. Afterward one can choose — not simply accept — the phrases that	

(continued)

"Politics and the English Language"	My Thought Processes

will best cover the meaning, and then switch round and decide what impressions one's words are likely to make on another person. This last effort of the mind cuts out all stale or mixed images, all prefabricated phrases, needless repetitions, and humbug and vagueness generally. But one can often be in doubt about the effect of a word or a phrase, and one needs rules that one can rely on when instinct fails. I think the following rules will cover most cases:
 	
   (i) Never use a metaphor, simile, or other figure of speech which you are used to seeing in print.
 	
   (ii) Never use a long word where a short one will do.
 	
   (iii) If it is possible to cut a word out, always cut it out.
 	
   (iv) Never use the passive where you can use the active.
 	
   (v) Never use a foreign phrase, a scientific word, or a jargon word if you can think of an everyday English equivalent.
 	
   (vi) Break any of these rules sooner than say anything outright barbarous.
 	
These rules sound elementary, and so they are, but they demand a deep change of attitude in anyone who has grown used to writing in the style now fashionable. One could keep all of them and still write bad English, but one could not write the kind of stuff that I quoted in those five specimens at the beginning of this article.
 	
I have not here been considering the literary use of language, but merely language as an instrument for expressing and not for concealing or preventing thought. Stuart Chase and others have come near to claiming that all abstract words are meaningless, and have used this as a pretext for advocating a kind of political quietism. Since you don't know what Fascism is, how can you struggle against Fascism? One need	

(continued)

"Politics and the English Language"	My Thought Processes
not swallow such absurdities as this, but one ought to recognize that the present political chaos is connected with the decay of language, and that one can probably bring about some improvement by starting at the verbal end. If you simplify your English, you are freed from the worst follies of orthodoxy. You cannot speak any of the necessary dialects, and when you make a stupid remark its stupidity will be obvious, even to yourself. Political language—and with variations this is true of all political parties, from Conservatives to Anarchists—is designed to make lies sound truthful and murder respectable, and to give an appearance of solidity to pure wind. One cannot change this all in a moment, but one can at least change one's own habits, and from time to time one can even, if one jeers loudly enough, send some worn-out and useless phrase—some jackboot, Achilles' heel, hotbed, melting pot, acid test, veritable inferno, or other lump of verbal refuse—into the dustbin, where it belongs.	

Thematic Messages

Text #2: "A Language"

"A Language"	My Thought Processes
I had heard the story before about the two prisoners, alone in the same cell, and one gives the other lessons in a language. Day after day, the pupil studies hard— what else does he have to do?—and year after year they practice, waiting for the hour of release. They tackle the nouns, the cases, and genders, the rules for imperatives and conjugations, but near the end of his sentence, the teacher suddenly dies and only the pupil goes back through the gate and into the open world. He travels to the country of his new language, fluent, and full of hope. Yet when he arrives he finds that the language he speaks is not the language that is spoken. He has learned a language one other person knew—its inventor, his cell-mate and teacher. And then the other evening, I heard the story again. This time the teacher was Gombrowicz, the pupil was his wife. She had dreamed of learning Polish and, hour after hour, for years on end, Gombrowicz had been willing to teach her a Polish that does not and never did exist. The man who told the story would like to marry his girlfriend. They love to read in bed and between them speak three languages. They laughed—at the wife, at Gombrowicz, it wasn't clear, and I wasn't sure that they themselves knew what was funny. I wondered why the man had told the story, and thought of the tricks enclosure can play. A nod, or silence, another nod, consent—or not, as a cloud drifts beyond the scene and the two stand pointing in different directions at the very same empty sky.	

(continued)

"A Language"	My Thought Processes

Even so, there was something
else about the story, like teaching
a stunt to an animal—a four-legged
creature might prance on two legs
or a two-legged creature might
fall onto four.
      I remembered,
then, the miscarriage, and before that
the months of waiting: like baskets filled
with bright shapes, the imagination
run wild. And then what arrived:
the event that was nothing, a mistaken idea,
a scrap of charred cloth, the enormous
present folding over the future,
like a wave overtaking
a grain of sand.
      There was a myth
I once knew about twins who spoke
a private language, though one
spoke only the truth and the other
only lies. The savior gets mixed
up with the traitor, but the traitor
stays as true to himself as a god.
 	
All night the rain falls here, falls there,
and the creatures dream, or drown, in the lair.	

Thematic Messages

Literary Analysis #2 Writing Prompt

Student Directions (80 Minutes)

Use what you have learned by reading the excerpt from George Orwell's "Politics and the English Language" and Susan Stewart's poem, "A Language," to write an essay that analyzes how both texts treat the issue of language.

Develop your essay by providing textual evidence from both sources. Be sure to follow the conventions of Standard English.

Prewriting

Issue of Death	
"Politics and the English Language"	"A Language"
Mini-theme #1 (fill in):	Mini-theme #1 (fill in):
Quotations (fill in):	Quotations (fill in):
Mini-theme #2 (fill in):	Mini-theme #2 (fill in):
Quotations (fill in)	Quotations (fill in)

(continued)

Thesis Statement:

Mini-themes	Topic Sentences

Write your essay in a notebook or on loose-leaf paper and utilize the Scoring Checklist and the Scoring Rubric found at the back of the book.

CHAPTER 5

The Research Simulation Task

Introduction
(Performance-Based Assessment)

Now that we have worked through the narrative and literary analysis tasks, we will begin working closely with the Research Simulation Task (RST). We mentioned this reading and writing activity in our introductory chapter; now we are going to start looking at it in more detail.

As we first look at the specifics of writing the Research Simulation Task, we want to stress the following point to you: When you take the PARCC, you will encounter numerous multiple-choice items before you actually write the Research Simulation Task. Our purpose in this chapter is not to focus on the multiple-choice but instead to concentrate on the skills necessary to successfully complete the Research Simulation Task. As we have discussed in our introductory chapter, each PBA will focus on a larger "anchor text" that will require students to answer related multiple-choice questions. For the purposes of this chapter, we are focusing on the larger writing task (that requires intensive reading as well), also known as the prose constructed-response.

First, we will look at one sample RST question. In doing so, we will introduce you to a step-by-step system to address the task, and we will walk you through the reading and analysis process of each of the question's sources from which you can extract information to support your essay's points. This chapter's goal is to get you familiarized with the structure of the task, especially the brainstorming and preparation piece before you begin writing your essay. We will not compose practice RST essays until Chapters 6, 7, 8, and 9.

The following activities align with the common core standards, as detailed below:

CCSS Alignment	
RL.1	Cite strong and textual evidence.
RL.5	Analyze how an author's choices contribute to its overall structure.
RI.7	Integrate and evaluate multiple sources of information presented in different media or formats (e.g., visually, quantitatively) as well as in words in order to address a question or solve a problem.
L.1	Demonstrate command of the conventions of standard English grammar and usage when writing.
L.3	Apply knowledge of language to understand how language functions in different contexts.
L.5	Demonstrate understanding of figurative language, word relationships, and nuances in word meanings.
W.1	Write arguments to support claims in an analysis of substantive topics or texts, using valid reasoning and relevant and sufficient evidence.
W.2	Write informative/explanatory texts to examine and convey complex ideas, concepts, and information clearly and accurately through the effective selection, organization, and analysis of content.
W.5	Develop and strengthen writing as needed by planning, revising, editing, and rewriting.
W.6	Use technology to produce, publish, and update individual writing products.

As we work through the following exercises, keep these eight steps in mind:

Step #1	Read through the question carefully. Make sure to decipher if the question is asking you to convey an opinion, or to convey information/research objectively.
Step #2	In the upper right-hand corner of your paper, simplify what the question is asking you to do. Put the question/task into your own words.
Step #3	Circle the minimum amount of sources that need to be addressed.

Step #4	Take notes with each of the sources. Address the source's main points. Underline actively.
Step #5	After you've addressed and highlighted the main point of the source, make separate notes on the reliability of these sources. Is the source reliable in general? Is it slanted in any way? Do logical fallacies or "holes in argument" exist?
Step #6	You've read through your sources. Choose the sources that you are most comfortable with, and put a star (*) in the upper right-hand corner of each source that you will be using in your research simulation task.
Step #7	In source chart, copy your notes from your sources into each.
Step #8	Now, look at the relationships of your sources. Do they agree with each other? Do they disagree? Use your source-relationship chart to begin thinking about how you will have your sources begin conversing with one another.

Now we will begin looking at our first RST. Then, we will look at a series of sources that will help us in supporting our points with information. Let's move through this process together.

Step #1	Read through the question carefully. Make sure to decipher if the question is asking you to convey an opinion, or to convey information/research objectively.

In the research simulation task shown below, we have two sources under each source. For example, there are two sources under Source A; two under Source B; etc. . . . We have set up this RST this way for one important reason. We want to model for you how to tackle the reading for the RST prompt about "Switching to E-books." We will show you how to interact with source 1, then you will practice independently for source 2. We have done this to emphasize that good writing unequivocally starts with good reading.

Moreover, we want you to become familiar with what the PARCC labels, the "anchor text." The anchor text for the RST is a text that serves as the "grounding point" or "orientation" for the topic introduced by the RST. For instance, in the RST below, the anchor text is found in Source A, in this case entitled, "Should Kids Get eBooks in School" and also, "A Short History of ebooks." For ease in navigating this test-prep book, we will assume that *all* sources in Source A of the sample research simulation tasks will serve as the anchor text.

Writing the Research Simulation Essay

Ready? Let's begin. Here is our first sample RST:

Sample RST Question: Going Electronic

85 minutes

We live in changing times. Technology is all around us, and electronics make up a great deal of our every day. From cell phone technology to gadgets and gizmos that make life easier and more accessible, advancements have slowly made their way into our classrooms. Many school districts feel that we should change with the times, replacing all paper-bound books with electronic copies instead.

You have reviewed four sources regarding eBook technology. These four pieces provide information to begin drafting your own argument.

Source A: "Should Kids Get eBooks in School?" (Erik Hellman) (1) / "A Short History of eBooks" (Marie Lebert) (2)

1. *www.libraryjournal.com/lj/home/886504-264/ebook_summit.html.csp*

2. *http://www.gutenberg.org/cache/epub/29801/pg29801.html*

Source B: E-Books in Schools Graph (1) / Budget Cuts Graph (2)

1. *www.thedigitalshift.com/2011/10/ebooks/ljslj-ebook*

2. *gothamschools.org/tag/the-chopping-block/*

Source C: Multimedia Video Clips — "On Education and Technology" (1) / "Challenges and Education" (2)

1. *http://watchmojo.com/video/id/7695/*

2. *http://watchmojo.com/video/id/7676/*

Source D: Image (1) / Image (2)

1. *http://www.publicdomainpictures.net/view-image.php?image=25033&picture=books*

2. *http://www.publicdomainpictures.net/view-image.php?image=44809&picture=girl-on-touch-screen-phone*

Should all eBooks replace our current paper copies in the high school classroom? Write a persuasive piece that addresses the question and supports your position with evidence from at least three of the four sources. Be sure to acknowledge competing views. You may give examples from past and current events or issues to illustrate and clarify your position. You may refer to the sources by their titles (Source A, Source B, Source C, Source D).

At this point, we have read through the question thoroughly before even moving onto the reading of our sources. This question is asking us to come up with an opinion, and support that opinion with information from our sources. We know what our objective is at this point.

So, let's move to Step #2:

Step #2	In the upper right-hand corner of your paper, simplify what the question is asking you to do. Put the question/task into your own words.

We know that the question is asking: Should we replace current paper-bound textbooks with eBooks?

Step #3	Circle the minimum amount of sources that need to be addressed.

We know that the question is asking us to use at least **three** of the four sources. This is important to note before we begin.

Step #4	Take notes with each of the sources. Address the source's main points. Underline actively.
Step #5	After you've addressed and highlighted the main point of the source, make separate notes on the reliability of these sources. Is the source reliable in general? Is it slanted in any way? Do logical fallacies or "holes in argument" exist?

We'll work through Steps #4 and #5 together. We are first looking at the source's main points and listing those appropriately. Then, when we talk about logical fallacies, we are looking to see if any "holes" or lapses exist in the source's reliability. Is the information slanted or biased in any way? Let's start with Source A:

SOURCE A — Traditional Text

Source A: "Should Kids Get eBooks in School?"	How Should We Analyze?
Searching for information is NOT like trolling for fish. You know the saying: "Give a man a fish and you have fed him for today. Teach a man to fish and you have fed him for life." Answer someone's question, and most likely they'll go away for today. Teach someone how to search for the answer, and they'll continually hunger for more. I thought about this when a librarian friend related to me how she loves working the reference desk. One of her favorite patrons is an elderly gentleman with a passion for baseball statistics. This patron will have nothing to do with the Internet, which is a shame, because we live in a golden age for baseball statistics thanks to the deluge of raw data made available online. My friend can answer her patron's question of the day by pulling up Baseball-Reference.com, the Baseball Cube or some other site. Over the course of his life Mr. Elderly Patron learned to use the reference desk in his library to answer his questions, and maybe it's unfair to ask him to change. But it seems to me that it would be a crime for anyone to be taught the same information-seeking strategy today. Kids need be taught to find the answers to the vast majority of their questions directly, without the mediation of a librarian. As one school librarian told me, "We're not the gatekeepers anymore. We have to train people to be their own gatekeepers." What could be more important than teaching our kids how to navigate a world of information that gets more complex every day? Library vs. Internet? Unfortunately, school librarians are under severe pressure as tight budgets cause administrators to cut any services perceived as non-essential (just look at the Nation without School Librarians map). In my own town, state budget cuts have led our district to eliminate library staff positions.	Step #4: • There is an obvious shift in generations when it comes to searching for information. This elderly patron, obviously, is not comfortable with the ways of the Internet. • Our students today must learn the way that is appropriate for their generation. Working with online resources makes sense for our contemporary youngsters.

(continued)

Source A: "Should Kids Get eBooks in School?"	How Should We Analyze?
My own high-school-age son expressed to me that he was relieved that it was school library staff and not teachers that got cut. He thinks that the high school library is useless when he has all of the Internet at his fingertips: why pay people to shelve books? I quizzed him about this, and he has a point. He recently wrote a paper for history class on the Philippine-American War. The school library has only the six brief paragraphs in Encyclopedia Britannica on this neglected episode of U.S. History, and the electronic databases that the school subscribes to weren't much help. He ended up using material from Google Books and public domain material in Wikisources for his paper, both of which are quite extensive, and don't cost the school anything. At the same time, my son wishes that his school offered more instruction on "how to get stuff."	• Books only have limited information. Imagine if the Internet was at their fingertips at all times!
The entry of ebook technology into schools will only increase budget pressures on school libraries. Declining prices for ebook readers will soon make it economically feasible for schools to issue ebook readers to all of their students. Each reader would be loaded with an array of textbooks, reference works and reading material tailored for the student's grade level, in quantities that surpass almost any physical library. School districts will inevitably be invited by educational publishing companies to compare the cost of these complete content packages with the cost of operating a physical library.	• Since ebooks are now much more accessible than they have been before, budgetary constraints may be lessened.
Difficult choices will present themselves. In the 1990s, parents demanded that schools incorporate computers into their curricula so their children would be computer-literate, long before anyone knew whether computers in schools really benefited students. In the 2010s, many parents will want their children to have all the advantages of ebook-based school libraries. How should school administrators respond to these pressures? What is best for the students?	• Must look at what is best for the students.

(continued)

Source A: "Should Kids Get eBooks in School?"	How Should We Analyze?
Libraries and Student Performance A careful look at the available research on the benefits of school libraries might give hints as to what's important. Most of the studies find correlations between student performance and school library services, but they're not much help in figuring out how school libraries should address changes in technology in the midst of budgetary pressures. In California, decades of budgetary pressure could provide insight into the effects of cutting services. One large-scale study on the effect of libraries in California schools gave inconsistent and contradictory results. The study, by education consultants Stacy Sinclair-Tarr and William Tarr Jr. found disappointingly small correlations between school libraries and student performance [PDF]; in some cases students with access to libraries were found to have done worse on standardized tests. What on earth was happening in California? These odd results led Douglas Achterman, a teacher librarian at Hollister High School in California and also an Adjunct at San Jose State SLIS, to go back and take a closer look at the California data for his dissertation research at the University of North Texas. His conclusion: Successful school library programs are much more than books, bytes and buildings. As results from this study demonstrate, the level of library staffing, both certificated and clerical, is directly related to the kinds and number of services such programs provide. And at the middle and high school level, where there is at least a critical mass of professional staffing, the levels of staffing are directly related to student achievement. At all grade levels, the levels of services regularly provided by the library program are significantly related to student achievement.	• Libraries are not used the same way they have in the past. We need to change the ways we deliver information to our children as well.

(continued)

Source A: "Should Kids Get eBooks in School?"	How Should We Analyze?
The previous study had problems with control methodology, but more importantly, it neglected staffing or funding levels. Achterman's re-analysis of the data showed that it's not having a library that helps students, it's having sufficient staff to allow librarians to have meaningful interaction with students and teachers. This is a conclusion that transcends the form of the library's content. Neither books nor ebooks will teach kids how to answer questions all by themselves.	• Staffing, funding, and training need to be active consideration when thinking about ebook technology.
A Reality Check	
Ph.D. dissertations are all well and good, but real sixth and seventh graders provided me a reality check. I interviewed two daughters of friends who live in another state. They love their school libraries. "The library is a great place to study. They have nice computers and everything. Our librarian is really nice, she doesn't get upset if we talk. She helps us find stuff." Both of them report that they alternate a library class every few weeks with a technology class, where they learn to use spreadsheets, word processors, and the like. They have research projects that require them to use books, websites and databases.	• Information from students themselves. Research projects are given that require students to seek out information.
My interview subjects, though both voracious readers, were not enthusiastic with the idea of replacing their print books with an ebook reader. They were both familiar with Kindles through their parents, and they don't like that Kindles don't tell you how much of a book you've read. They hated when the batteries ran out. They carry heavy backpacks to school, but not because of books. It's because they never clean out their backpacks.	

(continued)

Source A: "Should Kids Get eBooks in School?"	How Should We Analyze?
It's likely that ebook technology will be marketed to schools as replacement for print collections, backpack-emptiers, and cost-savers. But the available research shows that it's having sufficient staff—not sufficient content—that really works. Switching to ebooks will make sense for school libraries only when they result in savings of time and money that allow library staff to *increase* their focus on instruction and interaction with students and other teachers. Despite the benefits of putting large collections into student backpacks, stocking the pond just isn't that important. Once a young mind discovers how to fish the Internet for intellectual nourishment, the fish don't stand a chance.	• School districts will most likely not entirely make this shift unless sufficient measures are taken under consideration. **Step #5:** • In terms of reliability, this source is adequate. From *The Library Journal,* the credence behind its message is most likely legitimate. • The writer sees the usage of library as different from its traditional goals, and for this, they seem to also look at the eBook in a very realistic way as well. • Fortunately, this writer has considered both sides of the argument, and addresses both sides as he shared the information with the reader.

Research Simulation Essay Practice

Now that we have looked at a traditional text together, it is time for you to try out your own analysis as it relates to a similar informational text. Be sure to underline the passage and jot down notes in the appropriate area. Interacting with these sources will, most likely, be the easiest and most comfortable for you, especially since you have worked with very similar texts in your own classrooms throughout your years of being a student.

Step #4	Take notes with each of the sources. Address the source's main points. Underline actively.

| Step #5 | After you've addressed and highlighted the main point of the source, make separate notes on the reliability of these sources. Is the source reliable in general? Is it slanted in any way? Do logical fallacies or "holes in argument" exist? |

Source A — Traditional Text

"A Short History of eBooks" (Marie Lebert)	Analysis:
Introduction The book is no longer what it used to be. The electronic book (ebook) was born in 1971, with the first steps of Project Gutenberg, a digital library for books from public domain. It is nearly 40 years old, already. But this is a short life compared to the 5-century old print book. The internet went live in 1974, with the creation of the protocol TCP/IP by Vinton Cerf and Bob Kahn. It began spreading in 1983 as a network for research centers and universities. It got its first boost with the invention of the web by Tim Berners-Lee in 1990, and its second boost with the release of the first browser Mosaic in 1993. From 1994 onwards, the internet quickly spread worldwide. In Bookland, people were reluctant, curious or passionate. The internet didn't bring print media, movies, radio or television to an end. It created its own space as a new medium, to get information, access documents, broaden our knowledge and communicate across borders and languages. Booksellers began selling books online within and outside their home country, offering excerpts on their websites.	

(continued)

"A Short History of eBooks" (Marie Lebert)	Analysis:
Libraries began creating websites as a "virtual" window, as well as digital libraries stemming from their print collections. Librarians helped patrons to surf on the web without being drowned, and to find the information they needed at a time search engines were less accurate. Library catalogs went online. Union catalogs offered a common point for hundreds and then thousands of catalogs. Newspapers and magazines began being available online, as well as their archives. Some journals became "only" electronic to skip the costs of print publishing, while offering print on demand. Some newsletters, zines and journals started online from scratch, skipping a print version. Authors began creating websites to self-publish their work or post it while waiting to find a publisher. Communication with readers became easier through email, forums, chat and instant messaging. Some authors explored new ways of writing, called hypertext literature. More and more books were published with both a print version and a digital version. Some books were "only" digital. Other books were digitized from print versions. New online bookstores began selling "only" digital books. Aggregators partnered with publishers to produce and sell digital versions of their books. People no longer needed to run after information and to worry about living in a remote place with no libraries and bookstores. Information was there, by the numbers, available on our screen, often at no cost. In 2009, most of us would not be able to work, study, communicate and entertain without connecting with others through the internet.	

(continued)

"A Short History of eBooks" (Marie Lebert)	Analysis:
Here is the "virtual" journey we are going to follow: 1971: Project Gutenberg is the first digital library 1990: The web boosts the internet 1993: The Online Books Page is a list of free ebooks 1994: Some publishers get bold and go digital 1995: Amazon.com is the first main online bookstore 1996: There are more and more texts online 1997: Multimedia convergence and employment 1998: Libraries take over the web 1999: Librarians get digital 2000: Information is available in many languages 2001: Copyright, copyleft and Creative Commons 2002: A web of knowledge 2003: eBooks are sold worldwide 2004: Authors are creative on the net 2005: Google gets interested in ebooks 2006: Towards a world public digital library 2007: We read on various electronic devices 2008: "A common information space in which we communicate"	

Step #4	Take notes with each of the sources. Address the source's main points. Underline actively.
Step #5	After you've addressed and highlighted the main point of the source, make separate notes on the reliability of these sources. Is the source reliable in general? Is it slanted in any way? Do logical fallacies or "holes in argument" exist?

Source B — Visual Graph

Source B: e-Books in Schools (Graph)

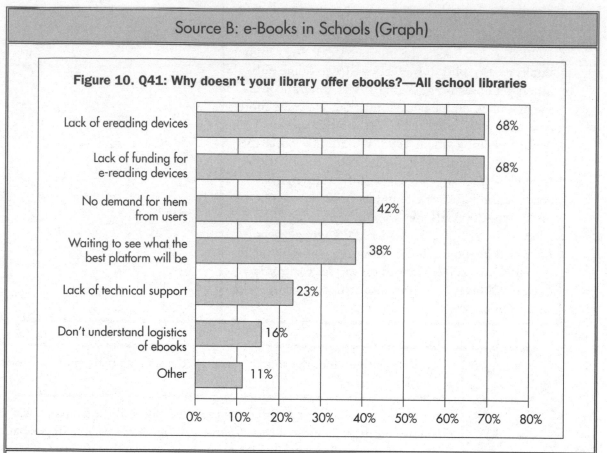

Figure 10. Q41: Why doesn't your library offer ebooks?—All school libraries

- Lack of ereading devices — 68%
- Lack of funding for e-reading devices — 68%
- No demand for them from users — 42%
- Waiting to see what the best platform will be — 38%
- Lack of technical support — 23%
- Don't understand logistics of ebooks — 16%
- Other — 11%

How should we analyze?

Step #4:

• The largest reasons include lack of funding or interest.

• As a result, some questions need to be asked of our school districts. How do we know the interest doesn't exist, and is it possible to move money around to make this sort of a change?

Step #5:

• While this source is not outright unreliable, it is important to ask ourselves some questions. How was this data collected? Who collected the data? How much of the school was actually surveyed?

• We must look at all variables that work with the graph. Be sure to do so as you read through the next example.

Step #4	Take notes with each of the sources. Address the source's main points. Underline actively.
Step #5	After you've addressed and highlighted the main point of the source, make separate notes on the reliability of these sources. Is the source reliable in general? Is it slanted in any way? Do logical fallacies or "holes in argument" exist?

SOURCE B — Visual Graph

Source B: School Budget Cuts — Gotham Schools (Graph)

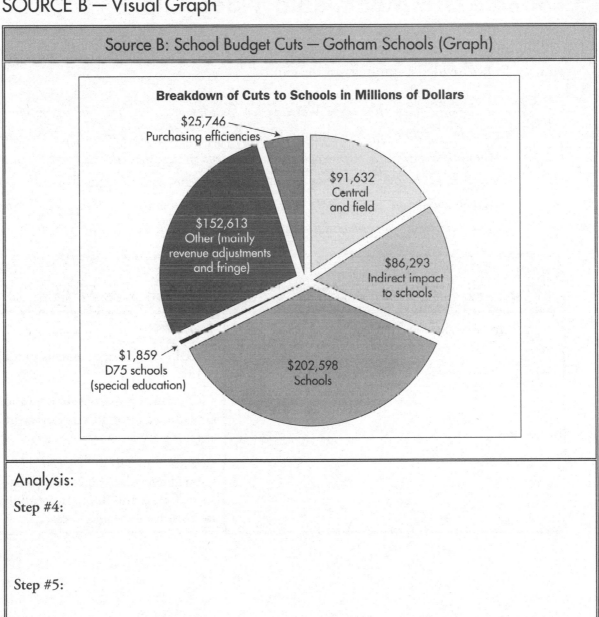

Breakdown of Cuts to Schools in Millions of Dollars

$25,746 — Purchasing efficiencies

$91,632 Central and field

$152,613 Other (mainly revenue adjustments and fringe)

$86,293 Indirect impact to schools

$1,859 D75 schools (special education)

$202,598 Schools

Analysis:

Step #4:

Step #5:

Step #4	Take notes with each of the sources. Address the source's main points. Underline actively.
Step #5	After you've addressed and highlighted the main point of the source, make separate notes on the reliability of these sources. Is the source reliable in general? Is it slanted in any way? Do logical fallacies or "holes in argument" exist?

 # Source C — Multimedia Video Clip

Summary: This source requires that you have access to the Internet. If this is an issue for you, we have provided a summary of the clip:

In this video clip, Steve Wozniak, co-founder of Apple, presents his vision of the role of technology in education in the future. Calling the computer "a teacher," Wozniak envisions a technological environment in which children learn through videogames. In this videogame environment, students, according to Wozniak, will become immersed and part of the learning process. According to Wozniak, "it's less important what you teach kids and more important that you motivate them."

Source C: Image http://watchmojo.com/video/id/7695/	How Should We Analyze?
http://watchmojo.com/video/id/7695/	**Step #4:** • Need to encourage students to want to read. • Reflecting on the craft of education: how can we integrate technology in an engaging way? • Makes comparison between classroom and a video game, using a balance of work and fun to successfully get students to meet objectives.

(continued)

Source C: Image http://watchmojo.com/video/id/7695/	How Should We Analyze?
	Step #5: Steve Wozniak is the co-founder of Apple, which gives him definite reliability when speaking about technology. He is now, however, an educator. He does not hold any degrees or diplomas in relation to education, so his discussion of engaging students in the classroom can only hold so much weight.

Step #4	Take notes with each of the sources. Address the source's main points. Underline actively.
Step #5	After you've addressed and highlighted the main point of the source, make separate notes on the reliability of these sources. Is the source reliable in general? Is it slanted in any way? Do logical fallacies or "holes in argument" exist?

SOURCE C — Multimedia Video Clip

Summary of Clip: Steve Wozniak on Challenges of the Information Age

In this video clip, Steve Wozniak, co-founder of Apple, discusses the overabundance of information in our present computer age. Wozniak feels that as consumers of this information, we need to be selective in what we read and view on the Internet. Additionally, Wozniak argues that while computers have made certain aspects of education simpler, in the bigger picture he says that computers in the classroom make learning and networking very complicated.

Source C: Image http://watchmojo.com/video/id/7676/	How Should We Analyze?
http://watchmojo.com/video/id/7676/	Step #4: Step #5:

Step #4	Take notes with each of the sources. Address the source's main points. Underline actively.
Step #5	After you've addressed and highlighted the main point of the source, make separate notes on the reliability of these sources. Is the source reliable in general? Is it slanted in any way? Do logical fallacies or "holes in argument" exist?

Source D — Visual/Image/Artwork/ Advertisement

Source D: Image

Analysis:

Step #4

• This library hallway can represent our intellectual past. E-books could possibly threaten the extinction of such centers.

• Libraries encourage intellectual community. E-books could challenge this very face-to-face learning experience.

• With libraries come librarians and media specialists that can help train many visitors in research skills.

Step #5

We are not aware of who has created this image, or where this is from. Our determination of its reliability will be minimal. This is OK since we will use it for surface analysis only.

Step #4	Take notes with each of the sources. Address the source's main points. Underline actively.
Step #5	After you've addressed and highlighted the main point of the source, make separate notes on the reliability of these sources. Is the source reliable in general? Is it slanted in any way? Do logical fallacies or "holes in argument" exist?

SOURCE D — Visual/Image/Artwork/Advertisement

Source D: Image	How Should We Analyze?
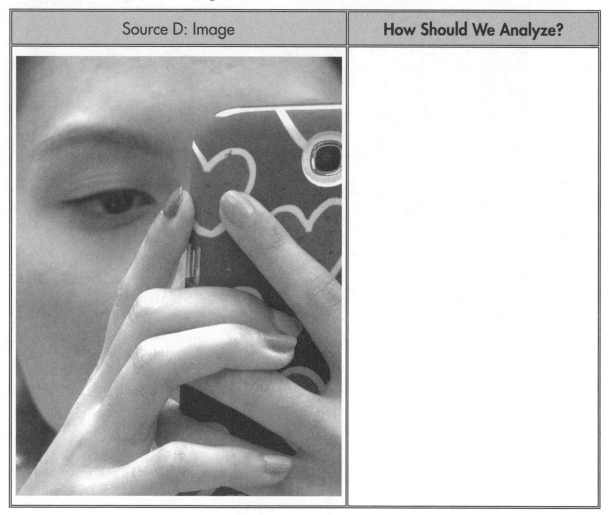	

(continued)

	You've read through your sources. Choose the sources that you are most comfortable with, and put a star (*) in the upper right-hand corner of each source that you will be using in your research simulation task.
Step #6	
Step #7	In source chart, copy your notes from your sources into each.
Step #8	Now, look at the relationships of your sources. Do they agree with each other? Do they disagree? Use your source-relationship chart to begin thinking about how you will have your sources begin conversing with one another.

At this point, you have been able to see our rationale and our thinking as we analyzed the sources provided and could also see how we looked at each source's possible reliability of information. You have taken the time to practice these skills as well.

Look at the following charts to continue organizing your thoughts before we tackle the writing of your responses in the following chapters. Use the information you have collected from these sources to organize in the graphic organizer on the next page.

Source A	Source B	Source C	Source D	

Now, look at the relationships among the sources. How do they relate to one another?

Use this graphic organizer to begin these conversations between and among your sources. This will help you as you integrate this information into your RST essays in the following chapters.

Source Relationships

Source _____	How does _____ interact with _____?	Source _____
	→	
Source _____	How does _____ interact with _____?	Source _____
	→	

At this point, you have been able to see our rationale and our thinking as we analyzed the sources provided. You also could see how we looked at each source's possible reliability of information. You have taken the time to practice these skills as well.

Look at the appropriate charts and graphic organizers to continue organizing your thoughts before we tackle the writing of your responses in the following chapters.

CHAPTER 6

Research Simulation Task: English

Introduction
(Performance-Based Assessment)

The Research Simulation Task (RST) represents a formidable challenge for three primary reasons: 1.) You will have to balance three or four separate sources as you consider your essay topic, 2.) You will have to deal with various media-type sources; for instance, the research simulation task might involve an article, a video, and a graph, and 3.) Perhaps most difficult of all, you will have to "synthesize" at least two of the three sources into a thesis-driven essay. On top of this, you will be tested on how well you can read and write in relation to a particular academic subject, such as English, history, or science. Does this sound tough? Yes, it certainly is, but not if you are prepared. With a little practice and a little know-how, the RST is not as difficult as it sounds.

The goal of this chapter is simple: We will show you, step-by-step, how to excel on the RST. We will give you a sample essay response to an RST prompt that will provide a model for you to follow as you practice further on in the chapter. Moreover, we will consider what an RST question looks like, specifically, in the content area of English.

CCSS Alignment	
RL.1	Cite strong and textual evidence.
RL.5	Analyze how an author's choices contribute to its overall structure.
RI.7	Integrate and evaluate multiple sources of information presented in different media or formats (e.g., visually, quantitatively) as well as in words in order to address a question or solve a problem.

(continued)

CCSS Alignment	
L.1	Demonstrate command of the conventions of standard English grammar and usage when writing.
L.3	Apply knowledge of language to understand how language functions in different contexts.
L.5	Demonstrate understanding of figurative language, word relationships, and nuances in word meanings.
W.1	Write arguments to support claims in an analysis of substantive topics or texts, using valid reasoning and relevant and sufficient evidence.
W.2	Write informative/explanatory texts to examine and convey complex ideas, concepts, and information clearly and accurately through the effective selection, organization, and analysis of content.
W.5	Develop and strengthen writing as needed by planning, revising, editing, and rewriting.
W.6	Use technology to produce, publish, and update individual writing products.

Writing the Research Simulation Essay for English

Let's get started. Below is the first RST sample question with which we will work. Our first RST deals with the topic of video games, the inspiration of which comes from the famous science fiction novel, *Ender's Game*, by Orson Scott Card. Those lucky enough to have read this book will appreciate the topic very much.

Here's the prompt:

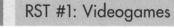

RST #1: Videogames

85 minutes

Sony PlayStation. Wii. X-Box. It seems as though videogames are becoming an ever-increasing form of entertainment in our country. Advocates of videogames claim that it is a harmless form of entertainment, while others view videogames as contributing to violence.

You have reviewed three sources regarding the benefits and drawbacks of videogames. These three pieces provide information to begin drafting your own argument.

- **Source A:** Video, History of Gaming
  http://vimeo.com/18743950

- **Source B:** Image

- **Source C:** Excerpt, *Youth* (G. Stanley Hall)

Do videogames contribute to violence among teens in America? Write a persuasive piece that addresses the question and supports your position with evidence from at least two of the three sources. Be sure to acknowledge competing views. You may give examples from past and current events or issues to illustrate and clarify your position. You may refer to the sources by their titles (Source A, Source B, Source C).

As we have shown you throughout this book, the writers of the PARCC view reading and writing as connected activities. Therefore, to begin, we will show you, as in Chapter 2, how you might interact with the sources in the RST prompt in a meaningful manner. Here are some questions that will guide us as we view and read the texts:

- What is the main idea the author wishes to convey?

- What statistics seem to be important, especially when I have to write the essay?

- What type of bias does the author have in writing the piece?

- Can the information be interpreted in a way different from the way the author presents it?

- How can I use the arguments presented to further my opinion on the matter?

Here is our first source in our quest to answer the question, "Do videogames contribute to violence among teens in America?" Since our text (our anchor text), "Source A," is a video, we have a graphic organizer that is an effective tool to utilize when interacting with videos. As you watch the video, notice the notes we have recorded in the chart. These notes represent the mental actions the mind is required to make when viewing media on the PARCC.

Source A: Anchor Text Graphic Organizer

Summary of "History of Games" video:

In this video clip, a variety of games are introduced to illustrate the evolution of videogames. Make note of the trends that exist from the beginning of this video to the ending segment. Be conscious of details to help support your argument.

RST Prompt: History of Videogames
Video notes
• The first contraption looks almost prehistoric.
• Pac-Man is a game that serves as a childhood memory for many.
• As the movie continues forward, one can see the change in technology, and especially, the major change in vibrant colors, graphics, and concepts upon the ever-evolving television screen.
• Characters become more and more lifelike.
• Violence exists, though, on a more and more detailed scale. What was once just a point-and-shoot game has turned into a more interactive battle between the player and the characters on their screen. This should be strongly noted.
• It is also obvious that such games, as in the golf video game, will help a teenager's dexterity and motor skills.

The chart above is an excellent example for you to learn from when taking notes on a video in an RST prompt on the PARCC. As we watched and listened to the video, we learned that the evolution of the videogame is quite long. We are taken through the gambit of genres that appear before our television set, flat-screen or otherwise. We learned that the graphics, sounds, and colors of the games have become more vibrant, intricate, and detailed. We also inferred from this video that the purpose of these videogames is also vast. From simple point-and-shoot games, to sporting games, and even more violent battle scenes, a teenager experiences a lot through the various genres of games that exists. These can easily help one to make an argument for either side of this question, utilizing information from this video to help as support.

Consider using the following graphic organizer to also help you in preparing notes as you view the video clip (or any video clip).

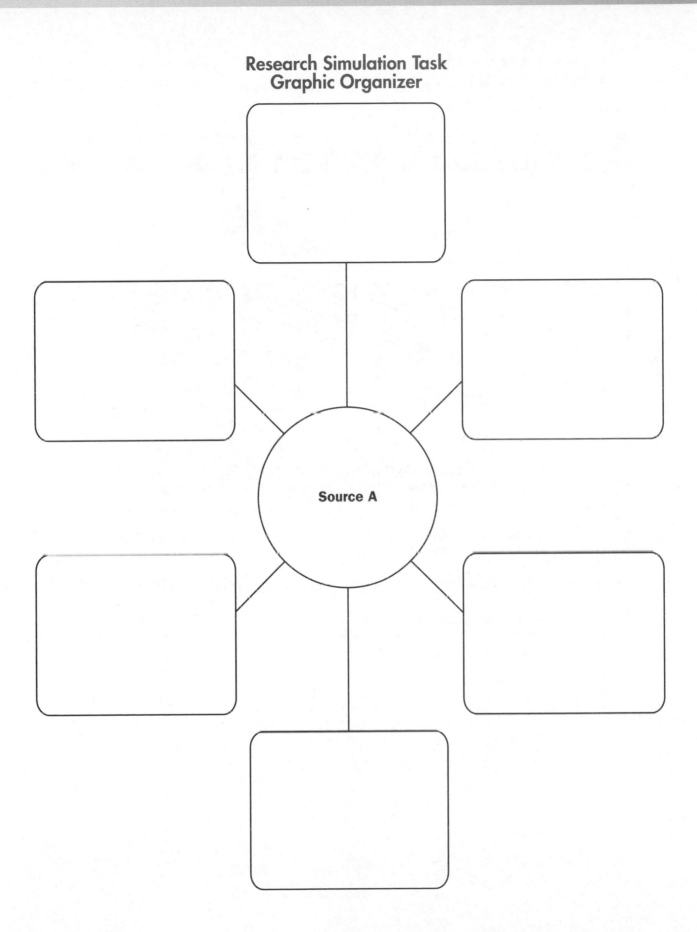

**Research Simulation Task
Graphic Organizer**

Source A

So, now that we have all this information at our disposal, it is still premature to take aside in the question, "Do videogames contribute to violence among teens in America?" Let's look at our next source.

Source B: Image

By Frits Ahlefeldt - HikingArtist.com

Image

• It is clear that the image portrays videogames in a very negative light. The blame is put on videogames and less on the player themselves. Instead, the videogame's content serves as the one in control, harming our teenagers as a result.

OK. So, what did we learn from our analysis of this source? First, we must remember that the artwork comes from only one person, Frits Ahlefeldt. While this fact does not invalidate the information present, it should give us some pause when considering the data in the text. Having said this, there are some interesting points to notice here: Two-thirds of Americans play videogames.

It is completely unrealistic, then, to make the argument that

    a.   all videogames are harmful, and

    b.   that people who play videogames, even violent ones, are automatically violent.

Keep these items in mind as you continue through the reading of your last and final source.

Source C: Excerpt, Youth (G. Stanley Hall)	Our Thoughts
Dancing is one of the best expressions of pure play and of the motor needs of youth. Perhaps it is the most liberal of all forms of motor education. Schopenhauer thought it the apex of physiological irritability and that it made animal life most vividly conscious of its existence and most exultant in exhibiting it. In very ancient times China ritualised it in the spring and made it a large part of the education of boys after the age of thirteen. Neale thinks it was originally circular or orbicular worship, which he deems oldest. In Japan, in the priestly Salic College of ancient Rome, in Egypt, in the Greek Apollo cult, it was a form of worship. St. Basil advised it; St. Gregory introduced it into religious services. The early Christian bishops, called præsuls, led the sacred dance around the altar; and only in 692, and again in 1617, was it forbidden in church. Neale and others have shown how the choral processionals with all the added charm of vestment and intonation have had far more	• It is clear that Hall explains the need to complete a variety of physical activities. • Games are strongly encouraged, at a very young age. While Hall does not explain videogames specifically, one could argue that videogames certainly serve as games themselves.

(continued)

Source C: Excerpt, Youth (G. Stanley Hall)	Our Thoughts
to do in Christianizing many low tribes, who could not understand the language of the church, than has preaching. Savages are nearly all great dancers, imitating every animal they know, dancing out their own legends, with ritual sometimes so exacting that error means death. The character of people is often learned from their dances, and Molière says the destiny of nations depends on them. The gayest dancers are often among the most downtrodden and unhappy people. Some mysteries can be revealed only in them, as holy passion-plays. If we consider the history of secular dances, we find that some of them, when first invented or in vogue, evoked the greatest enthusiasm. One writer says that the polka so delighted France and England that statesmen forgot politics. The spirit of the old Polish aristocracy still lives in the polonaise. The gipsy dances have inspired a new school of music. The Greek drama grew out of the evolution of the tragic chorus. National dances like the hornpipe and reel of Scotland, the *Reihen*, of Germany, the *rondes* of France, the Spanish tarantella and *chaconne*, the strathspey from the Spey Valley, the Irish jig, etc., express racial traits. Instead of the former vast repertory, the stately pavone, the graceful and dignified saraband, the wild *salterrelle*, the bourrée with song and strong rhythm, the light and skippy bolero, the courtly bayedere, the dramatic plugge, gavotte, and other peasant dances in costume, the fast and furious fandango, weapon and military dances; in place of the pristine power to express love, mourning, justice, and philosophical conceptions, and every industry or characteristic act of life in pantomime and gesture, we have in the dance of the modern ballroom only a degenerate relict, with at best but a very insignificant culture value, and too often stained with bad associations. This is most unfortunate for youth, and for their sake a work of rescue and revival is greatly needed; for it is perhaps, not excepting even music,	• The importance of physical activities remains paramount in a child's life. • This source certainly is a little confusing, due to its slightly outdated language. The sentiment remains the same, however. Physical activity and mentality of mind of work hand-in-hand with one another.

(continued)

Source C: Excerpt, Youth (G. Stanley Hall)	Our Thoughts
the most complete language of the emotions and can be made one of the best schools of sentiment and even will, inculcating good states of mind and exorcising bad ones as few other agencies have power to do. Right dancing can cadence the very soul, give nervous poise and control, bring harmony between basal and finer muscles, and also between feeling and intellect, body and mind. It can serve both as an awakener and a test of intelligence, predispose the heart against vice, and turn the springs of character toward virtue. That its present decadent forms, for those too devitalized to dance aright, can be demoralizing, we know in this day too well, although even questionable dances may sometimes work off vicious propensities in ways more harmless than those in which they would otherwise find vent. Its utilization for and influence on the insane would be another interesting chapter. Very interesting scientifically and suggestive practically is another correspondence which I believe to be new, between the mode of spontaneous activity in youth and that of labor in the early history of the race. One of the most marked distinctions between savage and civilized races is in the longer rhythm of work and relaxation. The former are idle and lazy for days, weeks, and perhaps months, and then put forth intense and prolonged effort in dance, hunt, warfare, migration, or construction, sometimes dispensing with sleep and manifesting remarkable endurance. As civilization and specialization advance, hours become regular. The cultured man is less desultory in all his habits, from eating and sleeping to performing social and religious duties, although he may put forth no more aggregate energy in a year than the savage. Women are schooled to regular work long before men, and the difficulty of imposing civilization upon low races is compared by Bücher[8] to that of training a eat to work when harnessed to a dog-cart. It is	• The writer here, Hall, explains the importance of performing one's social duties. Videogames can contribute to a teenager's social direction.

(continued)

Source C: Excerpt, Youth (G. Stanley Hall)	Our Thoughts
not dread of fatigue but of the monotony of method makes them hate labor. The effort of savages is more intense and their periods of rest more prolonged and inert. Darwin thinks all vital function bred to go in periods, as vertebrates are descended from tidal ascidian.[9] There is indeed much that suggests some other irregular rhythm more or less independent of day and night, and perhaps sexual in its nature, but not lunar, and for males. This mode of life not only preceded the industrial and commercial period of which regularity is a prime condition, but it lasted indefinitely longer than the latter has yet existed; during this early time great exertion, sometimes to the point of utter exhaustion and collapse, alternated with seasons of almost vegetative existence. We see abundant traces of this psychosis in the muscle habits of adolescents, and, I think, in student and particularly in college life, which can enforce regularity only to a limited extent. This is not reversion, but partly expression of the nature and perhaps the needs of this stage of immaturity, and partly the same instinct of revolt against uniformity imposed from without, which rob life of variety and extinguish the spirit of adventure and untrammeled freedom, and make the savage hard to break to the harness of civilization. The hunger for fatigue, too, can become a veritable passion and is quite distinct from either the impulse for activity for its own sake or the desire of achievement. To shout and put forth the utmost possible strength in crude ways is erethic intoxication at a stage when every tissue can become erectile and seems, like the crying of infants, to have a legitimate function in causing tension and flushing, enlarging the caliber of blood vessels, and forcing the blood perhaps even to the point of extravasation to irrigate newly growing fibers, cells, and organs which atrophy if not thus fed. When penalty, fear, anger, consolation, divine service, symbolic maturity is complete this need abates. If this be correct, the phenomenon of second breath, so	• Videogames can, perhaps, can keep teenagers mentally active, free from fatigue. • Exercise and physical activity can help keep the blood flowing in teenagers. • Teenage boys, naturally, may often fight. Videogames may either push a teenager to be more violent, or may help to inhibit this behavior, keeping these violent urges contained within the confines of a television or computer screen.

(continued)

Source C: Excerpt, Youth (G. Stanley Hall)	Our Thoughts
characteristic of adolescence, and one factor in the inebriate's propensity, is ontogenetic expression of a rhythm trait of a long racial period. Youth needs over-exertion to compensate for underexertion, to under-sleep in order to offset oversleep at times. This seems to be nature's provision to expand in all directions its possibilities of the body and soul in this plastic period when, without this occasional excess, powers would atrophy or suffer arrest for want of use, or larger pos-sibilities world not be realized without this regimen peculiar to nascent periods. This is treated more fully elsewhere. Perhaps next to dancing in phyletic motivation come personal conflicts, such as wrestling, fighting, box-ing, dueling, and in some sense, hunting. The animal world is full of struggle for survival, and primitive warfare is a wager of battle, of personal combat of foes contesting eye to eye and hand to hand, where victory of one is the defeat and perhaps death of the other, and where life is often staked against life. In its more brutal forms we see one of the most degrad-ing of all the aspects of human nature. Burk[10] has shown how the most bestial of these instincts survive and crop out irresistibly in boyhood, where fights are often engaged in with desperate abandon. Noses are bitten, ears torn, sensitive places kicked, hair pulled, arms twisted, the head stamped on and pounded on stones, fingers twisted, and hoodlums sometimes deliberately try to strangle, gouge out an eye, pull off an ear, pull out the tongue, break teeth, nose, or bones, or dislocate jaws or other joints, wring the neck, bite off a lip, and torture in utterly nameless ways. In unrestrained anger, man becomes a demon in love with the blood of his victim. The face is distorted, and there are yells, oaths, animal snorts and grunts, cries, and then exultant laughter at pain, and each is bruised, dirty, disheveled and panting with exhaustion. For coarser natures,	

(continued)

Source C: Excerpt, Youth (G. Stanley Hall)	Our Thoughts
the spectacle of such conflicts has an intense attraction, while some morbid souls are scared by a distinct phobia for everything suggestive of even lower degrees of opposition. These instincts, more or less developed in boyhood, are repressed in normal cases before strength and skill are sufficiently developed to inflict serious bodily injury, while without the reductives that orthogenetic growth brings they become criminal. Repulsive as are these grosser and animal manifestations of anger, its impulsion can not and should not be eliminated, but its expression transformed and directed toward evils that need all its antagonism. To be angry aright is a good part of moral education, and non-resistance under all provocations is unmanly, craven, and cowardly.[11] An able-bodied young man, who can not fight physically, can hardly have a high and true sense of honor, and is generally a milksop, a lady-boy, or sneak. He lacks virility, his masculinity does not ring true, his honesty can not be sound to the core. Hence, instead of eradicating this instinct, one of the great problems of physical and moral pedagogy is rightly to temper and direct it.	

It should be clear to you by this time that Source C is quite different from the previous two in that it seems to be written much longer ago that the more contemporary video and images in Sources A and B. We must remember that Hall's "facts" are certainly biased, but that does not mean that they are not useful. The success of G. Stanley Hall's piece is that he is able to appeal, quite successfully, to the reader's sense of logic. The phrases used throughout this excerpt are extremely scientific, and almost clinical in tone.

Moreover, Hall is also able to use firsthand observations of youth to make his assertions throughout his writing. Source A makes it clear that violence in our videogames can often be seen subjectively, as does Source B. Source B, moreover, addresses key opposite points that we must consider when developing an answer to the question, "Do videogames contribute to violence among teens in America?"

At this point in our analysis of the three pieces, it is time to come to a decision as to where we stand on the issue of violence in videogames. As we have suggested throughout this book, we think it is important, if not critical, that you answer this question based upon the facts of the sources rather than your own emotions. Therefore, in our analysis of the videogame texts, we choose to answer the question in the negative: Videogames do not cause teens in America to become more violent. This conclusion is based upon the observation that Sources A and B grapple with the question of videogames and violence by addressing the range that exists amongst the genres of videogames that exist, whereas Source C, while still persuasive, is centered more on observations that can be used to support one's point further as well.

Now that we have our thesis statement in mind, let's refer back to the writing prompt (reproduced below):

RSI #1: Videogames

85 minutes

Sony PlayStation. Wii. X-Box. It seems as though videogames are becoming an ever-increasing form of entertainment in our country. Advocates of videogames claim that it is a harmless form of entertainment, while others view videogames as contributing to violence.

You have reviewed three sources regarding the benefits and drawbacks of videogames. These three pieces provide information to begin drafting your own argument.

- **Source A:** Video, History of Gaming, *http://vimeo.com/18743950*

- **Source B:** Image, Frits Ahlefeldt, *HikingArtist.com*

- **Source C:** Excerpt, *Youth* (G. Stanley Hall)

Do videogames contribute to violence among teens in America? Write a persuasive piece that addresses the question and supports your position with evidence from at least two of the three sources. Be sure to acknowledge competing views. You may give examples from past and current events or issues to illustrate and clarify your position. You may refer to the sources by their titles (Source A, Source B, Source C).

At this point, we should be very ready to tackle this essay topic, but let's take a closer look at what the prompt is actually asking of us. In our many years of teaching, we have seen too many students do poorly on an assessment because they either (a) didn't understand the prompt, or (b) didn't do exactly what the prompt required. On the PARCC, we cannot afford to make these mistakes. Below are eleven specific steps you can take to ensure success.

11 Steps for Success on the RST

Before Writing Begins

Step #1:   Read through the question carefully. Make sure to decipher if the question is asking you to convey an opinion, or to convey information/research objectively.

- *The question is asking us to convey an opinion.*

Step #2:   Simplify what the question is asking you to do. Put the question/task into your own words.

- *The prompt is asking this: "Do I think that videogames contribute to teen violence in America?"*

Step #3:   Circle the minimum amount of sources that need to be addressed.

- *Two sources*

Step #4:   Take notes with each of the sources. Address the source's main points. Underline actively.

- *We completed this activity extensively in our two-column approach and when we took notes on the video.*

Step #5:   After you've addressed and highlighted the main point of the source, make separate notes on the reliability of these sources. Is the source reliable in general? Is it slanted in any way? Do logical fallacies or "holes in argument" exist?

- *We took notes on the reliability of sources in our active reading.*

Step #6: You've read through your sources. Choose the sources that you are most comfortable with, and put an asterisk (*) next to them.

- *Clearly, we will be primarily working with Sources A & B. We have asterisked them above.*

Writing the RST

Step #7: Copy the arguments—textual evidence—you will use in your essay into the prewriting chart. (shown below)

Step #8: Now, look at the relationships among your sources. Do they agree with each other? Do they disagree? Use your source-relationship chart to begin thinking about how you will have your sources begin conversing with one another. (shown below)

Step #9: Compose a quick outline of your essay (shown below)

Step #10: Complete your essay using the framework/outline as a guide. (shown below)

Step #11: After you have completed your essay, go back to check that your sources have a conversation, and replace the verbs you've used to integrate these sources with the action verbs from the sheet provided. (shown below)

Now that we have completed Steps 1–6, it is time for us to really start writing. For the RST, we have designed a graphic organizer for you to use to structure the writing process. We feel that this organizer is important because it serves one critical aspect of the RST writing task: Getting your sources "talking to each other." This skill of getting your sources "talking" is a key feature of the RST and is representative of all good writing that synthesizes information. Let's look at our prewriting chart:

Topic: Do videogames contribute to violence among teens in America?

My Thesis Statement: It is a false notion to believe that videogames contribute to violence in teens.

Source A	Source B	Source C
Video Evolution (video clip)	Videogame Image (photograph)	Excerpt, *Youth*
The first contraption looks almost prehistoric. Pac-man is a game that serves as a childhood memory for many. As the movie continues forward, one can see the change in technology, and especially, the major change in vibrant colors, graphics, and concepts upon the ever-evolving television screen. Characters become more and more lifelike. Violence exists, though, on a more and more detailed scale. What was once just a point-and-shoot game has turned into a more interactive battle between the player and the characters on their screen. This should be strongly noted. It is also obvious that such games, as in the golf video game, will help a teenager's dexterity and motor skills.	Image It is clear that the second image portrays videogames in a very negative light. The blame is put on videogames and less on the players themselves. So, the videogame's content is viewed as being in control, harming our teenagers as a result.	It is clear that Hall explains the need to complete a variety of physical activities. Games are strongly encouraged, at a very young age. While Hall does not explain videogames specifically, one could argue that videogames certainly serve as games themselves. The importance of physical activities remains paramount in a child's life. This source certainly is a little confusing, due to its slightly outdated language. The sentiment remains the same, however. Physical activity and mentality of mind of work hand-in-hand with one another. The writer here, Hall, explains the importance of performing one's social duties. Videogames can contribute to a teenager's social direction. Videogames can, perhaps, can keep teenagers mentally active, free from fatigue. Exercise and physical activity can help the blood flowing in teenagers. Teenage boys, naturally, may often fight. Videogames may either push a teenager to be more violent, or may help to inhibit this behavior, keeping these violent urges through the confines of a television or computer screen.

Exactly how do the sources talk with each other?

On the point of violence in America, Sources A and B both help the student infer that violence amongst American youth is quite subjective, and the answer is not clear. Therefore, both sources do a great job in relaying that videogames may do just the opposite, help with one's creativity, and the notion of violence may be a misperception. Consequently, it is easy and erroneous to make the claim that videogames are making our teens more violent.

A note on validity: All sources may be questionable in nature. While Source A seems to be created by technology workers in their field, we do not know who has created Source B, and Source C is obviously antiquated. We must remember how each addresses the topic in our contemporary perspective.

As you can see, we have tackled steps seven and eight. The amount of prewriting we completed with these steps will be of great benefit to us as we compose a response to the RST. For now, however, we must move on to Step 9: Making an Outline. Please note that our outline need not be "formal" or overly detailed. We just need to do enough in order to provide structure and organization to our own writing. Look at our sample below:

Sample Outline for Videogame RST

I. Introduction

    a. Attention grabber

    b. Thesis statement: It is a false notion to believe that videogames contribute to violence in teens.

II. Body

    a. Argument A: The Misperception of Violence

    b. Argument B: The Facts about Videogames and Violence

III. Conclusion

    a. Reworking of thesis

    b. Answering the So What? Question (What is really important about the thesis of this paper?)

Step 10: Writing the Essay

Now that we have completed all the necessary steps for the RST, it is time to actually do the essay writing. What we want you to note at this point in the process is that a majority of the work of our writing has already been completed. The actual writing of the RST essay should be quite easy. Here is our sample below.

Turn on the evening news and there you have it: another example of someone committing a violent crime. Turn on the news app on your handheld phone, and, once again, there you have it: an even more sad case of violent crime. In today's America, violence seems to be ubiquitous; it seems to be the norm. In the midst of this seeming chaos, it is human nature to find a scapegoat for our failings as a culture: that scapegoat would be videogames. However, when one looks at the research, it becomes clear that our media are creating a false reality and that, in fact, videogames do not make people more violent. Based upon the information presented, it is a false notion to believe that videogames contribute to violence in teens.

America lives in a false reality. We believe that violence is on the rise and that videogames are the culprit. A look at our sources, however, paints a different story. One can clearly note that Sources A and B can provide one with the benefits that exist as a result of videogames. How can it be that videogames are causing America's teens to be more violent when so many opportunities for creativity exist? From the growth in vibrant colors to the vast variety of genres, videogames truly provide something for every teenager. Teenagers may be introduced to new sports, can work on their own dexterity, and can build upon teenager's own strategic skills in using their own inference skills to solve virtual puzzles and to navigate through the twists and turns upon one's gaming world. Look at the vibrant colors and intricate details of each screen! If nothing else, videogames should provide interesting entertainment for all types of teenagers. As a result, the answer is clear: Videogames are not making teens violent. As much as one would like to blame videogames for our country's perceived violent tendencies, the facts do not coincide.

Further, by looking at through Hall's observation (Source C) of youngsters, it is clear that he makes an argument in support of the importance of physical activity for our youth. While he cites gymnastics and dancing as possible activities, he mentions the importance of playing games. One must keep in mind that it is very much possible for a teenager to find a balance between physical activity and mental activity through videogames. While the second image in Source B clearly depicts the violence in some videogames, this is certainly not an absolute. Source A exhibits the vast variety of game genres that exist to our current teenagers in America. They can learn how to play golf. They can work through puzzles. They can learn strategy. Videogames allow teenagers to apply their interests and creative explorations to this variety of gaming scenarios, and as a result, one is left to remember that things, especially for teenagers, are best in moderation. Finding a balance between physical and mental activities may be paramount to the development of the American teenager.

There is an old saying that goes, "Perception is reality." While to a certain degree this adage might be true, it is the purpose of science to find truth and to debunk myths. In the case of the misperception that violent videogames cause teenagers to be violent, the research is unequivocally clear: the answer is a resounding, "No!" Videogames do not cause teenagers to be violent; they do not even cause most students to have behavioral problems at school. As this essay has made clear, other factors are at play. If America wants to find the cause of the seemingly endless violence portrayed on the media, it needs to look someplace else.

Step 11: Looking at the Verbs

Now that we have completed the essay, it is time to consider our last step, number 11: the use of active verbs. After a combined 25 years in education, we have learned that the key to quality writing is contained within the verbs. Using precise, descriptive action verbs is a sure way to improve the value of what you have written. This list is presented to you in Appendix A. Look back through the sample essay. Did the author do an adequate job with the action verbs? Which ones would you change?

Analysis of Sample Essay

You may have been wondering through this entire process, "How will the PARCC grade my essay?" Well, we're glad you asked because we will address it now. In terms of the writing task you will complete on the test, the PARCC has defined quality written expression in four categories:

1. Development of Ideas,

2. Organization,

3. Clarity of Language,

4. Knowledge of Language and Conventions.

By "Development of Ideas," the makers of the PARCC refer to the ways in which arguments are developed and maintained throughout the course of the essay. Some questions might be:

> "Did the author use evidence from the text?"

> "Did this evidence come from more than one source?"

> "Did the author successfully have the two sources interact with each other?"

As you can see, these questions are quite difficult and will take time for you to master. However, you can see these principles in action if you read carefully through our sample essay above. We did cite evidence from both sources. We did have the two sources interact with each other. Both Source A (Video) and Source B (Images) are used together as evidence against violence and videogames. One source complements and feeds off the other.

Second, the PARCC will look at the organization of your writing. This, in fact, should come as no surprise at all for you. Organization is a key facet of all good writing, regardless of where it is done. By virtue of the fact that we meticulously followed our outline, we organized our work. The three main parts of the essay are clearly present:

> Introduction,

> body, and

> conclusion.

The next criterion, "clarity of language," will look at your writing style and the effectiveness of that style. "What is writing style?" you may ask? It deals with the author's ability to effectively use vocabulary, including content-specific words, to utilize vivid and proper description, and to appropriately use transitional words throughout the piece. Style, then, is nothing more than the writer's identity on paper. What the PARCC cares about most is simple: Is your style clear, concise, and to the point? There is nothing worse than reading an essay that lacks clarity and is difficult to read because the writer lacks a command of language.

Looking at our sample essay:

> What would you say of the style? Look back at our choice of vocabulary: Did we use vocabulary terms that were appropriate to research and statistics?

Were our descriptions of the research sources clear?

Was any of the wording ambiguous and difficult to comprehend?

Could something we wrote have been written clearer?

All of these questions are great starting points when looking at style.

Lastly, the PARCC will consider your knowledge of language and conventions. This is where your knowledge of grammar, mechanics, and usage will come to play.

Were there any mistakes in these three categories?

Did the author go back and edit the work? Does the work read effortlessly?

Does poor grammar become a distraction or a nuisance?

Our sample essay, we believe, does pretty well in this area, and provides to you, a RST essay that is free of grammatical issues and reads as thought it were edited (which it was!).

In order to assist you in the skill of evaluating writing, we have included a checklist for you based upon PARCC writing standards. In addition, we have also included the PARCC rubric. You might wish score our sample essay using the rubric.

Summary of the RST in English

We have covered a great many skills and issues in this chapter concerning the RST, including the skills involved, the necessary steps in terms of reading and prewriting, and the structure and organization of a model essay. We are under no delusions that this task is easy, but we are absolutely certain that the more you follow our 11 steps and the more you practice getting your sources "talking," the better you will be at the RST task.

In the interest of helping you achieve success on the RST in English, we are giving you three sample essay prompts with the accompanying graphic organizers for you to use. You are about to venture on a highly productive journey. Refer back often to our model essay and when you first start, try not to skip any of the 11 steps. One last thing: We have said this numerous times in this book: Your ability to write well depends upon your ability to read well. Make sure you read and understand the texts before you begin any of the writing work.

CCSS Alignment	
RL.1	Cite strong and textual evidence.
RL.5	Analyze how an author's choices contribute to its overall structure.
RI.7	Integrate and evaluate multiple sources of information presented in different media or formats (e.g., visually, quantitatively) as well as in words in order to address a question or solve a problem.
L.1	Demonstrate command of the conventions of standard English grammar and usage when writing.
L.3	Apply knowledge of language to understand how language functions in different contexts.
L.5	Demonstrate understanding of figurative language, word relationships, and nuances in word meanings.
W.1	Write arguments to support claims in an analysis of substantive topics or texts, using valid reasoning and relevant and sufficient evidence.
W.2	Write informative/explanatory texts to examine and convey complex ideas, concepts, and information clearly and accurately through the effective selection, organization, and analysis of content.
W.5	Develop and strengthen writing as needed by planning, revising, editing, and rewriting.
W.6	Use technology to produce, publish, and update individual writing products.

RST #2: Love at First Sight, inspired by Shakespeare's *Romeo and Juliet*

85 minutes

One of the enduring themes of Shakespeare's *Romeo and Juliet* is the idea of love at first sight. While Romeo and Juliet undoubtedly believe that they fell in love with each other, skeptics do have their doubts. 500 years after the play was written, people still contend with the idea of "love at first sight." What do you think?

You have reviewed four sources regarding love at first sight. These four texts provide information to begin drafting your own argument.

- **Source A:** On Courtship and Marriage, *www.gutenberg.org/files/35963*
- **Source B:** Five Good Reasons Why You Can Believe Love at First Sight
- **Source C:** Why Do People Divorce?
- **Source D:** Excerpt from *Romeo and Juliet*, William Shakespeare

Does love at first sight really exist? Write a persuasive piece that addresses the question and supports your position with evidence from at least three of the four sources. Be sure to acknowledge competing views. You may give examples from past and current events or issues to illustrate and clarify your position. You may refer to the sources by their titles (Source A, Source B, Source C, Source D).

SOURCE A: Anchor Text

"On Courtship and Marriage"	My Thought Processes
I do not feel that any apology is required for my desire to linger a little over that old-fashioned yet ever-new phase of life known as courting days. It is one which is oftener made a jest of than a serious study; yet such is its perennial freshness and interest for men and women, that it can never become threadbare; and though there cannot be much left that is new or original to say about it, yet a few thoughts from a woman's point of view may not be altogether unacceptable. We are constantly being told that we live in a hard, prosaic age, that romance has no place in our century, and that the rush and the fever of life have left but little time or inclination for the old-time grace and leisure with which our grandfathers and grandmothers loved, wooed, and wed.	

(continued)

"On Courtship and Marriage"	My Thought Processes
This study of human nature is my business, and it appears to me that the world is very much as it was—that Eden is still possible to those who are fit for it; and it is beyond question that love, courtship, and marriage are words to conjure with in the garden of youth, and that a love-story has yet the power to charm even sober men and women of middle age, for whom romance is mistakenly supposed to be over.	
Every man goes to woo in his own way, and the woman he woos is apt to think it the best way in the world; it would be superfluous for a mere outsider to criticise it. Examples might be multiplied; in the novels we read we have variety and to spare. We know the types well. Let me enumerate a few. The diffident youth, weighed down with a sense of his own unworthiness, approaching his divinity with a blush and a stammer; and in some extreme cases—these much affected by the novelists of an earlier decade—going down upon his knees; the bold wooer, who believes in storming the citadel, and is visited by no misgiving qualms; the cautious one, who counts the cost, and tries to make sure of his answer beforehand, —the only case in which I believe that a woman has a right to exercise the qualities of the coquette; then we have also the victim of extreme shyness, who would never come to the point at all without a little assistance from the other side. There are other types, —the schemer and the self-seeker, whose matrimonial ventures are only intended to advance worldly interests. We need not begin to dissect them—it would not be a profitable occupation.	
Well, while not seeking or attempting to lay down rules or offer any proposition as final, there are sundry large and general principles which may be touched upon to aid us in looking at this interesting subject from a sympathetic and common sense point of view.	
Most people, looking back, think their own romance the most beautiful in the world, even if it sometimes lacked that dignity which the onlooker thought desirable.	

(continued)

"On Courtship and Marriage"	My Thought Processes
It is a crisis in the life of a young maiden when she becomes conscious for the first time that she is an object of special interest to a member of the opposite sex; that interest being conveyed in a thousand delicate yet unmistakable ways, which cause a strange flutter at her heart, and make her examine her own feelings to find whether there be a responsive chord. The modest, sensible, womanly girl, who is not yet extinct, in spite of sundry croakers, will know much better than anybody can tell her how to adjust her own conduct at this crisis in her life. Her own innate delicacy and niceness of perception will guide her how to act, and if the attentions be acceptable to her she will give just the right need of encouragement, so that the course of true love may run smoothly towards consummation. Of course the usual squalls and cross currents must be looked for—else would that delightful period of life be robbed of its chief zest and charm, to say nothing of the unhappy novelist's occupation, which would undoubtedly be gone for ever. There have occasionally been discussions as to the desirability of long engagements, and there are sufficient arguments both for and against; but the best course appears to be, as in most other affairs of life, to try and strike the happy medium. Of necessity, circumstances alter cases. When the young pair have known each other for a long period of years, and there are no obstacles in the way, the long engagement is then superfluous.	

SOURCE B

Five Good Reasons Why You Can Believe Love at First Sight	My Thought Processes
Five Good Reasons Why You Can Believe Love at First Sight **Statistics Back Up Love at First Sight** By s.e. Jones You hear a lot about people falling in love at first sight; whether in a crowded room, on a busy sidewalk, sitting in a desolate park or simply doing nothing more than trying to get from one place to another. Becki Newton, the actress that plays Amanda on the television show "Ugly Betty," recently revealed that she met the man that would become her husband on a subway platform as the two were doing nothing more than passing one another on the way to somewhere else. But then their eyes met, and that was all it took. Now, Earl Naumann's book, *Love at First Sight: The Stories and Science Behind Instant Attraction*, takes a look at not only the social beliefs in instant attraction, but at some of the science behind the experiences that back up his claim that there truly is love at first sight, and it is something almost magical in that it's not only true, but it seems to be felt stronger and last longer than other types of love. Below are ten reasons given by Naumann and others working in the field on why you should believe in love at first sight. **1. Because of anecdotal evidence.** In other words, nearly everyone knows someone, or is someone that has seen it firsthand. **2. Because surveys have been done that show it to be true.** In the early 70's several surveys were done that when combined showed that nearly 30% of people in relationships claimed to have fallen in love at first sight. Twenty years later, Naumann did a similar survey and came up with even stronger results, finding that nearly two-thirds of respondents believed in love at first sight and more than half claimed to have experienced it.	

(continued)

Five Good Reasons Why You Can Believe Love at First Sight	My Thought Processes
3. Because science has shown that it's actually more than just love at first "sight." Social scientists and biologist have discovered over the years that instant attraction is more than just what one sees. It's a combination of many stimuli such as smell and the ingestion of pheromones as well as difficult to study, but easy to recognize, that special something one person discovers in another's eyes.	
4. Because it stays. While doing his research, Naumann discovered that not only do people find themselves very nearly instantly attracted to one another, but that the attraction they feel isn't fleeting. In fact, he found that 55% of those that were married had met that way, and over 75% of those were still married, which seems to imply that those that marry after falling in love at first sight, stay married longer and have happier marriages than those that do not.	
5. Because you believe in your heart that it's true. And that is nothing to be taken lightly.	
These five good reasons on why you can believe that falling in love at first sight is not just for those hopeless romantics out there pining away as they wait for that perfect someone to cross their path, but for anyone who holds faith in the human race, and are struggling to cling to the silly notion that there truly are magical and mysterious elements out there; things that can stop us dead in our tracks and make our heats skip a beat or two. If you are someone who has been fortunate to have fallen in love at first sight with someone, and vice-versa, I hope you keep it as the precious gift that it is.	

SOURCE C

Why Do People Divorce?	My Thought Processes
Why Do People Divorce? People who were seeking a divorce were asked to tell the most important reasons that brought them to this decision Don't know each other any more Little real conversations Money troubles Physical/mental illness Major negative event Cheating with someone else One person's selfishness Substance abuse Disagreements over children Mother-in-law problems Physical abuse Work more important	

SOURCE D

Excerpt from *Romeo and Juliet*	My thought Processes
ROMEO [To a Servingman] What lady is that, which doth enrich the hand Of yonder knight? 40 SERVENT I know not, sir. ROMEO O, she doth teach the torches to burn bright! It seems she hangs upon the cheek of night Like a rich jewel in an Ethiope's ear; Beauty too rich for use, for earth too dear! So shows a snowy dove trooping with crows, As yonder lady o'er her fellows shows. The measure done, I'll watch her place of stand, And, touching hers, make blessed my rude hand. Did my heart love till now? Forswear it, sight! For I ne'er saw true beauty till this night. 51	

Prewriting

RST Graphic Organizer

Topic:

My Thesis Statement:

Source A	Source B	Source C

Exactly how do the sources talk with each other?

Your Outline:

Write your essay in a notebook or on loose-leaf paper and then check the Scoring Checklist and the Scoring Rubric found at the back of the book.

CCSS Alignment	
RL.1	Cite strong and textual evidence.
RL.5	Analyze how an author's choices contribute to its overall structure.
RI.7	Integrate and evaluate multiple sources of information presented in different media or formats (e.g., visually, quantitatively) as well as in words in order to address a question or solve a problem.
L.1	Demonstrate command of the conventions of standard English grammar and usage when writing.
L.3	Apply knowledge of language to understand how language functions in different contexts.
L.5	Demonstrate understanding of figurative language, word relationships, and nuances in word meanings.
W.1	Write arguments to support claims in an analysis of substantive topics or texts, using valid reasoning and relevant and sufficient evidence.
W.2	Write informative/explanatory texts to examine and convey complex ideas, concepts, and information clearly and accurately through the effective selection, organization, and analysis of content.
W.5	Develop and strengthen writing as needed by planning, revising, editing, and rewriting.
W.6	Use technology to produce, publish, and update individual writing products.

RST #3: F. Scott Fitzgerald

85 minutes

Few writers of the 20th century had a more significant impact on American literary culture than F. Scott Fitzgerald. Through works such as *The Great Gatsby* and *This Side of Paradise*, Fitzgerald was able to capture the hopes and dreams of the 1920s, which he coined The Jazz Age.

- **Source A:** F. Scott Fitzgerald: Tales from the Jazz Age," *www.gutenberg.org/cache/epub/6695.html* (Anchor Text)

- **Source B:** F. Scott Fitzgerald biography (*www.biography.com/people/f-scott-fitzgerald-9296261*)

- **Source C:** F. Scott Fitzgerald: Encyclopedia of American Literature

Consider the arguments that these three texts use in their characterization of F. Scott Fitzgerald's contribution to American culture. Write an informative piece that addresses the question, "What is F. Scott Fitzgerald's contribution to American culture?" and supports your position with evidence from at least two of the three sources. Be sure to acknowledge competing views. You may give examples from past and current events or issues to illustrate and clarify your position. You may refer to the sources by their titles (Source A, Source B, Source C).

SOURCE A: Anchor Text

Excerpt: Tales from the Jazz Age	My Thought Processes
F. Scott Fitzgerald: "May Day" There had been a war fought and won and the great city of the conquering people was crossed with triumphal arches and vivid with thrown flowers of white, red, and rose. All through the long spring days the returning soldiers marched up the chief highway behind the strump of drums and the joyous, resonant wind of the brasses, while merchants and clerks left their bickerings and figurings and, crowding to the windows, turned their white-bunched faces gravely upon the passing battalions. Never had there been such splendor in the great city, for the victorious war had brought plenty in its train, and the merchants had flocked thither from the South and West with their households to taste of all the luscious feasts and witness the lavish entertainments prepared—and to buy for their women furs against the next winter and bags of golden mesh and varicolored slippers of silk and silver and rose satin and cloth of gold. So gaily and noisily were the peace and prosperity impending hymned by the scribes and poets of the conquering people that more and more spenders had gathered from the provinces to drink the wine of excitement, and faster and faster did the merchants dispose of their trinkets and slippers until they sent up a mighty cry for more trinkets and more slippers in order that they might give in barter what was demanded of them. Some even of them flung up their hands helplessly, shouting: "Alas! I have no more slippers! and alas! I have no more trinkets! May heaven help me for I know not what I shall do!"	

(continued)

Excerpt: Tales from the Jazz Age	My Thought Processes
But no one listened to their great outcry, for the throngs were far too busy—day by day, the foot-soldiers trod jauntily the highway and all exulted because the young men returning were pure and brave, sound of tooth and pink of cheek, and the young women of the land were virgins and comely both of face and of figure. So during all this time there were many adventures that happened in the great city, and, of these, several—or perhaps one—are here set down. **I** At nine o'clock on the morning of the first of May, 1919, a young man spoke to the room clerk at the Biltmore Hotel, asking if Mr. Philip Dean were registered there, and if so, could he be connected with Mr. Dean's rooms. The inquirer was dressed in a well-cut, shabby suit. He was small, slender, and darkly handsome; his eyes were framed above with unusually long eyelashes and below with the blue semicircle of ill health, this latter effect heightened by an unnatural glow which colored his face like a low, incessant fever. Mr. Dean was staying there. The young man was directed to a telephone at the side. After a second his connection was made; a sleepy voice hello'd from somewhere above. "Mr. Dean?"—this very eagerly—"it's Gordon, Phil. It's Gordon Sterrett. I'm down-stairs. I heard you were in New York and I had a hunch you'd be here." The sleepy voice became gradually enthusiastic. Well, how was Gordy, old boy! Well, he certainly was surprised and tickled! Would Gordy come right up, for Pete's sake!	

(continued)

Excerpt: Tales from the Jazz Age	My Thought Processes
A few minutes later Philip Dean, dressed in blue silk pajamas, opened his door and the two young men greeted each other with a half-embarrassed exuberance. They were both about twenty-four, Yale graduates of the year before the war; but there the resemblance stopped abruptly. Dean was blond, ruddy, and rugged under his thin pajamas. Everything about him radiated fitness and bodily comfort. He smiled frequently, showing large and prominent teeth.	
"I was going to look you up," he cried enthusiastically. "I'm taking a couple of weeks off. If you'll sit down a sec I'll be right with you. Going to take a shower."	
As he vanished into the bathroom his visitor's dark eyes roved nervously around the room, resting for a moment on a great English travelling bag in the corner and on a family of thick silk shirts littered on the chairs amid impressive neckties and soft woollen socks.	
Gordon rose and, picking up one of the shirts, gave it a minute examination. It was of very heavy silk, yellow, with a pale blue stripe—and there were nearly a dozen of them. He stared involuntarily at his own shirt-cuffs—they were ragged and linty at the edges and soiled to a faint gray. Dropping the silk shirt, he held his coat-sleeves down and worked the frayed shirt-cuffs up till they were out of sight. Then he went to the mirror and looked at himself with listless, unhappy interest. His tie, of former glory, was faded and thumb-creased—it served no longer to hide the jagged buttonholes of his collar. He thought, quite without amusement, that only three years before he had received a scattering vote in the senior elections at college for being the best-dressed man in his class.	
Dean emerged from the bathroom polishing his body.	
"Saw an old friend of yours last night," he remarked. "Passed her in the lobby and couldn't think of her name to save my neck. That girl you brought up to New Haven senior year."	

(continued)

Excerpt: Tales from the Jazz Age	My Thought Processes
Gordon started. "Edith Bradin? That whom you mean?" "'At's the one. Damn good looking. She's still sort of a pretty doll—you know what I mean: as if you touched her she'd smear." He surveyed his shining self complacently in the mirror, smiled faintly, exposing a section of teeth. "She must be twenty-three anyway," he continued. "Twenty-two last month," said Gordon absently. "What? Oh, last month. Well, I imagine she's down for the Gamma Psi dance. Did you know we're having a Yale Gamma Psi dance to-night at Delmonico's? You better come up, Gordy. Half of New Haven'll probably be there. I can get you an invitation." Draping himself reluctantly in fresh underwear, Dean lit a cigarette and sat down by the open window, inspecting his calves and knees under the morning sunshine which poured into the room. "Sit down, Gordy," he suggested, "and tell me all about what you've been doing and what you're doing now and everything." Gordon collapsed unexpectedly upon the bed; lay there inert and spiritless. His mouth, which habitually dropped a little open when his face was in repose, became suddenly helpless and pathetic. "What's the matter?" asked Dean quickly. "Oh, God!" "What's the matter?" "Every God damn thing in the world," he said miserably, "I've absolutely gone to pieces, Phil. I'm all in." "Huh?" "I'm all in." His voice was shaking. Dean scrutinized him more closely with appraising blue eyes.	

(continued)

Excerpt: Tales from the Jazz Age	My Thought Processes
"You certainly look all shot."	
"I am. I've made a hell of a mess of everything." He paused. "I'd better start at the beginning—or will it bore you?"	
"Not at all; go on." There was, however, a hesitant note in Dean's voice. This trip East had been planned for a holiday—to find Gordon Sterrett in trouble exasperated him a little.	
"Go on," he repeated, and then added half under his breath, "Get it over with."	
"Well," began Gordon unsteadily, "I got back from France in February, went home to Harrisburg for a month, and then came down to New York to get a job. I got one—with an export company. They fired me yesterday."	
"Fired you?"	
"I'm coming to that, Phil. I want to tell you frankly. You're about the only man I can turn to in a matter like this. You won't mind if I just tell you frankly, will you, Phil?"	
Dean stiffened a bit more. The pats he was bestowing on his knees grew perfunctory. He felt vaguely that he was being unfairly saddled with responsibility; he was not even sure he wanted to be told. Though never surprised at finding Gordon Sterrett in mild difficulty, there was something in this present misery that repelled him and hardened him, even though it excited his curiosity.	
"Go on."	
"It's a girl."	
"Hm." Dean resolved that nothing was going to spoil his trip. If Gordon was going to be depressing, then he'd have to see less of Gordon.	

(continued)

Excerpt: Tales from the Jazz Age	My Thought Processes
"Her name is Jewel Hudson," went on the distressed voice from the bed. "She used to be 'pure,' I guess, up to about a year ago. Lived here in New York—poor family. Her people are dead now and she lives with an old aunt. You see it was just about the time I met her that everybody began to come back from France in droves—and all I did was to welcome the newly arrived and go on parties with 'em. That's the way it started, Phil, just from being glad to see everybody and having them glad to see me." "You ought to've had more sense." "I know," Gordon paused, and then continued listlessly. "I'm on my own now, you know, and Phil, I can't stand being poor. Then came this darn girl. She sort of fell in love with me for a while and, though I never intended to get so involved, I'd always seem to run into her somewhere. You can imagine the sort of work I was doing for those exporting people—of course, I always intended to draw; do illustrating for magazines; there's a pile of money in it."	

SOURCE B

Summary of Video: F. Scott Fitzgerald biography

This video clip chronicles the life and works of a writer who has come to embody the 1920s, F. Scott Fitzgerald. Fitzgerald started his writing career at Princeton University, where eventually he was forced to drop out after three years due to poor academic performance. In 1917, Fitzgerald met his wife, Zelda. She refused to marry Fitzgerald until he proved he could support her financially. Moving to New York City, Fitzgerald published his first novel, This Side of Paradise, *which was an instant success and made him very wealthy. Next, Fitzgerald, with his wife, Zelda, and their daughter, Frances, moved to France, where he finished his greatest work,* The Great Gatsby. *Fitzgerald died of a heart attack on December 21st, 1940.*

F. Scott Fitzgerald biography:
http://www.biography.com/people/f-scott-fitzgerald-9296261

My Notes

SOURCE C

Scott Fitzgerald: Encyclopedia of American Literature	My Thought Processes
Fitzgerald, F. Scott **Also known as:** Francis Scott Key Fitzgerald **Born:** 1896 **Died:** 1940 American novelist, short story writer **From:** *Encyclopedia of American Literature: Into the Modern, 1896–1945*, vol. 3, Revised Edition.  *. . . sometimes I think the impersonal and objective quality of my talent, and the sacrifices of it, in pieces, to preserve its essential value has some sort of epic grandeur.* —letter to Scottie Fitzgerald The dominant influences on F. Scott Fitzgerald's life and career were literature, Princeton, aspiration, money, alcohol, and his wife, Zelda Sayre Fitzgerald. He grew up in St. Paul, Minnesota, and was raised a Catholic but left the Church in his twenties. The son of an unsuccessful businessman, Fitzgerald developed in his boyhood and at school intense feelings about wealth and the American class system, which he wrote into his fiction.	

(continued)

Scott Fitzgerald: Encyclopedia of American Literature	My Thought Processes
After Newman, a New Jersey Catholic prep school, Fitzgerald entered Princeton as a member of the Class of 1917. At college he neglected his studies in order to serve a literary apprenticeship. He wrote for the *Nassau Literary Magazine* and the *Tiger* humor magazine, and he provided the lyrics for three Triangle Club musicals. He was about to flunk out of college when he took an army commission in 1917; to his lasting regret he did not experience battle. In the army he wrote a novel, which he rewrote as *This Side of Paradise*. Stationed at Camp Sheridan, Alabama, he fell in love with an archetypal Southern belle, Zelda Sayre. [. . .] During his lifetime his fiction was underrated or dismissed as trivial because the reputation-makers regarded his characters and their values as trivial. He was better known and more widely read as the author of popular magazine stories—which provided most of his income—than as a novelist. His brilliant style, wit, warm tone, and the poetry of his prose were regarded as facile; he was labeled an irresponsible writer who had squandered his gifts to make money. But Fitzgerald was a painstaking writer and rewriter who labored to achieve readability and emotional power. He was a hard-working professional with high literary ambitions who published four novels, a play, and four volumes of short stories between 1920 and 1935. One of the glamor figures in American literature, Fitzgerald achieved success and celebrity with his first novel, *This Side of Paradise* (1920), set at Princeton, and embarked on an extravagant life with his eccentric wife. Despite his alcoholism and the strain of her eventual insanity, he published two masterpiece novels—one of which, *The Great Gatsby* (1925), is a leading contender for designation as "the great American novel." Jay Gatsby is the best-known figure in American fiction and is recognized by people who have not read the novel.	

(continued)

Scott Fitzgerald: Encyclopedia of American Literature	My Thought Processes
[. . .] *The Great Gatsby* (1925)—a short novel of 50,000 words, published before Fitzgerald was thirty—achieved a control of structure and point of view previously absent in his work. A study of romantic commitment and betrayal, it is also an examination of the American Dream and American society during the boom years. Fitzgerald's name and work are closely connected with the 1920s because he was a brilliant social historian who utilized details to evoke the feelings and moods associated with time and place. The description of Gatsby's party and the guest list evoke the excitement and vulgarity of "the greatest, gaudiest spree in history." The reviews for the novel were mixed, with the favorable ones very strong; but the sales of about 23,000 copies were disappointing. Fitzgerald's fourth and best novel, *Tender Is the Night* (1934), was published nine years after *The Great Gatsby;* and the delay, which partly resulted from the necessity to write commercial stories that would pay Zelda Fitzgerald's medical bills, damaged its reception when it appeared during the Depression. Most of the reviewers were unimpressed or unfriendly. The flashback structure was unappreciated, and the causes for the deterioration of the hero, Dick Diver, were largely misunderstood. James Dickey, who admired the novel, remarked that "If they could get Dick Diver, none of us is safe." Following the failure of *Tender Is the Night* to restore or advance Fitzgerald's literary standing, he experienced a physical and nervous breakdown, accompanied by financial worries, which he wrote about in the *Esquire* confessional essays posthumously collected in *The Crack-Up* (1945). Unable to continue writing popular magazine fiction, he went to Hollywood in 1937 to work for MGM on screenplays—at which he was not successful. At his death he was writing a Hollywood novel, published as a work in progress as *The Last Tycoon* in 1941. In its unfinished form it is one of the best novels inspired by the movie industry.	

(continued)

Scott Fitzgerald: Encyclopedia of American Literature	My Thought Processes
During his lifetime and into the twenty-first century Fitzgerald had two reputations: as a playboy and as a gifted writer—with his wastrel image predominating among general readers and Fitzgerald groupies. He became the subject of exaggerated or false anecdotes that interfered with the proper judgment of his work. Fitzgerald died believing himself a failure, and the obituaries treated him as a casualty of the 1920s: a writer who had wasted his ability and sold out. A spontaneous reappraisal generated by readers began in the mid 1940s with the reprinting of *The Great Gatsby;* this reappraisal became a revival in the 1950s. John O'Hara wrote in 1945, "All he was was our best novelist, one of our best novella-ists, and one of Write your essay in a notebook or on loose-leaf paperour finest writers of short stories." At the end of the 1960s F. Scott Fitzgerald was safely positioned among the greatest American writers. **Studying F. Scott Fitzgerald** F. Scott Fitzgerald's literary career covered two decades. In the 1920s he enjoyed celebrity and financial rewards; in the 1930s he experienced critical neglect and money troubles. Although he wrote that "there are no second acts in American lives," his career had two posthumous acts: the rediscovery or revival during the late 1940s and early 1950s, followed by the critical reappraisal of the 1960s and 1970s that made *The Great Gatsby* (1925) the most widely taught American novel and elevated Fitzgerald to a secure position among the major American writers.	

(continued)

Scott Fitzgerald: Encyclopedia of American Literature	My Thought Processes
Study of Fitzgerald properly starts with his first novel, *This Side of Paradise* (1920), which launched him as a key literary figure in what he christened "The Jazz Age." His astonishing technical development was proclaimed five years later in *The Great Gatsby* —which, nonetheless, was not a marked popular or critical success at the time of its publication. Fitzgerald's most substantial financial rewards and fame resulted from his 160 short stories published in the mass-circulation magazines. There was a close literary relationship between his commercial stories and his novels; he tested themes and characters in his magazine work for development in his novels. Fitzgerald's greatest novels, *The Great Gatsby* and *Tender is the Night* (1934), cannot be fully appreciated without knowledge of the stories connected with them. Fitzgerald's stories and novelettes merit close study apart from their connections with his novels. Fitzgerald published four volumes of stories during his lifetime, and nearly all of his previously uncollected stories have been republished. [. . .] Fitzgerald's manuscripts are at Princeton. The most comprehensive Fitzgerald research collection is described in the illustrated catalogue compiled by Park Bucker: *The Matthew J. and Arlyn Bruccoli Collection of F. Scott Fitzgerald at the University of South Carolina* (Columbia: University of South Carolina Press, 2004). The University of South Carolina Fitzgerald Centenary Website can be accessed at *<http://www.sc.edu/fitzgerald/index.html>*.	

(continued)

Scott Fitzgerald: Encyclopedia of American Literature	My Thought Processes
Image Citation (Chicago Manual of Style format): "Fitzgerald, F. Scott." Library of Congress. Prints and Photographs Division. Carl Van Vechten Photograph Collection. *Bloom's Literary Reference Online.* Facts On File, Inc. *http://www.fofweb.com/activelink2.asp?ItemID=WE54&SID=&iPin=EAmL1050&SingleRecord=True* (accessed February 8, 2013). **Text Citation (Chicago Manual of Style format):** Bruccoli, Matthew J. "Fitzgerald, F. Scott." In Anderson, George P., Judith S. Baughman, Matthew J. Bruccoli, and Carl Rollyson, eds. *Encyclopedia of American Literature, Revised Edition: Into the Modern: 1896–1945*, Volume 3. New York: Facts On File, Inc., 2008. *Bloom's Literary Reference Online.* Facts On File, Inc. *http://www.fofweb.com/activelink2.asp?ItemID=WE54&SID=&iPin=EAmL1050&SingleRecord=True* (accessed February 8, 2013).	

Prewriting

RST Graphic Organizer

Topic:

My Thesis Statement:

Source A	Source B	Source C

Exactly how do the sources talk with each other?

Your Outline:

Write your essay in a notebook or on loose-leaf paper. Make use of the Scoring Checklist and the Scoring Rubric found at the back of the book.

CCSS Alignment	
RL.1	Cite strong and textual evidence.
RL.5	Analyze how an author's choices contribute to its overall structure.
RI.7	Integrate and evaluate multiple sources of information presented in different media or formats (e.g., visually, quantitatively) as well as in words in order to address a question or solve a problem.
L.1	Demonstrate command of the conventions of standard English grammar and usage when writing.
L.3	Apply knowledge of language to understand how language functions in different contexts.
L.5	Demonstrate understanding of figurative language, word relationships, and nuances in word meanings.
W.1	Write arguments to support claims in an analysis of substantive topics or texts, using valid reasoning and relevant and sufficient evidence.
W.2	Write informative/explanatory texts to examine and convey complex ideas, concepts, and information clearly and accurately through the effective selection, organization, and analysis of content.
W.5	Develop and strengthen writing as needed by planning, revising, editing, and rewriting.
W.6	Use technology to produce, publish, and update individual writing products.

RST #4: Bullying

85 minutes

Recent events in the United States have caused politicians, educators, and law enforcement officials to rethink how they treat bullying. Some officials want to treat bullying as a crime. What do you think?

You have reviewed four sources regarding the causes and effects of bullying. These four texts provide information to begin drafting your own argument.

- **Source A:** School Ordeal: Being Bullied at School (Graph) (Anchor Text) *www. gao.gov/assets/600/591478.pdf*

- **Source B:** In Bullying Programs, A Call For Bystanders To Act (audio) *www.npr. org/2012/03/30/149606925*

- **Source C:** Teasing and Bullying, Boys and Girls *www.psychologytoday.com/ blog/thinking-about-kids/201010*

- **Source D:** Texting Graphic *http://middleschooladvisory101.blogspot. com/2009/02/are-you-cyber-bully.html*

Should bullying be treated as a crime? Write a persuasive piece that addresses the question and supports your position with evidence from at least two of the three sources. Be sure to acknowledge competing views. You may give examples from past and current events or issues to illustrate and clarify your position. You may refer to the sources by their titles (Source A, Source B, Source C, Source D).

SOURCE A

School Ordeal: Being Bullied at School (Graph)	My Thought Processes
Bullying A survey conducted by the GAO from April 2011 through May 2012, and reported on to a Senate committee, found that millions of middle school and high school students were being bullied (sometimes called harassment). They were asked to describe what they have experienced: Made fun of, called names or insulted — 19% Subject of rumors — 17% Pushed, hit, shoved, tripped or spit on — 9% Cyberbullied — 6% Taunted or threatened with harm — 6% Isolated from activities or other students on purpose — 28% Tried to make to do things they did not want to do — 28% Property destroyed on purpose — 28% Taken from Testimony before the Committee on Health, Education, Labor and Pensions, U.S. Senate: SCHOOL BULLYING by Linda M. Calbom, Western Regional Director, GAO (Government Accounting Office)	

(continued)

SOURCE B

Summary of "In Bullying Programs, A Call For Bystanders To Act"

In this audio clip, reporter Tovia Smith documents a new method for combatting bullying in schools. Developed at Harvard University, this new program encourages those who witness bullying to speak out when a bullying event is observed. In this shift, researchers want those who witness bullying to move from "bystanders" to "upstanders." Researchers argue that educators need to help kids create a "new social norm" where bullying is not accepted.

In Bullying Programs, A Call For Bystanders To Act (audio)
www.npr.org/2012/03/30/149606925

My Thought Processes

SOURCE C

Teasing and Bullying, Boys and Girls	**My Thought Processes**
Teasing and Bullying, Boys and Girls By Nancy Darling, Ph.D., Oberlin College, Oberlin, Ohio, published with author's permission Created Oct 26 2010 - 8:36pm I **Biff and George** Something is missing from the recent news stories focusing on bullying in our schools, teen suicide, and the words of support spoken by celebrities, politicians, and athletes in the It Gets Better campaign. **A definition of 'bullying'** Partly, I think that's because—like many psychological constructs—people think they know bullying when they see it. Just as we naturally judge those around us as intelligent or insecure or we judge ourselves to be in love or angry, the meaning of what it means to be bullied seems—and more importantly, feels—obvious. It hurts. [　] **Bullying v. Teasing** [. . .] First, a minority of adolescents overtly bully others—it isn't something that most kids do. Too many kids, yes (estimates vary by method and context). Most kids, no. Second, many bullies are low status and both bully others and are victimized themselves.	

(continued)

Teasing and Bullying, Boys and Girls	My Thought Processes
Third, and probably most disturbingly, most kids will stand by and watch a bully harass and hurt one of their peers without stepping in and stopping it. Moreover, they often make it worse by acting as an audience—or even laughing. All the estimates I have read that say that almost 75% of all children "bullied" have classified kids who watch or laugh when someone else hurts a peer as being the same as perpetrators. [. . .] FROM THE PERSPECTIVE OF THE PERPETRATOR and of an outside observer, teasing is different from bullying. From the perspective of the victim, this distinction may be unimportant. Teasing can also turn into bullying. But the distinction between bullying and teasing is important, because the way teasing and the way bullying work socially are very different. If we want to understand peer-on-peer aggression, it's important to keep that distinction clear. Two keep facts: Teasing is an AMBIGUOUS social exchange that can be friendly, neutral, or negative. How a teasing interchange proceeds really depends upon how the person BEING TEASED reacts. For example, if a girl walks into the cafeteria with a boy and a classmate says "OOO! Carmen's got a BOYfriend!", it's probably teasing. Carmen could smile, laugh, and say it's true. Then it might turn into a cheerful discussion. She could blush and deny it, in which case the other girls might laugh and more teasing might ensue or it could be dropped. Or she could get angry and treat the remark as if it were hostile, in which case the next remark would almost definitely be more overtly hostile and negative. Or, Carmen might just laugh, shake her head, ask the teaser if she's jealous, and never address the question at all.	

(continued)

Teasing and Bullying, Boys and Girls	My Thought Processes
Bullying doesn't work that way. Because the intention of bullying—including verbal harassment or aggression—is to hurt the victim, their reaction doesn't determine the meaning of the bully's action. It is overtly hostile and almost nothing the victim does will change that. The meaning of teasing depends on how the person being teased responds. If the teased laughs, it's a joke. If they take it seriously, it's serious. If they take it as an insult, it is, and the next interaction proceeds accordingly. Even youth who are often targeted by their peers—like students with developmental disabilities—are less likely to be teased or bullied over time if they respond to teasing as if it were a joke. Think of your classic Clint Eastwood movie, where he comes into a bar and one of the locals makes an aggressive statement disguised as a 'funny' remark. Clint responds AS IF the remark were a joke (i.e., as if he is being teased, not threatened). If the onlookers laugh, the aggressor can either back down and act as if he was joking (i.e., teasing) or he can turn the exchange into a straight confrontation by making another overtly aggressive remark. Failing to accept Clint's suggestion that the meaning of the initial remark was not serious (i.e., accept Clint's interpretation of the remark as teasing and non-aggressive) turns what Clint is saying is teasing into an attempt to bully. The interpretation of bullying is unambiguously hostile and will be treated as a challenge.	

(continued)

Teasing and Bullying, Boys and Girls	My Thought Processes
George McFly in Back to the Future In *Back to the Future*, you see an even more unambiguous example. Michael J. Fox plays the hero, Marty McFly, who travels to the past and meets his parents when they were in high school. In one painful exchange in the town malt shop, Marty's father (George McFly) tries to treat an overt act of bullying by the villain, Biff, as if it were a joke (i.e., as if it were a non-hostile exchange — teasing). Biff's refusal to accept George's interpretation is what makes you know that George is being victimized. The insults are not jokes. George is being insulted and abused. One of the high points of the movie is when George finally stands up to the bully. [. . .] **Boys and Girls** Classic observational research by Ritch Savin-Williams and by Donna Eder suggests that teasing tends to work differently for adolescent boys and girls. Among boys, teasing tends to establish a fairly strict and stable hierarchy — who's on top, who gets listened to, who makes decisions. Teasing includes small insults, physical bumps and pushes, and minor insults. When a new group of boys meets — as when everyone gets assigned to a new gym class or camp cabin — teasing is intense. Physical size, pubertal status, verbal ability, and attractiveness all determine who is on top in the status hierarchy. Interestingly, being liked isn't the same as having high status. Lots of boys who other kids like never get listened to and are often the butt of jokes. And those low status boys get reminded of their place in the pecking order A LOT in the first few days. Teasing is intense. On the other hand, things establish themselves quickly — in just a few days — and, as soon as they do, the teasing drops down to a low, stable level.	

(continued)

Teasing and Bullying, Boys and Girls	My Thought Processes
It doesn't work that way for girls. Girls' status hierarchies are much more unstable that are boys'. Girls tend to form triarchic friendships, which change, and thus who is on top changes as well. In addition to teasing, slights, and petty remarks, girls' status hierarchies are established by asking favors—high status girls impose on lower status ones—and giving compliments—low status girls compliment higher status ones. Girls' aggression is typically less physical and more subtle—sneaky—than the aggression of boys. **Boys attack when the person teased shows weakness.** Teasing functions differently as well. Boys tease to establish a hierarchy. And boys can be brutal. A boy is teased about his pants being too short. He responds with a laugh and it's over. The ability of boys to exchange insults and tease each other with no one getting mad is a critical sign that boys are real friends. But if the person teased responds by getting angry and looking upset, the other boy will intensify the attack immediately. The more upset he gets, the more and the harsher the teasing. The 'teaser' wins when the boy being teased loses his temper or loses his cool. And if it happens chronically, this can absolutely turn into harassment and bullying. **Girls diffuse tension within the clique. "Just teasing."** Girls tease to establish and enforce social norms. 'Your pants are too short.' 'Ooo, you decided to dress as a slut for Halloween?' 'Was there a wind tunnel in the hallway or did you decide to go for that just rolled out of bed look?' The message is clear—you aren't acting the way you're supposed to. As with boys, a laugh or a rueful acknowledgement will probably let the topic drop (if it really is teasing and not straight aggression). But, unlike boys, in typical female-on-female teasing, getting upset doesn't usually intensify teasing. If the girl being teased looks obviously upset the cutting remark, the typical response is that most hated of remarks.	

(continued)

Teasing and Bullying, Boys and Girls	My Thought Processes
"Just teasing!" What does 'just teasing' mean? It was all a joke. I didn't mean to hurt you. It might be true, but . . . In other words, this isn't serious and I don't really hate you. [. . .] © 2010 Nancy Darling. All Rights Reserved [. . .] Definitions are important. Source URL: *http://www.psychologytoday.com/node/49693*	

SOURCE D

Texting Graphic	My Thought Processes

Prewriting

RST Graphic Organizer

Topic:

My Thesis Statement:

Source A	Source B	Source C

Exactly how do the sources talk with each other?

Your Outline:

Write your essay in a notebook or on loose-leaf paper. Then, evaluate it by using the Scoring Checklist and the Scoring Rubric at the end of the book.

CHAPTER 7

Research Simulation Task: History

 Introduction

Congratulations! You have made it far in your progress on the Research Simulation Task. Chapter 6, the English RST, should have prepared you for the rigors of this new-type of synthesis-based writing. You have learned how to take notes while you read; to breakdown the RST prompt; to prewrite in the form of a graphic organizer; to create a workable outline; to execute a high-quality essay in the RST style; to get your sources talking to each other; and to edit your work using vivid, action verbs. All of these skills are no small accomplishment.

The good news is that you have all the necessary skills to perform at a high level on the PARCC's RST. Now, it's only a matter of you transferring these skills to different academic disciplines. The rest of the book, including this chapter, will take you through the process of completing the RST in a variety of academic subjects. This chapter will focus on history.

At this point, you might be tired of hearing that the PARCC views reading and writing as a combined literacy event, but we cannot emphasize the point enough. The better you read, the easier and more effective your writing will be. Therefore, in this chapter, we will take you, step-by-step, through the completion of an RST in history. First, we will actively read the texts, using our two-column approach. Afterward, we will use the 11-step process to complete the written portion of the RST. Next, we will provide you with a model essay. Finally, you will be given two practice RSTs in history. By the end of this chapter, you will be a pro when it comes to the RST in history.

Writing the Research Simulation Task for History

Let's begin with the model RST:

RST #1: The American Dream

85 minutes

According to Merriam-Webster, the American Dream is defined as an American social ideal that stresses social equality and especially material prosperity. For centuries, the American Dream attracted people to our country with the idea that if you work hard, you too can experience material success. There are those, however, who argue that the American Dream recently has come under attack and that the American Dream is in peril.

You have reviewed three sources regarding the American Dream. These four pieces provide information to begin drafting your own argument.

- **Source A:** Poem, "Chicago," by Carl Sandburg

- **Source B:** Video, "The Great Depression" *http://vimeo.com/63867463*

- **Source C:** Excerpt, "How We Made the First Flight," by Orville Wright

Is the American Dream still alive? Write a persuasive piece that addresses the question and supports your position with evidence from these three sources. Be sure to acknowledge competing views. You may give examples from past and current events or issues to illustrate and clarify your position. You may refer to the sources by their titles (Source A, Source B, Source C).

After reading the RST on the American Dream, you might be thinking that this is a difficult topic, and, yes, you would be right. The above prompt is difficult, in part, because of the number of sources involved. However, we will break it down for you. As you know, before we can attack the RST prompt, we must actively read our three sources. So, let's begin:

SOURCE A

Source A: Poem, "Chicago" (Carl Sandburg)	Our Thought Processes

Hog Butcher for the World,
    Tool Maker, Stacker of Wheat,
    Player with Railroads and the Nation's Freight
      Handler;
    Stormy, husky, brawling,
    City of the Big Shoulders:
	• This is Sandburg's description of the city of Chicago – each synonymous with the city itself.

They tell me you are wicked and I believe them, for I have seen your painted women under the gas lamps luring the farm boys. And they tell me you are crooked and I answer: Yes, it is true I have seen the gunman kill and go free to kill again. And they tell me you are brutal and my reply is: On the faces of women and children I have seen the marks of wanton hunger.	• Sandburg focuses on the negative aspects of the city of Chicago. He speaks directly to the city.

And having answered so I turn once more to those who sneer at this my city, and I give them back the sneer and say to them:
Come and show me another city with lifted head singing so proud to be alive and coarse and strong and cunning.
Flinging magnetic curses amid the toil of piling job on job, here is a tall bold slugger set vivid against the little soft cities;
Fierce as a dog with tongue lapping for action, cunning as a savage pitted against the wilderness,
    Bareheaded,
    Shoveling,
    Wrecking,
    Planning,
    Building, breaking, rebuilding,
Under the smoke, dust all over his mouth, laughing with white teeth,
Under the terrible burden of destiny laughing as a young man laughs,
	• A change of mood begins to exist into a more positive outlook of Chicago. Sandburg discusses the reality that all cities have their downfalls, and Chicago is no different.

(continued)

Source A: Poem, "Chicago" (Carl Sandburg)	Our Thought Processes
Laughing even as an ignorant fighter laughs who has never lost a battle, Bragging and laughing that under his wrist is the pulse, and under his ribs the heart of the people, Laughing! Laughing the stormy, husky, brawling laughter of Youth, half-naked, sweating, proud to be Hog Butcher, Tool Maker, Stacker of Wheat, Player with Railroads and Freight Handler to the Nation.	• The city has triumphed over a variety of struggles! • The beginning phrases have a much different connotation by this point of the poem.

As you can tell through our notes in the right column, this piece, by Carl Sandburg, is in support of the American Dream. Through citing important figures in America's turbulent past, Carl Sandburg argues that the American Dream is still alive and that it is worth fighting for. Overall, this piece sounds like a gem if we choose to write our response to the RST as in support of the American Dream being alive. However, that choice is very premature. We still have three sources to go! Here's number 2:

SOURCE B

Source B: Video, "The Great Depression" *http://vimeo.com/63867463*
Video notes   • The images of sad families and torn children are found throughout this video.   • The time of unrest during the Great Depression is clearly depicted, where the stability of family has been put into question.   • Children look saddened.   • Many people lost jobs.   • The Stock Market crashed, where families lost their entire savings. They were often left with nothing.   • Is their American Dream achievable? Or will this dream ever be a reality?

Compared to Source A, this video illustrating the Great Depression presents the dismal life of a terrible time. One may view this video, however, and look at such troubling times as an opportunity for hard work. One can move forward and achieve beyond the most sorrowful of times.

At this point, in our reading on the American Dream, we have one source, A, that argues in favor of the American Dream, and another source, B, that suggests the dream exists, but may also be out of reach. Let's now take a look at Source C:

SOURCE C

Source C: Excerpt, "How We Made the First Flight" (Orville Wright)	Our Thoughts
How We Made the First Flight *By Orville Wright* THE flights of the 1902 glider had demonstrated the efficiency of our system of maintaining equilibrium, and also the accuracy of the laboratory work upon which the design of the glider was based. We then felt that we were prepared to calculate in advance the performance of machines with a degree of accuracy that had never been possible with the data and tables possessed by our predecessors. Before leaving camp in 1902 we were already at work on the general design of a new machine which we proposed to propel with a motor. Immediately upon our return to Dayton, we wrote to a number of automobile and motor builders, stating the purpose for which we desired a motor, and asking whether they could furnish one that would develop eight brake-horsepower, with a weight complete not exceeding 200 pounds. Most of the companies answered that they were too busy with their regular business to undertake the building of such a motor for us; but one company replied that they had motors rated at 8 horse-power, according to the French system of ratings, which weighed only 135 pounds, and that if we thought this motor would develop enough power for our purpose they would be glad to sell us one. After an examination of the particulars of this motor, from which we learned that it had but a single cylinder of 4-inch bore and 5-inch stroke, we were afraid it was much over-rated. Unless the motor would develop a full 8 brake-horsepower, it would be useless for our purpose.	• With hard work, great things can happen, including even the invention of a flying machine! • Met various roadblocks along the way.

(continued)

Source C: Excerpt, "How We Made the First Flight" (Orville Wright)	Our Thoughts
Finally we decided to undertake the building of the motor ourselves. We estimated that we could make one of four cylinders with 4-inch bore and 4-inch stroke, weighing not over two hundred pounds, including all accessories. Our only experience up to that time in the building of gasoline motors had been in the construction of an air-cooled motor, 5-inch bore and 7-inch stroke, which was used to run the machinery of our small workshop. To be certain that four cylinders of the size we had adopted (4″ × 4″) would develop the necessary 8 horse-power, we first fitted them in a temporary frame of simple and cheap construction. In just six weeks from the time the design was started, we had the motor on the block testing its power. The ability to do this so quickly was largely due to the enthusiastic and efficient services of Mr. C. E. Taylor, who did all the machine work in our shop for the first as well as the succeeding experimental machines. There was no provision for lubricating either cylinders or bearings while this motor was running. For that reason it was not possible to run it more than a minute or two at a time. In these short tests the motor developed about nine horse-power. We were then satisfied that, with proper lubrication and better adjustments, a little more power could be expected. The completion of the motor according to drawing was, therefore, proceeded with at once. While Mr. Taylor was engaged with this work, Wilbur and I were busy in completing the design of the machine itself. The preliminary tests of the motor having convinced us that more than 8 horse-power would be secured, we felt free to add enough weight to build a more substantial machine than we had originally contemplated.	• Physical and mental labor played a large role in this dream becoming a reality.

(continued)

Source C: Excerpt, "How We Made the First Flight" (Orville Wright)	Our Thoughts
For two reasons we decided to use two propellers. In the first place we could, by the use of two propellers, secure a reaction against a greater quantity of air, and at the same time use a larger pitch angle than was possible with one propeller; and in the second place by having the propellers turn in opposite directions, the gyroscopic action of one would neutralize that of the other. The method we adopted of driving the propellers in opposite directions by means of chains is now too well known to need description here. We decided to place the motor to one side of the man, so that in case of a plunge headfirst, the motor could not fall upon him. In our gliding experiments we had had a number of experiences in which we had landed upon one wing, but the crushing of the wing had absorbed the shock, so that we were not uneasy about the motor in case of a landing of that kind. To provide against the machine rolling over forward in landing, we designed skids like sled runners, extending out in front of the main surfaces. Otherwise the general construction and operation of the machine was to be similar to that of the 1902 glider. When the motor was completed and tested, we found that it would develop 16 horse-power for a few seconds, but that the power rapidly dropped till, at the end of a minute, it was only 12 horse-power. Ignorant of what a motor of this size ought to develop, we were greatly pleased with its performance. More experience showed us that we did not get one-half of the power we should have had. With 12 horse-power at our command, we considered that we could permit the weight of the machine with operator to rise to 750 or 800 pounds, and still have as much surplus power as we had originally allowed for in the first estimate of 550 pounds.	• Specific, conscious decisions were needed, especially with each mechanism related to this invention. • A lot of experiments existed. Through trial-and-error, this hard work could be tested.

(continued)

Source C: Excerpt, "How We Made the First Flight" (Orville Wright)	Our Thoughts
Before leaving for our camp at Kitty Hawk we tested the chain drive for the propellers in our shop at Dayton, and found it satisfactory. We found, however, that our first propeller shafts, which were constructed of heavy gauge steel tubing, were not strong enough to stand the shocks received from a gasoline motor with light fly wheel, although they would have been able to transmit three or four times the power uniformly applied. We therefore built a new set of shafts of heavier tubing, which we tested and thought to be abundantly strong. We left Dayton, September 23, and arrived at our camp at Kill Devil Hill on Friday, the 25th. We found there provisions and tools, which had been shipped by freight several weeks in advance. The building, erected in 1901 and enlarged in 1902, was found to have been blown by a storm from its foundation posts a few months previously. While we were awaiting the arrival of the shipment of machinery and parts from Dayton, we were busy putting the old building in repair, and erecting a new building to serve as a workshop for assembling and housing the new machine. Just as the building was being completed, the parts and material for the machines arrived simultaneously with one of the worst storms that had visited Kitty Hawk in years. The storm came on suddenly, blowing 30 to 40 miles an hour. It increased during the night, and the next day was blowing over 75 miles an hour. In order to save the tar-paper roof, we decided it would be necessary to get out in this wind and nail down more securely certain parts that were especially exposed. When I ascended the ladder and reached the edge of the roof, the wind caught under my large coat, blew it up around my head and bound my arms till I was perfectly helpless. Wilbur came to my assistance and held down my coat while I tried to drive the nails. But the wind was so strong I could not guide the hammer and succeeded in striking my fingers as often as the nails.	

(continued)

Source C: Excerpt, "How We Made the First Flight" (Orville Wright)	Our Thoughts
The next three weeks were spent in setting the motor-machine together. On days with more favorable winds we gained additional experience in handling a flyer by gliding with the 1902 machine, which we had found in pretty fair condition in the old building, where we had left it the year before.	• Many steps were needed to be worked through in order to move forward with this project.
Mr. Chanute and Dr. Spratt, who had been guests in our camp in 1901 and 1902, spent some time with us, but neither one was able to remain to see the test of the motor-machine, on account of the delays caused by trouble which developed in the propeller shafts.	
While Mr. Chanute was with us, a good deal of time was spent in discussion of the mathematical calculations upon which we had based our machine. He informed us that, in designing machinery, about 20 percent. was usually allowed for the loss in the transmission of power. As we had allowed only 5 percent, a figure we had arrived at by some crude measurements of the friction of one of the chains when carrying only a very light load, we were much alarmed. More than the whole surplus in power allowed in our calculations would, according to Mr. Chanute's estimate, be consumed in friction in the driving chains. After Mr. Chanute's departure, we suspended one of the drive chains over a sprocket, hanging bags of sand on either side of the sprocket of a weight approximately equal to the pull that would be exerted on the chains when driving the propellers. By measuring the extra amount of weight needed on one side to lift the weight on the other, we calculated the loss in transmission. This indicated that the loss of power from this source would be only 5 percent, as we originally estimated. But while we could see no serious error in this method of determining the loss, we were very uneasy until we had a chance to run the propellers with the motor to see whether we could get the estimated number of turns.	

(continued)

Source C: Excerpt, "How We Made the First Flight" (Orville Wright)	Our Thoughts
The first run of the motor on the machine developed a flaw in one of the propeller shafts which had not been discovered in the test at Dayton. The shafts were sent at once to Dayton for repair, and were not received again until November 20, having been gone two weeks. We immediately put them in the machine and made another test. A new trouble developed. The sprockets which were screwed on the shafts, and locked with nuts of opposite thread, persisted in coming loose. After many futile attempts to get them fast, we had to give it up for that day, and went to bed much discouraged. However, after a night's rest, we got up the next morning in better spirits and resolved to try again. While in the bicycle business we had become well acquainted with the use of hard tire cement for fastening tires on the rims. We had once used it successfully in repairing a stop watch after several watchsmiths had told us it could not be repaired. If tire cement was good for fastening the hands on a stop watch, why should it not be good for fastening the sprockets on the propeller shaft of a flying machine? We decided to try it. We heated the shafts and sprockets, melted cement into the threads, and screwed them together again. This trouble was over. The sprockets stayed fast.	

Source C: Excerpt, "How We Made the First Flight" (Orville Wright)	Our Thoughts
Just as the machine was ready for test bad weather set in. It had been disagreeably cold for several weeks, so cold that we could scarcely work on the machine for some days. But now we began to have rain and snow, and a wind of 25 to 30 miles blew for several days from the north. While we were being delayed by the weather we arranged a mechanism to measure automatically the duration of a flight from the time the machine started to move forward to the time it stopped, the distance traveled through the air in that time, and the number of revolutions made by the motor and propeller. A stop watch took the time; an anemometer measured the air traveled through; and a counter took the number of revolutions made by the propellers. The watch, anemometer and revolution counter were all automatically started and stopped simultaneously. From data thus obtained we expected to prove or disprove the accuracy of our propeller calculations. On November 28, while giving the motor a run indoors, we thought we again saw something wrong with one of the propeller shafts. On stopping the motor we discovered that one of the tubular shafts had cracked!	• This was not an easy process. Many "wrongs" occurred before such an invention could be an eventual success.

OK. So where do we stand now with our third source on the American Dream? Wright's trials and tribulations prove that the American Dream could, indeed, be achieved.

Let's review our three sources: A, pro-American Dream; B includes information that can work towards con-American Dream, and now C, pro-American Dream. In terms of responding to our RST prompt, we are leaning toward writing an essay about the American Dream being alive. Let's continue to analyze our notes.

As you can undoubtedly tell, after reading all four sources, we are well on our way to writing a response to the RST prompt that shows that the American Dream is alive and well, but that it has changed. This idea is supported by at least two of the three sources. So, it's time to begin.

11 Steps for Success on the RST

Before Writing Begins	
Step #1:	Read through the question carefully. Make sure to decipher if the question is asking you to convey an opinion, or to convey information/research objectively. • The question is asking us to convey an opinion
Step #2:	Simplify what the question is asking you to do. Put the question/task into your own words. • The prompt is asking this: "Is the American Dream Alive?"
Step #3:	Circle the minimum amount of sources that need to be addressed. • Three sources
Step #4:	Take notes with each of the sources. Address the source's main points. Underline actively. • We completed this activity extensively in our two-column approach and when we took notes on the video
Step #5:	After you've addressed and highlighted the main point of the source, make separate notes on the reliability of these sources. Is the source reliable in general? Is it slanted in any way? Do logical fallacies or "holes in the argument" exist? • We took notes on the reliability of sources in our active reading.
Step #6:	You've read through your sources. Choose the sources that you are most comfortable with, and put an asterisk (*) next to them. • We will be primarily working with Sources A, B, and C. We have asterisked them above.
Writing the RST	
Step #7:	Copy the arguments—textual evidence—you will use in your essay into the pre-writing chart. (shown below)
Step #8:	Now, look at the relationships of your sources. Do they agree with each other? Do they disagree? Use your source-relationship chart to begin thinking about how you will have your sources begin conversing with one another. (shown below)
Step #9:	Compose a quick outline of your essay. (shown below)
Step #10:	Complete your essay using the framework/outline as a guide. (shown below)
Step #11:	After you have completed your essay, go back to check that your sources have a conversation, and replace the verbs you've used to integrate these sources with the action verbs from the sheet provided. (Shown below.)

So, let's get started on doing the prewriting for our response. Here is the RST graphic organizer:

RST Graphic Organizer

My Thesis Statement: The American Dream is alive and well, although it is a changed dream from the past.

Topic: The American Dream

Source A	Source B	Source C
"Chicago," Carl Sandburg	The Great Depression (Video)	Excerpt, *"How We Made the First Flight"* (Orville Wright)
This is Sandburg's description of the city of Chicago — each synonymous with the city itself.	The images of sad families and torn children are found throughout this video.	With hard work, great things can happen, including that of the invention of flight!
Sandburg focuses on the negative aspects of the city of Chicago. He speaks directly to the city.	The time of unrest during the Great Depression is clearly depicted, where the stability of family has been put into question.	Met various roadblocks along the way.
A change of mood begins to exist into a more positive outlook of Chicago. Sandburg discusses the reality that all cities have their downfalls, and Chicago is no different.	Children look saddened.	Physical and mental labor played a large role in this dream becoming a reality.
The city has triumphed over a variety of struggles!	Many people lost jobs.	Specific, conscious decisions were needed, especially with each mechanism related to this invention.
The beginning phrases, while repeated, have a much different connotation by this point of the poem.	The Stock Market crashed; where families lost their entire savings. They were often left with nothing.	A lot of experiments existed. Through trial-and-error, this hard work could be tested.
	Is their American Dream achievable? Or will this dream ever be a reality?	Many steps were needed to be worked through in order to move forward with this project.
		This was not an easy process. Many "wrongs" occurred before such an invention could be an eventual success.

How can the Sources talk to each other?

At the core of each of these sources is the idea that the American Dream, with its previous emphasis on material wealth and material success, has undoubtedly changed. Source A, for instance, argues that the American Dream is an inextricable part of our national identity, as mirrored through the city of Chicago, but that this dream must be renewed through attention to the poor, to violence, to immigration, to natural disasters, and to our entitlement programs. Similarly, the video, in Source B, argues that we can renew ourselves through overcoming the low points in life. Similarly, Source C argues that America must renew itself through focused hard work and detailed planning, as explained in Orville Wright's written piece.

As you can see, we did a fairly good job tackling Step 7 and Step 8. At the bottom of our chart, we pre-wrote a bit on how our sources share a common theme of American renewal. That work, undoubtedly, will become useful as we write our essay. For now, though, we must head to Step 9, the outline. As discussed previously, we want to keep our outline brief, focusing on the major themes of the essay. Here we go:

I. Introduction

    a. Attention Grabber

    b. Thesis: The American Dream is alive and well, although it is a changed dream from the past

II. Body

    a. Theme 1: American Renewal

    b. Theme 2: America's Future

III. Conclusion

    a. Rework thesis statement

    b. Answer to the So What? question

Let's just take brief look at our outline. Did you notice the two major themes in the body: American Renewal and America's Future? These two ideas will guide us as we write our essay. What we want you to know: Our very close reading of the three sources has served us very well. We are in a good position to write an excellent response to the RST prompt because we have a high degree of knowledge about the writing topic. Heed this advice: The better you read, the better you will write. Here's our sample essay:

> With the poverty rate in our country has recently increased, it is easy to conclude that if it is not dead, the American Dream, as President Clinton says, is under assault. It seems as though there isn't a family left in our country that hasn't suffered the loss of a job or hasn't taken another job for less pay and fewer benefits. Do these realities mean that the American Dream is dead? No! Americans are much more resilient than that. Instead of dying, the American Dream is evolving and is alive and quite well.

In this current time in our history, America in undergoing a profound renewal. At one's lowest point, there is significant room to grow. Chicago acts as a representation of America as a whole. America is poised to renew and revitalize itself. As per Sandburg's poem, "Chicago," this renewal is deeply tied to two factors: 1.) Economics and 2.) Spirituality. Tied closely to each remains the importance of pride. While we move forward, we cannot certainly forget where we have come from. Only then will the American Dream be kept alive and well. Look at the Great Depression video of Source B, when a time exists that success is no longer a possibility, Americans are known to not be defined by their struggles, as depicted in these images. Far from dead, the American Dream simply has changed.

As the American Dream adapts and changes, one might ask, "What will this dream look like in the future?" With a new world comes a new outlook. We cannot, though, simply deny the origins of success. Source C explains the plan through which Orville Wright used to begin his outcome of flight and flying motors. Just as Carl Sandburg struggled through hard years in Chicago, and those of the Great Depression met unexplainable strife, the idea that things will get better (or even "best") sometime thereafter. For instance, through Sources A, B, and C, an America exists that focuses on solving problems such as violence, immigration reform, funding entitlement programs, and helping communities rebound from the increase in natural disasters. It is a struggle that cannot be done without hard work and dedication, while also remembering the times that held us back in the first place.

In the face of ever-increasing income disparity, one would logically conclude that Americans would become resentful of the super-rich and ultimately bitter. The American character, however, is not that shallow. Far from being dead, the American Dream is evolving, morphing into something few would have expected: As a country, we see a brighter economic future as we become better stewards of our environment through the development of green technologies and green jobs. Moreover, Americans are less likely now to define success in materialistic terms. Perhaps, we wonder, "Success is not to be counted in money but to be determined in how we help and serve others."

Step 11: Looking at the Verbs

Now that we have completed our written response to the RST topic, it is time to pay close attention to our verb choice. Look through the essay above and circle the verb choices. Do you find them "boring" or "tiresome?" If so, use the Vivid Verb Chart in Appendix A to find replacements.

Analysis of Sample Essay

As we did in the previous chapter, we will provide to you an analysis of the sample essay according to the four criteria identified in our Scoring Checklist Chart (reproduced below). We also include the PARCC's writing rubric. Be sure to rate the sample essay using the 4-point scale.

By "Development of Ideas," the makers of the PARCC refer to the ways in which arguments are developed and maintained throughout the course of the essay. Some questions might be: "Did the author use evidence from the text?" "Did this evidence come from more than one source?" "Did the author successfully have the two sources interact with each other?" As you can see, these questions are quite difficult and will take time for you to master. However, you can see these principles in action if you read carefully our sample essay above. We did cite evidence from all three sources, and we did have the three sources interact, or "talk." For instance, we looked closely at the features of the American Dream by utilizing details from Sandburg's poem, the video, as well as Wright's article to explain that the American Dream is indeed possible.

Second, the PARCC will look at the organization of your writing. This, in fact, should come as no surprise at all for you. Organization is a key facet of all good writing, regardless of where it is done. By virtue of the fact that we meticulously followed our outline, we organized our work. The three main parts of the essay are clearly present: Introduction, body, and conclusion.

The next criterion, "clarity of language," will look at your writing style and the effectiveness of that style. "What is writing style?" you may ask? It deals with the author's ability to effectively use vocabulary, including content-specific words, to utilize vivid and proper description, and to appropriately use transitional words throughout the piece. Style, then, is nothing more than the writer's identity on paper. What the PARCC cares about most is simple: Is your style clear, concise, and to the point? There is nothing worse than reading an essay that lacks clarity and is difficult to read because the writer lacks a command of language.

Looking at our sample essay: What would you say of the style? Look back at our choice of vocabulary: Did we use vocabulary terms that were appropriate to research and statistics? Were our descriptions of the research sources clear? Was any of the wording ambiguous and difficult to comprehend? Could something we wrote have been written clearer? All of these questions are great starting points when looking at style.

Lastly, the PARCC will consider your knowledge of language and conventions. This is where your knowledge of grammar, mechanics, and usage will come to play. Were there any mistakes in these three categories? Did the author go back and edit the work? Does the work read fluidly and effortlessly? Does poor grammar become a distraction or a nuisance? Our sample essay, we believe, does pretty well in this area, and provides a sample RST essay that is free of grammatical issues and reads as though it was edited (which it was!).

Summary of the RST in History

At this point in the chapter, now that the skills of the RST are mastered—particularly the active reading and the 11 Steps to Success— your success only becomes a matter of learning new content. We have shown you how difficult texts, such as the ones on the American Dream, can become manageable when formulating a quality written response. Can you guess the idea that we want to impress upon you the most? You got it! The better you read, the better you will write.

Practice RSTs in History

Now, it's your turn. We will give you two sample RST tasks in history with accompanying organizers. Please be sure, as you go through this process to use the 11 Steps of Success, and, as always, read well; your writing depends upon it.

RST #2: President Franklin D. Roosevelt

85 minutes

Faced with the Great Depression and with World War II, a war fought on two fronts, Franklin Delano Roosevelt stands out as one of America's greatest presidents.

- **Source A:** Franklin Delano Roosevelt: Fireside Chats: Franklin Delano Roosevelt

- **Source B:** Franklin D. Roosevelt: Biography, R. Brayton: *www.watchmojo.com/ index.php?id=10839*

- **Source C:** Franklin D. Roosevelt First Inaugural Address: *http://www.bartleby. com/124/pres49.html*

What about FDR's character made him a truly outstanding president? Consider the arguments that these three texts use in their characterization of President Roosevelt. Write an informative piece that addresses the question and supports your position with evidence from at least two of the three sources. Be sure to acknowledge competing views. You may give examples from past and current events or issues to illustrate and clarify your position. You may refer to the sources by their titles (Source A, Source B, Source C).

SOURCE A

Fireside Chats: Franklin Delano Roosevelt	My Thought Processes
March 12, 1933. I want to talk for a few minutes with the people of the United States about banking—with the comparatively few who understand the mechanics of banking but more particularly with the overwhelming majority who use banks for the making of deposits and the drawing of checks. I want to tell you what has been done in the last few days, why it was done, and what the next steps are going to be. I recognize that the many proclamations from state capitols and from Washington, the legislation, the treasury regulations, etc., couched for the most part in banking and legal terms should be explained for the benefit of the average citizen. I owe this in particular because of the fortitude and good temper with which everybody has accepted the inconvenience and hardships of the banking holiday. I know that when you understand what we in Washington have been about I shall continue to have your cooperation as fully as I have had your sympathy and help during the past week. First of all let me state the simple fact that when you deposit money in a bank the bank does not put the money into a safe deposit vault. It invests your money in many different forms of credit— bonds, commercial paper, mortgages and many other kinds of loans. In other words, the bank puts your money to work to keep the wheels of industry and of agriculture turning around. A comparatively small part of the money you put into the bank is kept in currency— an amount which in normal times is wholly sufficient to cover the cash needs of the average citizen. In other words, the total amount of all the currency in the country is only a small fraction of the total deposits in all of the banks.	

(continued)

Fireside Chats: Franklin Delano Roosevelt	My Thought Processes
What, then, happened during the last few days of February and the first few days of March? Because of undermined confidence on the part of the public, there was a general rush by a large portion of our population to turn bank deposits into currency or gold—a rush so great that the soundest banks could not get enough currency to meet the demand. The reason for this was that on the spur of the moment it was, of course, impossible to sell perfectly sound assets of a bank and convert them into cash except at panic prices far below their real value.	
By the afternoon of March 3d scarcely a bank in the country was open to do business. Proclamations temporarily closing them in whole or in part had been issued by the governors in almost all the states.	
It was then that I issued the proclamation providing for the nation-wide bank holiday, and this was the first step in the government's reconstruction of our financial and economic fabric.	
The second step was the legislation promptly and patriotically passed by the Congress confirming my proclamation and broadening my powers so that it became possible in view of the requirement of time to extend the holiday and lift the ban of that holiday gradually. This law also gave authority to develop a program of rehabilitation of our banking facilities. I want to tell our citizens in every part of the nation that the national Congress— Republicans and Democrats alike—showed by this action a devotion to public welfare and a realization of the emergency and the necessity for speed that it is difficult to match in our history.	
The third stage has been the series of regulations permitting the banks to continue their functions to take care of the distribution of food and household necessities and the payment of payrolls.	

(continued)

Fireside Chats: Franklin Delano Roosevelt	My Thought Processes
This bank holiday, while resulting in many cases in great inconvenience, is affording us the opportunity to supply the currency necessary to meet the situation. No sound bank is a dollar worse off than it was when it closed its doors last Monday. Neither is any bank which may turn out not to be in a position for immediate opening. The new law allows the twelve Federal Reserve Banks to issue additional currency on good assets and thus the banks which reopen will be able to meet every legitimate call. The new currency is being sent out by the Bureau of Engraving and Printing in large volume to every part of the country. It is sound currency because it is backed by actual, good assets. A question you will ask is this: why are all the banks not to be reopened at the same time? The answer is simple. Your government does not intend that the history of the past few years shall be repeated. We do not want and will not have another epidemic of bank failures. As a result, we start tomorrow, Monday, with the opening of banks in the twelve Federal Reserve Bank cities—those banks which on first examination by the treasury have already been found to be all right. This will be followed on Tuesday by the resumption of all their functions by banks already found to be sound in cities where there are recognized clearing houses. That means about 250 cities of the United states. On Wednesday and succeeding days banks in smaller places all through the country will resume business, subject, of course, to the government's physical ability to complete its survey. It is necessary that the reopening of banks be extended over a period in order to permit the banks to make applications for necessary loans, to obtain currency needed to meet their requirements and to enable the government to make common sense checkups.	

(continued)

Fireside Chats: Franklin Delano Roosevelt	My Thought Processes
Let me make it clear to you that if your bank does not open the first day you are by no means justified in believing that it will not open. A bank that opens on one of the subsequent days is in exactly the same status as the bank that opens tomorrow. I know that many people are worrying about state banks not members of the Federal Reserve System. These banks can and will receive assistance from members banks and from the Reconstruction Finance Corporation. These state banks are following the same course as the national banks except that they get their licenses to resume business from the state authorities, and these authorities have been asked by the Secretary of the Treasury to permit their good banks to open up on the same schedule as the national banks. I am confident that the state banking departments will be as careful as the national government in the policy relating to the opening of banks and will follow the same broad policy. It is possible that when the banks resume a very few people who have not recovered from their fear may again begin withdrawals. Let me make it clear that the banks will take care of all needs—and it is my belief that hoarding during the past week has become an exceedingly unfashionable pastime. It needs no prophet to tell you that when the people find that they can get their money—that they can get it when they want it for all legitimate purposes—the phantom of fear will soon be laid. People will again be glad to have their money where it will be safely taken care of and where they can use it conveniently at any time. I can assure you that it is safer to keep your money in a reopened bank than under the mattress. The success of our whole great national program depends, of course, upon the cooperation of the public—on its intelligent support and use of a reliable system.	

(continued)

Fireside Chats: Franklin Delano Roosevelt	My Thought Processes
Remember that the essential accomplishment of the new legislation is that it makes it possible for banks more readily to convert their assets into cash than was the case before. More liberal provision has been made for banks to borrow on these assets at the Reserve Banks and more liberal provision has also been made for issuing currency on the security of those good assets. This currency is not fiat currency. It is issued only on adequate security—and every good bank has an abundance of such security. One more point before I close. There will be, of course, some banks unable to reopen without being reorganized. The new law allows the government to assist in making these reorganizations quickly and effectively and even allows the government to subscribe to at least a part of new capital which may be required. I hope you can see from this elemental recital of what your government is doing that there is nothing complex, or radical, in the process.	

SOURCE B

Franklin D. Roosevelt	My Thought Processes
Franklin D. Roosevelt Assuming the Presidency at the depth of the Great Depression, Franklin D. Roosevelt helped the American people regain faith in themselves. He brought hope as he promised prompt, vigorous action, and asserted in his Inaugural Address, "the only thing we have to fear is fear itself." Born in 1882 at Hyde Park, New York—now a national historic site—he attended Harvard University and Columbia Law School. On St. Patrick's Day, 1905, he married Eleanor Roosevelt.	

(continued)

Franklin D. Roosevelt	My Thought Processes
Following the example of his fifth cousin, President Theodore Roosevelt, whom he greatly admired, Franklin D. Roosevelt entered public service through politics, but as a Democrat. He won election to the New York Senate in 1910. President Wilson appointed him Assistant Secretary of the Navy, and he was the Democratic nominee for Vice President in 1920.	
In the summer of 1921, when he was 39, disaster hit—he was stricken with poliomyelitis. Demonstrating indomitable courage, he fought to regain the use of his legs, particularly through swimming. At the 1924 Democratic Convention he dramatically appeared on crutches to nominate Alfred E. Smith as "the Happy Warrior." In 1928 Roosevelt became Governor of New York.	
He was elected President in November 1932, to the first of four terms. By March there were 13,000,000 unemployed, and almost every bank was closed. In his first "hundred days," he proposed, and Congress enacted, a sweeping program to bring recovery to business and agriculture, relief to the unemployed and to those in danger of losing farms and homes, and reform, especially through the establishment of the Tennessee Valley Authority.	
By 1935 the Nation had achieved some measure of recovery, but businessmen and bankers were turning more and more against Roosevelt's New Deal program. They feared his experiments, were appalled because he had taken the Nation off the gold standard and allowed deficits in the budget, and disliked the concessions to labor. Roosevelt responded with a new program of reform: Social Security, heavier taxes on the wealthy, new controls over banks and public utilities, and an enormous work relief program for the unemployed.	

(continued)

Franklin D. Roosevelt	My Thought Processes
In 1936 he was re-elected by a top-heavy margin. Feeling he was armed with a popular mandate, he sought legislation to enlarge the Supreme Court, which had been invalidating key New Deal measures. Roosevelt lost the Supreme Court battle, but a revolution in constitutional law took place. Thereafter the Government could legally regulate the economy. Roosevelt had pledged the United States to the "good neighbor" policy, transforming the Monroe Doctrine from a unilateral American manifesto into arrangements for mutual action against aggressors. He also sought through neutrality legislation to keep the United States out of the war in Europe, yet at the same time to strengthen nations threatened or attacked. When France fell and England came under siege in 1940, he began to send Great Britain all possible aid short of actual military involvement. When the Japanese attacked Pearl Harbor on December 7, 1941, Roosevelt directed organization of the Nation's manpower and resources for global war. Feeling that the future peace of the world would depend upon relations between the United States and Russia, he devoted much thought to the planning of a United Nations, in which, he hoped, international difficulties could be settled. As the war drew to a close, Roosevelt's health deteriorated, and on April 12, 1945, while at Warm Springs, Georgia, he died of a cerebral hemorrhage. The Presidential biographies on WhiteHouse.gov are from "The Presidents of the United States of America," by Michael Beschloss and Hugh Sidey. Copyright 2009 by the White House Historical Association	

(continued)

SOURCE C

Franklin D. Roosevelt First Inaugural Address	My Thought Processes
I AM certain that my fellow Americans expect that on my induction into the Presidency I will address them with a candor and a decision which the present situation of our Nation impels. This is preeminently the time to speak the truth, the whole truth, frankly and boldly. Nor need we shrink from honestly facing conditions in our country today. This great Nation will endure as it has endured, will revive and will prosper. So, first of all, let me assert my firm belief that the only thing we have to fear is fear itself—nameless, unreasoning, unjustified terror which paralyzes needed efforts to convert retreat into advance. In every dark hour of our national life a leadership of frankness and vigor has met with that understanding and support of the people themselves which is essential to victory. I am convinced that you will again give that support to leadership in these critical days. In such a spirit on my part and on yours we face our common difficulties. They concern, thank God, only material things. Values have shrunken to fantastic levels; taxes have risen; our ability to pay has fallen; government of all kinds is faced by serious curtailment of income; the means of exchange are frozen in the currents of trade; the withered leaves of industrial enterprise lie on every side; farmers find no markets for their produce; the savings of many years in thousands of families are gone. More important, a host of unemployed citizens face the grim problem of existence, and an equally great number toil with little return. Only a foolish optimist can deny the dark realities of the moment.	

(continued)

Franklin D. Roosevelt First Inaugural Address	My Thought Processes
Yet our distress comes from no failure of substance. We are stricken by no plague of locusts. Compared with the perils which our forefathers conquered because they believed and were not afraid, we have still much to be thankful for. Nature still offers her bounty and human efforts have multiplied it. Plenty is at our doorstep, but a generous use of it languishes in the very sight of the supply. Primarily this is because the rulers of the exchange of mankind's goods have failed, through their own stubbornness and their own incompetence, have admitted their failure, and abdicated. Practices of the unscrupulous money changers stand indicted in the court of public opinion, rejected by the hearts and minds of men. True they have tried, but their efforts have been cast in the pattern of an outworn tradition. Faced by failure of credit they have proposed only the lending of more money. Stripped of the lure of profit by which to induce our people to follow their false leadership, they have resorted to exhortations, pleading tearfully for restored confidence. They know only the rules of a generation of self-seekers. They have no vision, and when there is no vision the people perish. The money changers have fled from their high seats in the temple of our civilization. We may now restore that temple to the ancient truths. The measure of the restoration lies in the extent to which we apply social values more noble than mere monetary profit. Happiness lies not in the mere possession of money; it lies in the joy of achievement, in the thrill of creative effort. The joy and moral stimulation of work no longer must be forgotten in the mad chase of evanescent profits. These dark days will be worth all they cost us if they teach us that our true destiny is not to be ministered unto but to minister to ourselves and to our fellow men.	

(continued)

Franklin D. Roosevelt First Inaugural Address	My Thought Processes
Recognition of the falsity of material wealth as the standard of success goes hand in hand with the abandonment of the false belief that public office and high political position are to be valued only by the standards of pride of place and personal profit; and there must be an end to a conduct in banking and in business which too often has given to a sacred trust the likeness of callous and selfish wrongdoing. Small wonder that confidence languishes, for it thrives only on honesty, on honor, on the sacredness of obligations, on faithful protection, on unselfish performance; without them it cannot live.	
Restoration calls, however, not for changes in ethics alone. This Nation asks for action, and action now.	
Our greatest primary task is to put people to work. This is no unsolvable problem if we face it wisely and courageously. It can be accomplished in part by direct recruiting by the Government itself, treating the task as we would treat the emergency of a war, but at the same time, through this employment, accomplishing greatly needed projects to stimulate and reorganize the use of our natural resources.	
Hand in hand with this we must frankly recognize the overbalance of population in our industrial centers and, by engaging on a national scale in a redistribution, endeavor to provide a better use of the land for those best fitted for the land. The task can be helped by definite efforts to raise the values of agricultural products and with this the power to purchase the output of our cities. It can be helped by preventing realistically the tragedy of the growing loss through foreclosure of our small homes and our farms. It can be helped by insistence that the Federal, State, and local governments act forthwith on the demand that their cost be drastically reduced. It can be helped by the unifying of relief activities which today are often scattered, uneconomical, and unequal. It can be helped by national planning for and supervision of all forms of transportation and of communications and other utilities which have a definitely public character. There are many ways in which it can be helped, but it can never be helped merely by talking about it. We must act and act quickly.	

(continued)

Franklin D. Roosevelt First Inaugural Address	My Thought Processes
Finally, in our progress toward a resumption of work we require two safeguards against a return of the evils of the old order; there must be a strict supervision of all banking and credits and investments; there must be an end to speculation with other people's money, and there must be provision for an adequate but sound currency.	
There are the lines of attack. I shall presently urge upon a new Congress in special session detailed measures for their fulfillment, and I shall seek the immediate assistance of the several States.	
Through this program of action we address ourselves to putting our own national house in order and making income balance outgo. Our international trade relations, though vastly important, are in point of time and necessity secondary to the establishment of a sound national economy. I favor as a practical policy the putting of first things first. I shall spare no effort to restore world trade by international economic readjustment, but the emergency at home cannot wait on that accomplishment.	
The basic thought that guides these specific means of national recovery is not narrowly nationalistic. It is the insistence, as a first consideration, upon the interdependence of the various elements in all parts of the United States—a recognition of the old and permanently important manifestation of the American spirit of the pioneer. It is the way to recovery. It is the immediate way. It is the strongest assurance that the recovery will endure.	
In the field of world policy I would dedicate this Nation to the policy of the good neighbor—the neighbor who resolutely respects himself and, because he does so, respects the rights of others—the neighbor who respects his obligations and respects the sanctity of his agreements in and with a world of neighbors.	

(continued)

Franklin D. Roosevelt First Inaugural Address	My Thought Processes
If I read the temper of our people correctly, we now realize as we have never realized before our interdependence on each other; that we can not merely take but we must give as well; that if we are to go forward, we must move as a trained and loyal army willing to sacrifice for the good of a common discipline, because without such discipline no progress is made, no leadership becomes effective. We are, I know, ready and willing to submit our lives and property to such discipline, because it makes possible a leadership which aims at a larger good. This I propose to offer, pledging that the larger purposes will bind upon us all as a sacred obligation with a unity of duty hitherto evoked only in time of armed strife.	
With this pledge taken, I assume unhesitatingly the leadership of this great army of our people dedicated to a disciplined attack upon our common problems.	
Action in this image and to this end is feasible under the form of government which we have inherited from our ancestors. Our Constitution is so simple and practical that it is possible always to meet extraordinary needs by changes in emphasis and arrangement without loss of essential form. That is why our constitutional system has proved itself the most superbly enduring political mechanism the modern world has produced. It has met every stress of vast expansion of territory, of foreign wars, of bitter internal strife, of world relations.	
It is to be hoped that the normal balance of executive and legislative authority may be wholly adequate to meet the unprecedented task before us. But it may be that an unprecedented demand and need for undelayed action may call for temporary departure from that normal balance of public procedure.	
I am prepared under my constitutional duty to recommend the measures that a stricken nation in the midst of a stricken world may require. These measures, or such other measures as the Congress may build out of its experience and wisdom, I shall seek, within my constitutional authority, to bring to speedy adoption.	

(continued)

Franklin D. Roosevelt First Inaugural Address	My Thought Processes
But in the event that the Congress shall fail to take one of these two courses, and in the event that the national emergency is still critical, I shall not evade the clear course of duty that will then confront me. I shall ask the Congress for the one remaining instrument to meet the crisis—broad Executive power to wage a war against the emergency, as great as the power that would be given to me if we were in fact invaded by a foreign foe. For the trust reposed in me I will return the courage and the devotion that befit the time. I can do no less. We face the arduous days that lie before us in the warm courage of the national unity; with the clear consciousness of seeking old and precious moral values; with the clean satisfaction that comes from the stern performance of duty by old and young alike. We aim at the assurance of a rounded and permanent national life. We do not distrust the future of essential democracy. The people of the United States have not failed. In their need they have registered a mandate that they want direct, vigorous action. They have asked for discipline and direction under leadership. They have made me the present instrument of their wishes. In the spirit of the gift I take it. In this dedication of a Nation we humbly ask the blessing of God. May He protect each and every one of us. May He guide me in the days to come.	

Prewriting

RST Graphic Organizer

RST Graphic Organizer

Topic:

My Thesis Statement:

Source A	Source B	Source C

Exactly how do the sources talk with each other?

Your Outline:

Write your Essay Response in a notebook or on a sheet of loose-leaf paper.

RST #3: Should Puerto Rico Become a State?

85 minutes

Since 1917, the people living in Puerto Rico have been United States citizens, yet their land is not an official State of the United States of America. Puerto Rico, therefore, lives in a state of limbo, partly independent and partly American. There are some that believe Puerto Rico should become on official state, while there are others who disagree. What is your opinion? Should Puerto Rico become a state?

You have reviewed three sources regarding the issue of Puerto Rico. These three pieces provide information to begin drafting your own argument.

- **Source A:** Excerpt, "The History of Puerto Rico" (R.A. Van Middeldyk)

- **Source B:** Image, Humacao, Puerto Rico *www.flickr.com/photos/themarbellaclub/5528418143/*

- **Source C:** Excerpt, *A Little Journey to Puerto Rico* (Marian M. George)

Should Puerto Rico become a state? Write a persuasive piece that addresses the question and supports your position with evidence from at least two of the three sources. Be sure to acknowledge competing views. You may give examples from past and current events or issues to illustrate and clarify your position. You may refer to the sources by their titles (Source A, Source B, Source C).

SOURCE A

Excerpt, "The History of Puerto Rico" (R.A. Van Middeldyk)	My Thought Processes
SITUATION AND GENERAL APPEARANCE OF PUERTO RICO The island of Puerto Rico, situated in the Atlantic Ocean, is about 1,420 miles from New York, 1,000 miles from Havana, 1,050 miles from Key West, 1,200 miles from Panama, 3,450 miles from Land's End in England, and 3,180 from the port of Cadiz. It is about 104 miles in length from east to west, by 34 miles in average breadth, and has an area of 2,970 square miles. It lies eastward of the other greater Antilles, Cuba, Haiti, and Jamaica, and although inferior even to the last of these islands in population and extent, it yields to none of them in fertility. By its geographical position Puerto Rico is peculiarly adapted to become the center of an extensive commerce. It lies to the windward of Cuba, Santo Domingo, and Jamaica, and of the Gulf of Mexico and Bay of Honduras. It is contiguous to all the English and French Windward Islands, only a few hours distant from the former Danish islands Saint Thomas, Saint John, and Santa Cruz, and a few days' sail from the coast of Venezuela. Puerto Rico is the fourth in size of the greater Antilles. Its first appearance to the eye of the stranger is striking and picturesque. Nature here offers herself to his contemplation clothed in the splendid vesture of tropical vegetation. The chain of mountains which intersects the island from east to west seems at first sight to form two distinct chains parallel to each other, but closer observation makes it evident that they are in reality corresponding parts of the same chain, with upland valleys and tablelands in the	

(continued)

Excerpt, "The History of Puerto Rico" (R.A. Van Middeldyk)	My Thought Processes
center, which again rise gradually and incorporate themselves with the higher ridges. The height of these mountains is lofty, if compared with those of the other Antilles. The loftiest part is that of Luguillo, or Loquillo, at the northeast extremity of the island, which measures 1,334 Castilian yards, and the highest point, denominated El Yunque, can be seen at the distance of 68 miles at sea. The summit of this ridge is almost always enveloped in mist, and when its sides are overhung by white fleecy clouds it is the certain precursor of the heavy showers which fertilize the northern coast. The soil in the center of the mountains is excellent, and the mountains themselves are susceptible of cultivation to their summits. Several towns and villages are situated among these mountains, where the inhabitants enjoy the coolness of a European spring and a pure and salubrious atmosphere. The town of Alboníto, built on a table-land about eight leagues from Ponce, on the southern coast, enjoys a delightful climate. To the north and south of this interior ridge of mountains, stretching along the seacoasts, are the fertile valleys which produce the chief wealth of the island. From the principal chain smaller ridges run north and south, forming between them innumerable valleys, fertilized by limpid streams which, descending from the mountains, empty themselves into the sea on either coast. In these valleys the majestic beauty of the palm-trees, the pleasant alternation of hill and dale, the lively verdure of the hills, compared with the deeper tints of the forest, the orange trees, especially when covered with their golden fruit, the rivers winding through the dales, the luxuriant fields of sugar-cane, corn, and rice, with here and there a house peeping through a grove of plantains, and cattle grazing in the green pasture, form altogether a landscape of rural beauty scarcely to be surpassed in any country in the world.	

(continued)

Excerpt, "The History of Puerto Rico" (R.A. Van Middeldyk)	My Thought Processes
The valleys of the north and east coasts are richest in cattle and most picturesque. The pasturage there is always verdant and luxuriant, while those of the south coast, richer in sugar, are often parched by excessive drought, which, however, does not affect their fertility, for water is found near the surface. This same alternation of rain and drought on the north and south coasts is generally observed in all the West India islands. Few islands of the extent of Puerto Rico are watered by so many streams. Seventeen rivers, taking their rise in the mountains, cross the valleys of the north coast and fall into the sea. Some of these are navigable for two or three leagues from their mouths for small craft. Those of Manati, Loisa, Trabajo, and Arecibo are very deep and broad, and it is difficult to imagine how such large bodies of water can be collected in so short a course. Owing to the heavy surf which continually breaks on the north coast, these rivers have bars across their embouchures which do not allow large vessels to enter. The rivers of Bayamón and Rio Piedras flow into the harbor of the capital, and are also navigable for boats. At Arecibo, at high water, small brigs may enter with perfect safety, notwithstanding the bar. The south, west, and east coasts are also well supplied with water. From the Cabeza de San Juan, which is the northeast extremity of the island, to Cape Mala Pascua, which lies to the southeast, nine rivers fall into the sea. From Cape Mala Pascua to Point Aguila, which forms the southwest angle of the island, sixteen rivers discharge their waters on the south coast. On the west coast, three rivers, five rivulets, and several fresh-water lakes communicate with the sea. The rivers of the north coast are well stocked with edible fish.	

(continued)

Excerpt, "The History of Puerto Rico" (R.A. Van Middeldyk)	My Thought Processes
The roads formed in Puerto Rico during the Spanish administration are constructed on a substantial plan, the center being filled with gravel and stones well cemented. Each town made and repaired the roads of its respective district. Many excellent and solid bridges, with stone abutments, existed at the time of the transfer of the island to the American nation. The whole line of coast of this island is indented with harbors, bays, and creeks where ships of heavy draft may come to anchor. On the north coast, during the months of November, December, and January, when the wind blows sometimes with violence from the east and northeast, the anchorage is dangerous in all the bays and harbors of that coast, except in the port of San Juan. On the western coast the spacious bay of Aguadilla is formed by Cape Borrigua and Cape San Francisco. When the southeast winds prevail it is *not* a safe anchorage for ships. Mayaguez is also an open roadstead on the west coast formed by two projecting capes. It has good anchorage for vessels of large size and is well sheltered from the north winds. The south coast also abounds in bays and harbors, but those which deserve particular attention are the ports of Guánica and Hobos, or Jovos, near Guayama. In Guánica vessels drawing 21 feet of water may enter with perfect safety and anchor close to the shore. Hobos or Jovos is a haven of considerable importance; sailing vessels of the largest class may anchor and ride in safety; it has 4 fathoms of water in the shallowest part of the entrance, but it is difficult to enter from June to November as the sea breaks with violence at the entrance on account of the southerly winds which prevail at this season.	

(continued)

Excerpt, "The History of Puerto Rico" (R.A. Van Middeldyk)	My Thought Processes
All the large islands in the tropics enjoy approximately the same climate. The heat, the rains, the seasons, are, with trifling variations, the same in all, but the number of mountains and running streams, the absence of stagnant waters and general cultivation of the land in Puerto Rico do, probably, powerfully contribute to purify the atmosphere and render it more salubrious to Europeans than it otherwise would be. In the mountains one enjoys the coolness of spring, but the valleys, were it not for the daily breeze which blows from the northeast and east, would be almost uninhabitable for white men during part of the year. The climate of the north and south coasts of this island, though under the same tropical influence, is nevertheless essentially different. On the north coast it sometimes rains almost the whole year, while on the south coast sometimes no rain falls for twelve or fourteen months. On the whole, Puerto Rico is one of the healthiest islands in the West Indies, nor is it infested to the same extent as other islands by poisonous snakes and other noxious reptiles. The laborer may sleep in peace and security in the midst of the forest, by the side of the river, or in the meadow with his cattle with no other fear than that of an occasional centipede or guabuá (large hairy spider). Unlike most tropical islands there are no indigenous quadrupeds and scarcely any of the feathered tribe in the forests. On the rivers there are a few water-fowl and in the forests the green parrot. There are neither monkeys nor rabbits, but rats and mongooses infest the country and sometimes commit dreadful ravages in the sugar-cane. Ants of different species also abound.	

SOURCE B

Image, Humacao, Puerto Rico
http://www.flickr.com/photos/themarbellaclub/5528418143/

My Thoughts

SOURCE C

Excerpt, *A Little Journey to Puerto Rico* (Marian M. George)	My Thought Processes
San Juan While we are learning of the plant and animal life about and beneath us, the good ship bears us swiftly on, and all too soon we are at our journey's end. We seem hardly to have left the shadow of Liberty's towering torch in New York harbor, before the gray walls of Morro Castle appear above the horizon. Far out at sea, this massive stone fort with its beacon light attracts our attention. Across the harbor entrance the white-capped waves rush furiously over each other in a mad race toward the shore. Passing through this narrow channel, the ship glides into the harbor under the guns of the two picturesque old forts which guard it, and we get our first glimpse of San Juan. Our first view of this beautiful old city fills us with anticipations of pleasure. We find that the ground upon which the city lies slopes upward from the calm, broad harbor to the forts that guard its heights. Here and there a tall palm-tree rears its graceful head above the tops of the gayly colored buildings that glisten in the sunlight. Our guide tells us that San Juan is one of the most perfectly fortified cities in the world. It is easy to believe this when, from the ocean and from the bay, we see the massive walls and battlements of the forts that guard the north and east. We learn that they are cut from the solid rock which crowns the crest of the narrow peninsula. The steep walls of the vast castle of San Cristobal overshadow the whole city. The city is built on an island, connected with the mainland by a bridge.	

(continued)

Excerpt, *A Little Journey to Puerto Rico* (Marian M. George)	My Thought Processes
It is surrounded by a high, thick stone wall: that is, it was once upon a time; but the city is now extended far beyond the walls. Inside is the city proper, or old San Juan. Outside are the more modern buildings and the suburbs.	
San Juan is not only the seat of government, but it is considered the first city of Puerto Rico in interest and in importance. Ponce, however, disputes this claim. It has the best harbor, and the best public buildings, churches and schools on the island.	
The palace of the governor-general and the headquarters of the American administration we find located in San Juan.	
Over thirty thousand people make their homes in this city, and a goodly number of them we find at the shore to meet our vessel. They do not wait for us to land. They come out to meet us.	
Dusky natives in landing boats are soon alongside, and we learn to our surprise that our ship does not go to the dock. We are to go ashore in these small awning-covered boats. This is a new experience for us, but it is an old Spanish custom.	
The steward of the ship tells us that we may retain our rooms and use the ship as a hotel during the stay in port, going ashore for sight-seeing when we like.	
We have heard that the hotels in San Juan are very poor; but of course we wish to see for ourselves what they are like, and so we decide to give them a trial.	
We are in no hurry to seek the hotels, however. The streets of San Juan present so many novel sights to our wandering eyes that we wish to look about first.	

(continued)

Excerpt, *A Little Journey to Puerto Rico* (Marian M. George)	**My Thought Processes**
Street Scenes We have been told that we could walk all over the town in an hour, and we resolve to try it. The streets are narrow and dark, but well paved and clean. They ought to be clean, for they are swept by hand every day. The sidewalks are so narrow that only two of us can walk abreast, so we take to the road. This is used as a highway for people as well as vehicles. Naked little children of all ages and colors play about the streets and on the sidewalks. Colored men and women, smoking black cigars, saunter idly about. Street venders carrying their stores upon their heads or backs, or in large panniers upon tiny ponies, fill the air with cries announcing their wares. Judging from the number of the venders of drinks we see on the streets, every one in San Juan is thirsty. We are, at any rate, and very delicious we find their ices and sherbets, their iced orange, lemon and strawberry waters, iced cherries, milk, coffee and chocolate. Fruit sellers under the arcades and in stalls tempt us with their attractive wares; but the fruits are new and strange to us, and we hesitate about buying. The hack drivers are asleep on closed carriages at the hack stand. Long lines of clumsy carts, with high wheels, rumble over the cobblestone pavements with a dreadful clatter. In the open doorways of shops we see men and women manufacturing articles for sale. Some are making chairs, some shoes, some jewelry, some boxes, and, in one place, we see a number of workmen making coffins.	

(continued)

Excerpt, *A Little Journey to Puerto Rico* (Marian M. George)	My Thought Processes
We are interested in observing that flags of different colors are used as signs, and that the walls are painted with brilliant pictures. In the quarter near the sea, the brandy stores, built of reeds, have round them swarms of beggars of every degree.	
The laundry shop we find just outside the city, beside a large creek. A laundry not built by hands! Here women stand knee-deep in the stream, with the hot sun beating down upon their heads. They are doing their laundry work. The clothes are cleaned by soaking them in water and pounding them with stones. We wonder if there are any buttons left on the clothes after this treatment, and resolve not to trust our clothes to this laundry.	
We note outside the city wall a broad concrete walk; along this walk seats, trees, and rude statues; and between the walk and the wall an ornamental garden.	
Having now taken a general stroll, we will rest up preparatory to our visit to the points of special interest.	
Points of Interest in San Juan	
We are now ready to visit the places of unusual interest about the capital city. The most noted buildings are the governor's palace, the cathedral, the city hall, the arsenal, the buildings used as quarters for the troops, the forts, the castles of Morro and San Cristobal, the house which Ponce de Leon built, the palace of the bishop, the theater, the hospital, the orphan asylum, the poorhouse, the jail, the library, and the colleges.	
In the heart of the town, facing the City Hall, the guide shows us a public plaza; and under the frowning walls of San Cristobal, on the outskirts of the city, he points out another. These plazas are flat, open spaces, paved with cement and surrounded by rows of shade trees.	

(continued)

Excerpt, *A Little Journey to Puerto Rico* (Marian M. George)	My Thought Processes
In the plaza of Columbus, on the outskirts of the city, is a handsome statue of Columbus. Facing this plaza is the grand theater. In the cool of the evening, the people gather in these plazas, and listen to the music of the band. One of the most interesting buildings in the, city to us is the "White House of Ponce de Leon." It is still standing where it looked northward over the sea so long ago. On the side toward the bay is an old wall, and beyond this is a beautiful garden and rows of palm trees. From the windows we get a fine view of the bay. The people of San Juan have honored its founder with a statue, which stands in the center of one of its plazas. His remains are preserved in a leaden box in the church of Santo Domingo. We find the famous Morro Castle to be a small military town in itself, with houses, chapel, barracks, dungeons, water tanks, warehouses, and also a light tower, a signal station, and a light-saving station. This ancient fort is the beginning of the wall which surrounds the city.	

▎ **Prewriting**

RST Graphic Organizer

RST Graphic Organizer

Topic:

My Thesis Statement:

Source A	Source B	Source C

Exactly how do the sources talk with each other?

Your Outline:

Write your Essay in your notebook or in your loose-leaf binder.

CHAPTER 8

Research Simulation Task: Science

 Introduction

You've done some great work so far in moving through the research simulation task, as you have worked through the English and history-based questions! You have practiced how to:

- take notes while you read;

- break down the RST prompt;

- pre-write in the form of a graphic organizer;

- create a workable outline;

- develop a high-quality essay in the RST style;

- get your sources talking to each other; and

- edit your work using vivid action verbs.

We will now focus on how we can use these same skills to tackle the science RST. Read through the following research simulation task question and its accompanying sources. While you have to think about scientific pieces of this question, you may also (and often) have to address the social implications of these scientific topics as well. Keep both in mind as you work through the RSTs in this chapter.

As we have done in the previous three chapters, we will take you, step-by-step, through the completion of a RST in science. First, we will actively read the texts, using our two-column approach. Afterward, we will use the 11-step process to complete the written portion of the RST. Next, we will give you a model essay. Finally, you will be given two practice RSTs in science. By the end of this chapter, you will be that much more prepared when it comes to the RST in science.

Let's begin with the model RST:

RST #1: How Do I Look?

85 minutes

We live in a world that stresses the importance of physical appearance; in fact, scientific advancements have been so momentous in the progress of cosmetic and plastic surgery that it has become almost commonplace. Look around at our American society. Turn on any television station. Read any magazine. Americans have not only become physically obsessed with their reflection in the mirror, but cosmetic and plastic surgery are also becoming an engrained norm.

You have reviewed four sources regarding cosmetic surgery. These four pieces provide information to begin drafting your own argument.

- **Source A:** Cellulite Treatments: Do They Work? *http://abcnews.go.com/ Health/SkinCare/story?id=4964279&page=1*

- **Source B:** Plastic Surgery for Men, informal survey

- **Source C:** "Risking Your Health for Beauty" (fashion magazine)

- **Source D:** "The Importance of Self-Confidence" (from a doctor's notebook)

Write a well-written essay discussing the benefits or detriments concerning the popularity and ever-increasing scientific advancements of plastic or cosmetic surgery in our contemporary society. In this argumentative piece, address the question and support your position with evidence from at least three of the four sources. Be sure to acknowledge competing views. You may give examples from past and current events or issues to illustrate and clarify your position. You may refer to the sources by their titles (Source A, Source B, Source C, Source D).

After reading the RST on the progress of cosmetic and plastic surgery, you might be thinking that this particular topic has a lot of layers, and you're right, it absolutely does. The above prompt is difficult, in part, because you not only have to address the scientific advancements of cosmetic surgery, but you also must look closely at the social implications of this scientific advancement. We will break this task down for you, though. As you know, before we can attack the RST prompt, we must actively read our four sources. So, let's begin:

SOURCE A

Source A: Cellulite Treatments: Do They Work?	Our Thought Processes
By AINA HUNTER June 4, 2008 I've recently completed my sixth cellulite treatment at a spa in New York's speedily gentrifying Hell's Kitchen neighborhood—about 10 blocks from Times Square. It cost $1,200 to get my thighs and butt slathered in cold jelly, wrapped in plastic, heated up, chilled to the bone, and pressed with a hand-held device emitting lasers and ultrasound waves. At the end of each hour-and-a-half long session my adipose tissue—loaded with watery toxins, I was informed—was kneaded by a Brazilian woman's tiny but preternaturally forceful hands. Did I mention I'm getting married next month? That could explain why I've gone temporarily insane. "In Brazil these treatments are much cheaper," Iriana had confided as she kneaded. "And girls start young. Before they even develop cellulite." I've seen the famous behinds on the beaches of Rio and Bahia, and Iriana's words might have depressed me. But now I knew the girl from Ipanema's secret. Or rather, the skinny brat's grossly unfair advantage. Last month, before our first session, Iriana took pictures of me from all angles and measured my waist and thighs. Plus that area just above my knees caps which has grown increasingly hateful over the past couple of years.	• While on the surface this may be a reliable source, because it is Hunter's *personal* account, it could be severely slanted. Be careful as you read through the information that follows. • The cost, $1,200, is high. This can contribute to our argument in looking at the monetary facet of our perspective. • Girls start cellulite treatment even before they develop any cellulite at all.

(continued)

Source A: Cellulite Treatments: Do They Work?	Our Thought Processes
At this point I'd like to say that if you're ready to deliver me a lecture about women and body-image the evils of self-loathing, know this: I am aware that my physical obsessions are petty and psychologically destructive. I simply choose to indulge them in my free time. Onward. Know that there are no studies in medical literature to prove that any laser, sonar, lymphatic massage, electric shock, injections, or creams will get rid of cellulite. Still, spa-goers and estheticians say that intense manipulation with the help of various scientific advances can make lumpy fat appear smoother. That's what we really want. The airbrushed look of magazine models. Even the rounded models of Dove's "Real Beauty" campaign. If we can't be thin, we want to be sleek and tight like porpoises. I wanted the treatments to work. I felt that they should work. They were uncomfortable enough. To be fair, Iriana asked me several times if she was pressing too hard. I shook my head no as she dug her little hands into my screaming flesh. I covered my face with a pillow and bit into it. I wanted results, not coddling. The type of massage which is said to work by loosening the tight tissue that refuses to bend with the fat cells it connects (and instead stays rigid, forcing the fat cells to squeeze through and around), is not of the Swedish variety. Expect cellulite treatment involving tissue manipulation—be it Endermologie, Vela Smooth, Syneron or some combination—to make you feel like the victim in a pre-code, post-mod Hollywood cult film. You will lie on a slab under fluorescent light in paper underwear and accept your expensive punishment. A few days later you'll return for more.	• This very process, where pictures are taken of problematic areas, can be detrimental to a patient's psyche. On the other hand, this could also provide the patient with the confidence to tackle these problematic areas. • While scientific advancements are progressing, there is no cure-all. • We are a product of such social expectations to look a certain way.

(continued)

Source A: Cellulite Treatments: Do They Work?	Our Thought Processes
Read into it what you will, but that was part of the appeal. And I don't believe I am alone here. My thinking goes like this: cellulite is bad. It is the result of a decade of wasted gym memberships, a failure to take the stairs, a stubborn refusal to give up Godiva chocolate clams or cocktails or much else in my quest for beauty. The cellulite must be punished. This thinking is wrong-headed of course. Not to mention a psychologist's dream (how many years of therapy might it take to break through this ring of pathology? I'll never know—I've spent all my money on cellulite treatments!) Anyway. Google "cellulite" and you'll find conflicting information as to its origin. Many say it's metabolic waste—the result of poor circulation and ineffective lymphatic drainage. Others say it stems from wearing tight clothes and high heels. It can be hard for doctors to argue with these ideas, but they are only ideas. There's absolutely no scientific data behind them. What dermatologists do know is that cellulite can be genetic (shout-outs to my Grandmas on both sides). In addition, many researchers also believe there is a strong hormonal component to cellulite development. Dr. Bruce Katz, Director of New York's JUVA Skin and Laser Center and member of the American Academy of Dermatology, says that it's the thickness of your dermis—the inner layer of skin—and the pattern of the connective tissue beneath it which holds your fat cells together that matters. If you are lucky enough to have a sort of cross-hatch pattern, your fat cells are held in with double reinforcements. Regrettably, this pattern is most often seen in men. Most women have connective tissue patterned like columns, says Katz. It's easier for fat cells to bulge out of columns than small openings.	• Regardless of these social implications, science still moves us ahead, looking closely at fat cells and how to manipulate these scientifically. • While Hunter's experience is indeed common, there are plenty of people out there who can fight cellulite the right way. For example, using their gym memberships.

(continued)

Source A: Cellulite Treatments: Do They Work?	Our Thought Processes
In addition, men generally have a thicker dermis, which serves as a more effective natural girdle.	• Such methods are looked at closely by doctors. This should be noted in our research simulation writing task.
Taking Katz's words at face value, I have to assume that any results I might have observed from my treatment package were just temporary. I lost about an inch and a half from my waist, hips, and thighs—but that was only after being wrapped in plastic and sweating for over half an hour before the final measurements were taken.	
Katz says something called "Laser-Lipo" is far more effective than the combination laser and fat manipulation technique he no longer likes to schedule. No clinical studies have been completed yet, but Katz says the relatively new liposuction technique not only dissolves fat, but the deeply penetrating lasers tighten and thicken the skin. This a very different from regular lipo, which can make cellulite look worse.	• So, a lot also has to do with natural genetics as well.
If Katz is right, it seems there might be real, lasting, hope—if you're ready to go under the knife.	
Now that it's over, I'm thinking less about the (negligible) results and more about the psychological process I went through. The twice-weekly unveiling of parts of myself I'd never before consider unveiling to a stranger.	• Results are temporary from such an expensive, extensive procedure.
Although at first the deep massage did feel like a pummeling, as the treatments went on it stopped hurting *bad* and started hurting *good*. I fell asleep more than once.	
My most shameful fat (and I use that word with full knowledge of all its Freudian implications) was scrubbed, squeezed, covered in goo and lasered by three cheerful estheticians. All that attention was surreal and, in the end, liberating.	• Advancements are in the works, in terms of the procedure and its results.
What had been hidden all winter long, swathed in thick cotton tights and Spanx, was now exposed.	
And no one was injured, no one laughed, the camera lens didn't crack.	

As you can see through our notes in the right column, this piece, by Aina Hunter, a patient, looks at both sides of cosmetic surgery. By looking closely at her cellulite treatment as both invasive and liberating, we, as the writer, can use this source to argue either side. Overall, looking at this source by itself, we would use it to address the frivolous squandering of money, along with the need to do cosmetic enhancements the natural way. Especially since this patient discusses how these procedures are occurring with younger and younger patients, this is also something to note. Keep this in mind as we move forward. We still have three sources to go! Here's our second:

SOURCE B

Source B: Men's Health Graph	Our Thought Processes
An informal survey of men's thinking on plastic surgery resulted in the following feedback: Eyelift 27% Stomach reduction 25% Hair transplant 20% Facelift 20% Thigh reduction 13% Nose change 10% Hair removal 5% Reduce breast size 5%	• We are not exactly sure what these numbers represent, how many men were surveyed, etc. The numbers, though, still are worthwhile to back up either side of this argument. • This issue is not just one that exists with women, as we commonly see through social media, men also find the need to look better. • Many men surveyed thought even if they had plastic surgery, that they still do not feel as if they are fit as it is. Perhaps if men hit the gym harder, cosmetic surgery wouldn't even be considered.

Compared to Source A, this graph still looks at information on the surface. How do we use it then? Now that we know that not all information provided is going to be entirely reliable, it is important to sort through our data to use it to our advantage. The chart recognizes three valuable observations:

1. Cosmetic surgery is not only a consideration for women.

2. Men's self-image of themselves, according to this survey, is not exactly high.

3. A vast variety of possible cosmetic surgery procedures exist.

With this mind, let's take a look at Source C.

SOURCE C

"Risking Your Health for Beauty" (extracted from a fashion magazine)	Our Thought Processes
The Real Botox Facts While recent reports discuss Botox as causing botulism and being unsafe, many still use it to fight wrinkles. According to the American Society for Aesthetic Plastic Surgery, cosmetic Botox procedures totaled an estimated $1.2 billion last year. While reports share that this toxin may be unsafe, the statistics prove that many have chosen to ignore such reports. Perusing Botox's prescribing information, which states that there have been "rare spontaneous reports of death…after treatment with botulinum toxin," isn't part of the usual treatment visit. It also states that those who have an allergy to the albumin in eggs probably shouldn't receive Botox, since the toxin is mixed with amounts of human albumin. It's worth stating that the cases recently reported in the news did not involve Botox Cosmetic, which is manufactured by Allergan. The Florida cases resulting in paralysis involved raw botulinum toxin made for research purposes in extremely high concentrations. While the short-term impact is limited, what about the long term effects?	• Some of this information should be reliable, as it has been researched to include certain statistics from reputable organizations, but be careful not to take all of this fashion magazine's article as complete truth. • Botulism and paralysis are obvious concerns that are being ignored as botox gains in popularity. • The toxins in some botox could be deadly. Is it really worth the risk? • Allergan's Botox works in the short-term, but the reality of the long-term effects is still not known.

(continued)

"Risking Your Health for Beauty" (extracted from a fashion magazine)	Our Thought Processes
A 1990 statement from the National Institutes of Health asserted that "the long-term effects [greater than five years] of chronic treatment with botulinum toxin remain unknown." Since then, an Allergan-supported meta-analysis published in 2004 indicates that Botox has had "a favorable safety and tolerability profile" for a range of uses over a 15-year period.	• The very presence of botulinum toxin should deter Americans from trying this out at all!
Too much Botox can lead to some unflattering effects as well. If Botox is placed incorrectly around the eyes or spreads to nearby muscles, things get more unsavory. Upper eyelids may droop and lower lids can pull away from the eyeball. It's also not uncommon for Botox to cause drooping and drooling when injected near the mouth. Most problems occur when Botox is used in areas other than the brow and crow's-feet because it can interfere with a functional element of the face. Kathleen Harron, 40, experienced problems when she had Botox injected on either side of her mouth to lessen her marionette lines. "I just wanted to lift the downturned corners of my mouth. The result was I couldn't chew properly," says Harron. Food would collect at the corners of Harron's mouth, requiring her to use a finger to push it further back, followed by cheek massaging to help break the food down. "I couldn't go out to dinner or anywhere, but the worst of it was when the plastic surgeon who injected me said, 'Well, at least you don't have the lines anymore,'" says Harron, who suffered these egregious effects for months until the Botox wore off.	• A resistance to botox exists, and should be noted in our essay.

• We live in a society of excess. Botox and beauty improvement is no different. |
| When administered correctly, Botox temporarily paralyzes or weakens muscles to keep them from contracting. However, when pressed, some dermatologists admit there can be a domino effect with Botox. Other muscles will contract to compensate for injected areas, often forming new wrinkles. "Bunny lines" across the bridge of the nose have already entered into the pop-culture lexicon as a telltale sign of Botox use. | • Yes, when Botox is administered correctly, but what if it isn't? Why take this chance? Is it worth the risk?

• New wrinkles may be created, making this a counterproductive procedure in the first place. |
| A safer alternative: Try Clarins Instant Smooth ($26), a cosmetic version of spackle that you dab onto wrinkles before putting on makeup to create a smooth surface. | • A look at alternatives, but really, are these creams as impactful in terms of seeing results? |

With our third source read, it is important to note that, again, while this source is leaning heavily in one direction (science advancements of cosmetic surgery are detrimental to our contemporary society), much more exists than meets the eye. Arguments for benefits may also exist, such as this idea of results. The article also mentions a cream as a safer alternative, but the results may not nearly compare to those of the Botox (non-bogus) itself. Keep these two perspectives in mind as we move forward.

Let's review our three sources—unlike those reviewed in our past RSTs, it is important to keep in mind that each can be used for completely opposite arguments. Be careful in selecting your supporting details. In terms of responding to our RST prompt, we are leaning toward writing an essay about the scientific advancements of cosmetic surgery being detrimental to our contemporary society. However, we still need to analyze our fourth, and final, source:

SOURCE D

"The Importance of Self-Confidence" (from a doctor's notebook)	Our Thought Processes
A variety of treatments now exist to help many of us in our 20s, 30s, 40s, 50s, and even older, to look and feel younger.	• A link exists between physical appearance and our emotions.
And with those treatments, we have found that these are not accessible to just Hollywood stars anymore.	• Plastic surgery is now accessible to many more people than just the rich and privileged.
With facial cosmetic procedures at an all-time high, even during a recession and economic upheaval in our country, beauty remains as an important part of our American society.	
Statistics reported by the American Society of Plastic Surgeons (ASPS) earlier this year indicate another 5% increase in total cosmetic procedures year-over-year, with cosmetic surgical procedures including nose reshaping, eyelid surgery and facelift reaching nearly 1.6 million in 2011, up 2% from last year while cosmetic minimally invasive procedures such as Botox injections, soft tissue fillers and chemical peels grew to 12.2 million last year, up 6% from 2010.	• Increase in cosmetic procedures.

(continued)

"The Importance of Self-Confidence" (from a doctor's notebook)	Our Thought Processes
And with the rise in interest, and rise in number of patients who want similar procedures, more and more treatments are being offered by more and more doctors in order to satisfy patients' demands. Both males and females are undergoing such treatments, and because of this popularity, more detail-oriented surgeries are occurring more readily.	• Advancements focus on more subtle, natural changes for patients.
What it comes down to is that such surgery is to promote self-confidence in the patient. The better a person looks, often indicates the better a person feels about themselves, and in general. Consequently, as one of northwest Indiana's most accomplished ear, nose, and throat surgeons, Dr. Cataldi brings a vast amount of expertise in facial plastic surgery and cosmetic enhancement procedures to her patients.	• ***This is the key point of the article. Physical image = self-esteem.
The most recent requests from patients focuses on the need to have such treatments be subtle, and less "overdone." The goal is to have the patient leave improved, without obvious notice of treatment being done – an obviously difficult task. The goal is for the patient to look as natural as possible.	• The goal of cosmetic surgery is no longer to look like cosmetic surgery, but to simply make physical improvement.
In an office setting, many doctors use chemical peels, Juviderm, and Botox on patients so that the setting feels as invasive as it looks—minimally. Private, open dialogue between the doctor and patient is necessary in dealing with the patient's needs and desires for the outcome of the process.	• Goal: a natural look. • Focus on individualized consultation. • Partnership of doctor and patient is important to delicately guide the patient through these procedures.

Now that we have read our final source, let's think for a moment how it fits with the previous three. Source D clearly argues the benefits scientific advancements have contributed to cosmetic surgery. Dr. Cataldi looks closely at the self-confidence cosmetic surgery can provide to a patient. Scientific advancements, however, contribute to this very crucial social implication.

As you can undoubtedly tell, after reading all four sources, we are well on our way to writing a response to the RST prompt that shows that scientific advancements are detrimental to our contemporary today. This idea can be supported by three of the four sources. So, it's time to begin. Keep in mind that when we write this model essay, while three sources will be used, the fourth source can be referenced to make a counterargument. We'll talk about this further as we move ahead together.

Let's take a look at our 11-step process:

 # 11 Steps for Success on the RST

Before Writing Begins	
Step #1:	Read through the question carefully. Make sure to decipher if the question is asking you to convey an opinion, or to convey information/research objectively. • The question is asking us to convey an opinion
Step #2:	Simplify what the question is asking you to do. Put the question/task into your own words. • The prompt is asking this: "Is plastic/cosmetic surgery good or bad?"
Step #3:	Circle the minimum amount of sources that need to be addressed. • Three sources
Step #4:	Take notes with each of the sources. Address the source's main points. Underline actively. • We completed this activity extensively in our two-column approach and when we took notes on the video

(continued)

Step #5:	After you've addressed and highlighted the main point of the source, make separate notes on the reliability of these sources. Is the source reliable in general? Is it slanted in any way? Do logical fallacies or "holes in argument" exist? • We took notes on the reliability of sources in our active reading.
Step #6:	You've read through your sources. Choose the sources that you are most comfortable with, and put an asterisk (*) next to them. • We will be primarily working with Sources A, B, and C.
	Writing the RST
Step #7:	Copy the arguments—textual evidence—you will use in your essay into the prewriting chart. (shown below)
Step #8:	Now, look at the relationships of your sources. Do they agree with each other? Do they disagree? Use your source-relationship chart to begin thinking about how you will have your sources begin conversing with one another. (shown below)
Step #9:	Compose a quick outline of your essay. (shown below)
Step #10:	Complete your essay using the framework/outline as a guide. (shown below)
Step #11:	After you have completed your essay, go back to check that your sources have a conversation, and replace the verbs you've used to integrate these sources with the action verbs from the sheet provided. (shown below)

So, let's get started on doing the prewriting for our response. Following is the RST graphic organizer:

RST Graphic Organizer

Topic: Cosmetic Surgery

My Thesis Statement: Cosmetic surgery is detrimental to our contemporary society.

Source A	Source B	Source C
Cellulite Treatments: Do They Work?	Men's Survey	Are You Risking Your Health for Beauty?
$1,200 for cellulite treatment = can become costly	We are not exactly sure what these numbers represent, how many men were surveyed, etc. The numbers, though, still are worthy to show that most mean see themselves as "average." What exactly does average look like?	Allergan's Botox works in the short-term, but the reality of the long-term effects are still not known.
Girls start cellulite treatment even before they develop any cellulite at all.		The very presence of botulinum toxin should deter Americans from trying this out at all!
Regardless of scientific advancements, no one can stop the aging process.	This issue is not just one that exists with women, as we commonly see through social media, men also find the need to look better.	A resistance to botox exists, and should be noted in our essay.
We are a product of such social expectations to look a certain way.	Many men surveyed, though, that regardless of considerations of plastic surgery, they still do not feel as if they are fit as it is. Perhaps if men hit the gym harder, cosmetic surgery wouldn't even need to be a consideration.	We live in a society of excess. Botox and beauty improvement is no different.
While Hunter's experience is indeed common, there are plenty of people out there who can fight cellulite the right way. For example, using their gym memberships, or eating healthy.		Yes, when Botox is administered correctly, but what if it isn't? Why take this chance? Is it worth the risk?
Natural genetics play a role in success of procedures.		New wrinkles may be created, making this a counter-productive procedure in the first place.
Results are temporary.		A look at alternatives, but really, are these creams as impactful in regards to seeing results?

How can the sources talk to each other?

At the core of each of these sources is the idea that cosmetic surgery plays a major role in our contemporary time. Mostly, a very natural conversation exists between Source A and Source C, looking closely at cellulite and Botox treatments. We have already addressed the fact that Source B can easily be used for both sides of the argument. Since we are looking at the detriments of the scientific advancements of cosmetic surgery, Source A and Source C can work with ease. Source B and converse with both Source A and Source C as well. Men's perspectives regarding cosmetic surgery, focusing on physical appearance, may completely overshadow the health risks discussed in Source A and Source C. This will be a good place to start.

As you can see, we again did a fairly good job tackling Step 7 and Step 8. At the bottom of our chart, we pre-wrote a bit on how our sources share a common theme that works towards crafting our argument on the detriments of cosmetic surgery. That work, undoubtedly, will become useful as we write our essay. For now, though, we must head to Step 9, the outline. As discussed previously, we want to keep our outline brief, focusing on the major themes of the essay. Here we go:

I. Introduction

    a. Attention Grabber

    b. Thesis: Cosmetic surgery is detrimental to our contemporary society.

II. Body

    a. Theme 1: Cosmetic Surgery / Health Concerns

    b. Theme 2: Cosmetic Surgery / Social Implications

III. Conclusion

    a. Rework thesis statement

    b. Answer to the So What? question

As you can see in the outline above, our essays will be working through the concept of how scientific advancements present health concerns and also have long-lasting social implications. What we want you to know: Our very close reading of the four texts has worked. We are ready to write an excellent response to the RST prompt because we have plenty of knowledge about the writing topic. **Heed this advice: The better you read, the better you will write.** Here's our sample essay:

> Lip injections. Nose jobs. Steroids. Eye lifts. Cellulite treatments. We live in a society that has become obsessed with our reflections in the mirror, and due to scientific advancements, we can now alter that reflection any way that we see fit. We tuck, suck, cut, and lift only to look like magazine covers. The contemporary reality is that in order to be a beauty queen, there will always be a price to pay that has no return policy.

> Going "under the knife" has its costs that go far beyond dollars and cents. Psychological effects undoubtedly impact patients, warping an overly obsessed

self-image into problems that lay deep beneath the surface. According to Source A, "I am aware that my physical obsessions are petty and psychologically destructive. I simply choose to indulge them in my free time." While sarcastic in tone, Aina Hunter's account has an echoing ring of truth that is no laughing matter. If we cannot be happy with ourselves, if we cannot accept our flaws, we will be left to try to attempt in achieving the impossible. Perfection is unattainable, and psychologically, if we do not understand this from an early age, our American population will be in trouble. Unfortunately, we already are. Source C addresses the impact scientific advancements have had on the bodies patients seem to hold so superficially dear. Simply put, toxins, lethal poisons, and paralysis contribute to a series of Botox procedures. If not done correctly, such a process can end up deadly. All that will be left is a pretty corpse. Focusing on Americans' laziness, Source A candidly declares, "My thinking goes like this: cellulite is bad. It is the result of a decade of wasted gym memberships, a failure to take the stairs, a stubborn refusal to give up Godiva chocolate, clams or cocktails…" Defying the gravity and gain that comes with age is indeed a possibility, but it takes a lot of hard work — doable work. Let's not forget that many of these procedures are not even FDA-approved (Source B). How can we put our health in jeopardy when highly effective creams exist and exercise and diet regimens are obviously the more healthy option? (Source C)

The social implications of cosmetic surgery remain long lasting, almost forcing American society to question every glance in the mirror. This obsession does not leave any gender spared, however; in fact, both men and women are spending their hard-earned money (Source C) and considering altering everything from their eyebrows to their hair (Source B). Our contemporary society is obsessed with image. From reality television to magazine covers, it seems as if every young girl wants to grow up to be the *Housewife of Some Town*, and modifying their appearance to do so. What happened to our pride? Why have we spent so much time on using our scientific advancements towards superficial changes, when diseases need to be cured and lives need to be changed? This ridiculous reality alone should make us think twice about wasting our money, our time, our dignity, or our hours in front of the mirror, scouring our face for every wrinkle, scar, and asymmetrical curve.

The quest for physical perfection will never be achieved, and the ways in which we attempt to gain this impossible goal will leave our American society that much more forever flawed. The mirror will be left fractured because it turns out that these supposed scientific advancements are only holding us back from accepting the physical nuances that make us who we are.

Step 11: Looking at the Verbs

Now that we have completed our written response to the RST topic, it is time to pay close attention to our verb choice. Look through the essay above and circle the verb choices. Do you find them "boring" or "tiresome?" If so, use the Action Verb Chart in Appendix A to find replacements. In our experiences with holistic scoring for high-stakes tests, action verbs often acted as the tipping point between a lower score and a higher score. Keep this in mind as you revise your own work.

Analysis of Sample Essay

As we did in the previous chapter, we are giving you an analysis of the sample essay according to the four criteria identified in our Scoring Checklist Chart (reproduced below). In addition, we have included the writing rubric from the PARCC. You might also wish to check our sample essay against the writing rubric in the back of the book.

Scoring Checklist

Development of Ideas
❏ Did the author use evidence from the text?
❏ Did this evidence come from more than one source?
❏ Did the author successfully have the two sources interact with each other?

Organization
❏ Is there a clearly expressed introduction, body, and conclusion?
❏ Does the introduction have an attention-grabber and a clearly stated thesis?
❏ Do each of the body paragraphs support the thesis?
❏ Does the conclusion successfully answer the So What? question?

(continued)

Written Expression
❏ Does the author effectively use vocabulary, including content-specific words?
❏ Does the author utilize vivid and proper description?
❏ Does the author appropriately use transitional words throughout the piece?
❏ Is the style clear, concise, and to the point?
❏ Are any points in the essay ambiguous and unclear?

Knowledge of Language Conventions
❏ Were there any mistakes in grammar, mechanics, and usage?
❏ Did the author go back and edit the work?
❏ Does the work read effortlessly?
❏ Does poor grammar become a distraction or a nuisance?

By "Development of Ideas," the makers of the PARCC refer to the ways in which arguments are developed and maintained throughout the course of the essay. Some questions might be: "Did the author use evidence from the text?" "Did this evidence come from more than one source?" "Did the author successfully have the two sources interact with each other?" As you can see, these questions are quite difficult and will take time for you to master. However, you can see these principles in action if you read carefully our sample essay above. We did cite evidence from three of the four sources, and we did have the three sources interact, or "talk." For instance, in the first body paragraph, we looked at how Source A and Source C both look at the detriments of cellulite and Botox procedures. The sources "interacted" or "talked" with each other in the sense that both sources were used to talk about the negativities of alternating one's appearance.

Second, the PARCC will look at the organization of your writing. This, in fact, should come as no surprise at all for you. Organization is a key to all good writing, regardless of where it is done. Because we carefully followed our outline, we organized our work. The three main parts of the essay are clearly present: Introduction, body, and conclusion.

The next criteria, "clarity of language" will look at your writing style and the effectiveness of that style., then, is nothing more than the writer's identity on paper. What the PARCC cares about most is simple: Is your style clear, concise, and to the point? There is nothing worse than reading an essay that lacks clarity and is difficult to read. What would you say of the style of our sample essay? Look back at our choice of vocabulary: Did we use vocabulary terms that were appropriate to research and statistics? Were our descriptions of the research sources clear? Were any of the words we used confusing? Could we have been clearer? These questions are helpful when looking at style.

The PARCC will look at your knowledge of language and conventions—your grammar, mechanics, and usage. Were there any mistakes in these three categories? Did the author go back and edit the work? Does the work read effortlessly? Does poor grammar make it difficult to understand what you are reading? We think that our sample essay is pretty good and gives you a RST essay that has no grammatical issues and reads well. Use the PARCC rubric in the back of the book to see how you would score it.

Summary of the RST in Science

As you know by this point in the chapter, once you master the skills of the RST—the active reading and the 11 Steps to Success—all you have to do is learn new content. We have shown you how difficult texts, such as the ones dealing with contemporary scientific-related issues, can be managed when putting together a quality, written response. Can you guess the idea that we want to impress upon you the most? You got it! The better you read, the better you will write!

Practice RSTs in Science

Now, it's your turn. We will give you two sample RST tasks in science with accompanying organizers and space to write. Please be sure, as you go through this process to utilize the 11 Steps of Success, and, as always, read well; your writing depends upon it!

RTS #2: Genetic Engineering and Ethics

85 minutes

We live in a world that is uncertain. When it comes to our children, parents undoubtedly feel this way throughout the duration of pregnancy. Many want to control their child's gene pool, including the way that they will look, act, and think.

- **Source A:** "Taboo and Genetics" by Melvin Moses Knight, Iva Lowther Peters, and Phyllis Mary Blanchard, *www.gutenberg.org/files/14325/14325-h/14325-h.htm*

- **Source B:** "Species and Varieties, Their Origin by Mutation," by Hugo DeVries, *www.gutenberg.org/files/7234.htm*

- **Source C:** Graph of results of survey of medical students regarding bioengineering

- **Source D:** Newborn Child (Image), Caroline Krueger

Is the process of genetic engineering ethical? Consider the arguments that these four sources use in their observations of genetic engineering. Write an informative piece that addresses the question and supports your position with evidence from at least three of the four sources. Be sure to acknowledge competing views. You may give examples from past and current events or issues to illustrate and clarify your position. You may refer to the sources by their titles (Source A, Source B, Source C, Source D).

SOURCE A

From "Taboo and Genetics"	My Thought Processes
Neither the ovum nor the spermatozoon (the human race is referred to) is capable alone of developing into a new individual. They must join in the process known as fertilization. The sperm penetrates the egg (within the body of the female) and the 23 chromosomes from each source, male and female, are re-grouped in a new nucleus with 46 chromosomes—the full number.	
The chances are half and half that the new individual thus begun will be of a given sex, for the following reason: There is a structural difference, supposed to be fundamentally chemical, between the cells of a female body and those of a male. The result is that the gametes (sperm and eggs) they respectively produce in maturation are not exactly alike as to chromosome composition. All the eggs contain what is known as the "X" type of sex chromosome. But only half the male sperm have this type—in the other half is found one of somewhat different type, known as "Y." (This, again, is for the human species—in some animals the mechanism and arrangement is somewhat different.) If a sperm and egg both carrying the X-type of chromosome unite in fertilization, the resulting embryo is a female. If an X unites with a Y, the result is a male. Since each combination happens in about half the cases, the race is about half male and half female.	
Thus sex is inherited, like other characters, by the action of the chromatin material of the cell nucleus. As Goldschmidt remarks, this theory of the visible mechanism of sex distribution "is to-day so far proven that the demonstration stands on the level of an experimental proof in physics or chemistry." But why and how does this nuclear material determine sex? In other words, what is the nature of the process of differentiation into male and female which it sets in motion?	

(continued)

From "Taboo and Genetics"	My Thought Processes
To begin with, we must give some account of the difference between the cells of male and female origin, an unlikeness capable of producing the two distinct types of gametes, not only in external appearance, but in chromosome makeup as well. It is due to the presence in the bodies of higher animals of a considerable number of glands, such as the thyroid in the throat and the suprarenals just over the kidneys. These pour secretions into the blood stream, determining its chemical quality and hence how it will influence the growth or, when grown, the stable structure of other organs and cells. They are called endocrine glands or organs, and their chemical contributions to the blood are known as *hormones*. Sometimes those which do nothing but furnish these secretions are spoken of as "ductless glands," from their structure. The hormones (endocrine or internal secretions) do not come from the ductless glands alone—but the liver and other glands contribute hormones to the blood stream, in addition to their other functions. Some authorities think that "every cell in the body is an organ of internal secretion", and that thus each influences all the others. The sex glands are especially important as endocrine organs; in fact the somatic cells are organized around the germ cells, as pointed out above. Hence the sex glands may be considered as the keys or central factors in the two chemical systems, the male and the female type.	

SOURCE B

From "Species and Varieties, Their Origin by Mutation" (excerpt)	My Thought Processes
Five-Leaved Clover Every one knows the "four-leaved" clover. It is occasionally found on lawns, in pastures and by the roadsides. Specimens with five leaflets may be found now and then in the same place, or on the same plant, but these are rarer. I have often seen isolated plants with quaternate leaves, but only rarely have I observed individuals with more than one such leaf. The two cases are essentially dissimilar. They may appear to differ but little morphologically, but from the point of view of heredity they are quite different. Isolated quaternate leaves are of but little interest, while the occurrence of many on the same individual indicates a distinct variety. In making experiments upon this point it is necessary to transplant the divergent individuals to a garden in order to furnish them proper cultural conditions and to keep them under constant observation. When a plant bearing a quaternate leaf is thus transplanted however, it rarely repeats the anomaly. But when plants with two or more quaternate leaves on the same individual are chosen it indicates that it belongs to a definite race, which under suitable conditions may prove to become very rich in the anomalies in question. Obviously it is not always easy to decide definitely whether a given individual belongs to such a race or not. Many trials may be necessary to secure the special race. I had the good fortune to find two plants of clover, bearing one quinate and several quaternate leaves, on an excursion in the neighborhood of Loosdrecht in Holland. After transplanting them into my garden, I cultivated them during three years and observed a slowly increasing number of anomalous leaves. This number in one summer amounted to 46 quaternate and 16 quinate leaves, and it was evident that I had secured an instance of the rare "five-leaved" race which I am about to describe.	

(continued)

From "Species and Varieties, Their Origin by Mutation" (excerpt)	My Thought Processes
Before doing so it seems desirable to look somewhat closer into the morphological features of the problem. Pinnate and palmate leaves often vary in the number of their parts. This variability is generally of the nature of a common fluctuation, the deviations grouping themselves around an average type in the ordinary way. Ash leaves bear five pairs, and the mountain-ash (*Sorbus Aucuparia*) has six pairs of leaflets in addition to the terminal one. But this number varies slightly, the weaker leaves having less, the stronger more pairs than the average. Such however, is not the case, with ternate leaves, which seem to be quite constant. Four leaflets occur so very rarely that one seems justified in regarding them rather as an anomaly than, as a fluctuation. And this is confirmed by the almost universal absence of two-bladed clover-leaves. Considering the deviation as an anomaly, we may look into its nature. Such an inquiry shows that the supernumerary leaflets owe their origin to a splitting of one or more of the normal ones. This splitting is not terminal, as is often the case with other species, and as it may be seen sometimes in the clover. It is for the most part lateral. One of the lateral nerves grows out becoming a median nerve of the new leaflet. Intermediate steps are not wanting, though rare, and they show a gradual separation of some lateral part of a leaflet, until this division reaches the base and divides the leaflet into two almost equal parts. If this splitting occurs in one leaflet we get the "four-leaved" Clover, if it occurs in two there will be five leaflets. And if, besides this, the terminal leaflet produces a derivative on one or both of its sides, we obtain a crown of six or seven leaflets on one stalk. Such were often met with in the race I had under cultivation, but as a rule it did not exceed this limit.	

(continued)

From "Species and Varieties, Their Origin by Mutation" (excerpt)	My Thought Processes
The same phenomenon of a lateral doubling of leaflets may of course be met with in other instances. The common laburnum has a variety which often produces quaternate and quinate leaves, and in strawberries I have also seen instances of this abnormality. It occurs also in pinnate leaves, and complete sets of all the intermediate links may often be found on the false or bastard-acacia (_Robinia Pseud_Acacia_). Opposed to this increase of the number of leaflets, and still more rare and more curious is the occurrence of "single-leaved" varieties among trees and herbs with pinnate or ternate leaves. Only very few instances have been described, and are cultivated in gardens. The ashes and the bastard-acacia may be quoted among trees, and the "one-leaved" strawberry among herbs. Here it seems that several leaflets have been combined into one, since this one is, as a rule, much larger than the terminal leaflet of an ordinary leaf of the same species. These monophyllous varieties are interesting also on account of their continuous but often incomplete reversion to the normal type.	

SOURCE C

The following graph illustrates information regarding the results related to a survey given to a 2013 graduating class of medical students in reference to their professional beliefs about bioengineering:

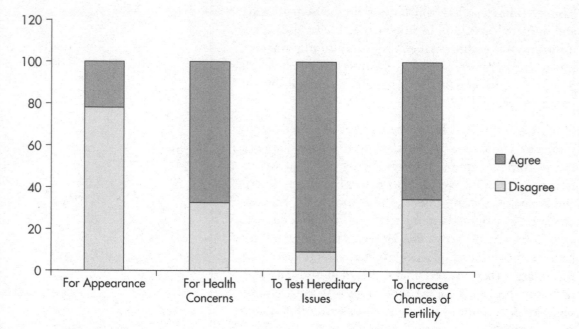

My Thought Processes:

SOURCE D

Image — Newborn Child

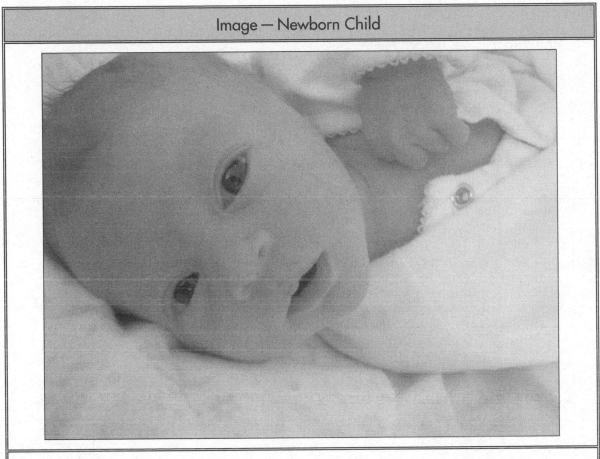

My Thought Processes

Prewriting

RST Graphic Organizer

RST Graphic Organizer

Topic:

My Thesis Statement:

Source A	Source B	Source C

Exactly how do the sources talk with each other?

Your Outline:

Write your Essay in your notebook or in your loose-leaf binder.

Scoring Checklist

Development of Ideas
❏ Did the author use evidence from the text?
❏ Did this evidence come from more than one source?
❏ Did the author successfully have the two sources interact with each other?

Organization
❏ Is there a clearly expressed introduction, body, and conclusion?
❏ Does the introduction have an attention-grabber and a clearly stated thesis?
❏ Do each of the body paragraphs support the thesis?
❏ Does the conclusion successfully answer the So What? question?

Written Expression
❏ Does the author effectively use vocabulary, including content-specific words?
❏ Does the author utilize vivid and proper description?
❏ Does the author appropriately use transitional words throughout the piece?
❏ Is the style clear, concise, and to the point?
❏ Are any points in the essay ambiguous and unclear?

Knowledge of Language Conventions
❏ Were there any mistakes in grammar, mechanics, and usage?
❏ Did the author go back and edit the work?
❏ Does the work read effortlessly?
❏ Does poor grammar become a distraction or a nuisance?

RST #3: The Science Behind Diet

85 minutes

With new fad diets, people of all ages are constantly looking to slim down and live a healthier lifestyle. A variety of diets exist today, labeled by catchy names and promised results. The science behind dieting can be complex, looking closely at how food intake can affect the process of fat loss.

You have reviewed three sources regarding the complexity of science behind dieting. These three pieces provide information to begin drafting your own argument.

- **Source A:** Excerpt, *No Animal Food* (Rupert H. Wheldon)
- **Source B:** "Health Myths Debunked: Are Carbs Bad for You?" *http://watch-mojo.com/video/id/10780/*
- **Source C:** Excerpt, *Diet and Health* (Lulu Hunt Peters, M.D.)

Write a well-written essay that addresses the considerations when changing one's daily diet. Be sure to address the question and support your position with evidence from the three sources. You may give examples from past and current events or issues to illustrate and clarify your position. You may refer to the sources by their titles (Source A, Source B, Source C).

SOURCE A

Excerpt, *No Animal Food* (Rupert H. Wheldon)	Our Thought Processes
Ethical Considerations The primary consideration in regard to the question of diet should be, as already stated, the hygienic. Having shown that the non-flesh diet is the more natural, and the more advantageous from the point of view of health, let us now consider which of the two—vegetarianism or omnivorism—is superior from the ethical point of view.	

(continued)

Excerpt, *No Animal Food* (Rupert H. Wheldon)	Our Thought Processes
The science of ethics is the science of conduct. It is founded, primarily, upon philosophical postulates without which no code or system of morals could be formulated. Briefly, these postulates are, (a) every activity of man has as its deepest motive the end termed Happiness, (b) the Happiness of the individual is indissolubly bound up with the Happiness of all Creation. The truth of (a) will be evident to every person of normal intelligence: all arts and systems aim consciously, or unconsciously, at some good, and so far as names are concerned everyone will be willing to call the Chief Good by the term Happiness, although there may be unlimited diversity of opinion as to its nature, and the means to attain it. The truth of (b) also becomes apparent if the matter is carefully reflected upon. Everything that is *en rapport* with all other things: the pebble cast from the hand alters the centre of gravity in the Universe. As in the world of things and acts, so in the world of thought, from which all action springs. Nothing can happen to the part but the whole gains or suffers as a consequence. Every breeze that blows, every cry that is uttered, every thought that is born, affects through perpetual metamorphoses every part of the entire Cosmic Existence.	
We deduce from these postulates the following ethical precepts: a wise man will, firstly, so regulate his conduct that thereby he may experience the greatest happiness; secondly, he will endeavour to bestow happiness on others that by so doing he may receive, indirectly, being himself a part of the Cosmic Whole, the happiness he gives. Thus supreme selfishness is synonymous with supreme egoism, a truth that can only be stated paradoxically.	
Applying this latter precept to the matter in hand, it is obvious that since we should so live as to give the greatest possible happiness to all beings capable of appreciating it, and as it is an indisputable fact that animals can suffer pain, *and that men who slaughter animals needlessly suffer from atrophy of all*	

(continued)

Excerpt, *No Animal Food* (Rupert H. Wheldon)	Our Thought Processes
finer feelings, we should therefore cause no unnecessary suffering in the animal world. Let us then consider whether, knowing flesh to be unnecessary as an article of diet, we are, in continuing to demand and eat flesh-food, acting morally or not. To answer this query is not difficult. It is hardly necessary to say that we are causing a great deal of suffering among animals in breeding, raising, transporting, and killing them for food. It is sometimes said that animals do not suffer if they are handled humanely, and if they are slaughtered in abattoirs under proper superintendence. But we must not forget the branding and castrating operations; the journey to the slaughter-house, which when trans-continental and trans-oceanic must be a long drawn-out nightmare of horror and terror to the doomed beasts; we must not forget the insatiable cruelty of the average cowboy; we must not forget that the animal inevitably spends at least some minutes of instinctive dread and fear when he smells and sees the spilt blood of his forerunners, and that this terror is intensified when, as is frequently the case, he witnesses the dying struggles, and hears the heart-rending groans; we must not forget that the best contrivances sometimes fail to do good work, and that a certain percentage of victims have to suffer a prolonged death-agony owing to the miscalculation of a bad workman. Most people go through life without thinking of these things: they do not stop and consider from whence and by what means has come to their table the flesh-food that is served there. They drift along through a mundane existence without feeling a pang of remorse for, or even thought of, the pain they are accomplices in producing in the sub-human world. And it cannot be denied, hide it how we may, either from our eyes or our conscience, that however skilfully the actual killing may usually be carried out, there is much unavoidable suffering caused to the beasts that have to be transported by sea and rail to the slaughter-house.	

(continued)

Excerpt, *No Animal Food* (Rupert H. Wheldon)	Our Thought Processes
The animals suffer violently from sea-sickness, and horrible cruelty (such as pouring boiling oil into their ears, and stuffing their ears with hay which is then set on fire, tail-twisting, etc.,) has to be practised to prevent them lying down lest they be trampled on by other beasts and killed; for this means that they have to be thrown overboard, thus reducing the profits of their owners, or of the insurance companies, which, of course, would be a sad calamity. Judging by the way the men act it does not seem to matter what cruelties and tortures are perpetuated; what heinous offenses against every humane sentiment of the human heart are committed; it does not matter to what depths of Satanic callousness man stoops provided always that—this is the supreme question—*there is money to be made by it.* A writer has thus graphically described the scene in a cattle-boat in rough weather: 'Helpless cattle dashed from one side of the ship to the other, amid a ruin of smashed pens, with limbs broken from contact with hatchway combings or winches—dishorned, gored, and some of them smashed to mere bleeding masses of hide-covered flesh. Add to this the shrieking of the tempest, and the frenzied moanings of the wounded beasts, and the reader will have some faint idea of the fearful scenes of danger and carnage ... the dead beasts, advanced, perhaps, in decomposition before death ended their sufferings, are often removed literally in pieces.' And on the railway journey, though perhaps the animals do not experience so much physical pain as travelling by sea, yet they are often deprived of food, and water, and rest, for long periods, and mercilessly knocked about and bruised. They are often so injured that the cattle-men are surprised they have not succumbed to their injuries. And all this happens in order that the demand for *unnecessary* flesh-food may be satisfied.	

(continued)

Excerpt, *No Animal Food* (Rupert H. Wheldon)	Our Thought Processes
Those who defend flesh-eating often talk of humane methods of slaughtering; but it is significant that there is considerable difference of opinion as to what *is* the most humane method. In England the pole-axe is used; in Germany the mallet; the Jews cut the throat; the Italians stab. It is obvious that each of these methods cannot be better than the others, yet the advocates of each method consider the others cruel. As Lieut. Powell remarks, this 'goes far to show that a great deal of cruelty and suffering is inseparable from all methods.' It is hard to imagine how anyone believing he could live healthily on vegetable food alone, could, having once considered these things, continue a meat-eater. At least to do so he could not live his life in conformity with the precept that we should cause no unnecessary pain. How unholy a custom, how easy a way to murder he makes for himself Who cuts the innocent throat of the calf, and hears unmoved its mournful plaint! And slaughters the little kid, whose cry is like the cry of a child, Or devours the birds of the air which his own hands have fed! Ah, how little is wanting to fill the cup of his wickedness! What unrighteous deed is he not ready to commit.	

SOURCE B

"Health Myths Debunked: Are Carbs Bad for You?"
http://watchmojo.com/video/id/10780/

Introduction to Video:

Due to a variety of new and trendy diets, carbohydrates have certainly received a bad reputation in terms of the process of weight loss! The video will provide you with information on the truth behind carbohydrates. In fact, not all carbohydrates are as terrible as we've always thought. Carbohydrates, due to our central nervous system, which runs by glucose breakdown and carbohydrates, play a major role in that process. Through this video interview, we find out that carbohydrates help our bodies actually "run," which means that carbohydrates aid in creating energy that help our bodies keep active. This interview distinguishes between the characteristics that make a "good" carbohydrate that impacts our body in a positive way as opposed to the characteristics that make a "bad" carbohydrate impacts our body in a negative way. It seems, though, that with most health topics, everything should occur in moderation. Carbohydrates are no different.

SOURCE C

Excerpt, *Diet and Health* (Lulu Hunt Peters, M.D.)	**Our Thought Processes**
Vegetarianism vs. Meat Eating **Protein** As protein is the only food which builds and repairs tissue, it is the food which has caused the most controversy. **First:** As to the amount needed. **Second:** As to whether animal flesh protein is necessary. **Chittenden** **Amount Needed:** It was thought for many years that 150 grams or 5 ounces of dry protein (equivalent to about 1½ pounds lean meat) per day was necessary. But experiments of Chittenden and others have proved that considerably less is sufficient, and that the health is improved if less is taken.	

(continued)

Excerpt, *Diet and Health* (Lulu Hunt Peters, M.D.)	Our Thought Processes
Chittenden's standard is 50 grams, or 1⅔ ounces, dry protein (equivalent to ½ pound meat per day). This is considered by many as insufficient. A variation from 1⅔ to 3 ounces dry protein per day will give a safe range. (ROSE.) **Approx. 240 to 360 C Per Day** *The amount of protein needed is comparatively independent of the amount of physical exertion,* thus differing from the purely fuel foods, carbohydrates and fats, which should vary in direct proportion to the amount of physical exertion. In general, 10 to 15 per cent of the total calories per day should be taken as protein. An excess is undoubtedly irritant to the kidneys, blood vessels, and other organs, and if too little is taken the body tissues will suffer. Not all of the protein should be taken in the form of animal protein; at least one-half should be taken from the vegetable kingdom. *Animal Flesh Protein* Necessary? The following are a few of the chief reasons given by those who object to its use: **The Negative Side** **First:** The animal has just as much right to life, liberty, and pursuit of happiness as we have. **Second:** They may be diseased, and there is the possibility of their containing animal parasites, such as tapeworms and trichinæ. I would like to tell you more about worms, they are so interesting, but He says not to try to tell all I know in this little book; that maybe he will let me write another sometime, although it is a terrible strain on him, and that I have given enough of the family history, anyway.	

(continued)

Excerpt, *Diet and Health* (Lulu Hunt Peters, M.D.)	Our Thought Processes
Some Word **Third:** The tissues of animals contain excrementitious material, which may cause excess acidity, raise the blood pressure, and so forth. **Fourth:** More apt to putrefy and thus give ptomaine poisoning. **Fifth:** Makes the disposition more vicious. (Honest,—animals eating meat exclusively are more vicious.) **The Affirmative Side** Those who believe that animal protein should be eaten answer these points as follows: **First:** Survival of the fittest. **Second:** If you give decent support to your health departments they can furnish enough inspectors to prevent the marketing of diseased meat; and if some should slip through, if you thoroughly bake, boil, or fry your animal parasites they will lose their pep. **Third:** Most of the harmful products are destroyed by the intestines and liver. **Fourth:** True, but see that you get good meat, and don't eat it in excess. **Fifth:** Unanswerable—to be proved later by personal experiments. In addition, they say that animal protein is more easily digested, that 97 percent is assimilated because it is animal, and so it is much more to be desired, especially by children and convalescents; that vegetable protein is enclosed in cellulose, and only 65 to 75 percent is used by the system; thus the diet is apt to be too bulky if the proper amount is taken.	

(continued)

Excerpt, *Diet and Health* (Lulu Hunt Peters, M.D.)	Our Thought Processes
Strong Vegetarians It has been proved, however, by several endurance tests, that the vegetarian contestants had more strength and greater endurance than their meat-eating competitors, so there is no reason why we should be worried by one or two, or even more, meatless days, especially when animal product protein, such as milk, eggs, cheese, and the vegetable proteins, as in the legumes and the nuts, are available. **A Confession** I confess that for quite a while after studying vegetarian books I took a dislike to meat, but now I am in the comfortable state described by Benjamin Franklin in his autobiography. It seems that he had been converted to vegetarianism and had decided that he never again would eat the flesh of animals that had been ruthlessly slaughtered, when they so little deserved that fate. But he was exceedingly fond of fish, and while on a fishing party, as some fish were being fried, he found they did smell most admirably well, and he was greatly torn between his desire and his principle. Finally he remembered that when the fish were opened he saw some smaller fish in their stomachs, and he decided that if they could eat each other he could eat them.	

(continued)

Excerpt, *Diet and Health* (Lulu Hunt Peters, M.D.)		Our Thought Processes
Protein Calories in 100 C Portions of Food		
In 100 C's Bread, 1 slice, (W.W. the highest)	12 to 16 C's P	
In 100 C's Cooked Cereals, 1 sm. cup, (oatmeal highest)	10 to 18 C's P	
In 100 C's Rice, 1 small cup	10 C's P	
In 100 C's Macaroni, 1 small cup	15 C's P	
In 100 C's Whole milk, 5 oz.	20 C's P	
In 100 C's Skim and buttermilk, 10 oz.	35 C's P	
In 100 C's Cheese, 3 heaping tbsp. Cottage cheese	75 C's P	
In 100 C's Eggs 1⅓	36 C's P	
In 100 C's Meat or fish, Very lean 2–3 oz.	50 to 75 C's P	
In 100 C's Nuts, peanuts, almonds, walnuts. Peanuts the highest	10 to 20 C's P	
In 100 C's Beans ⅓ cup average	20 C's P	
In 100 C's Green peas ¾ cup average	28 C's P	
In 100 C's Corn ⅓ cup average	12 C's P	
In 100 C's Onions 3 to 4 medium	12 C's P	
In 100 C's Potato 1 medium	12 C's P	
In 100 C's Tomatoes 1 lb	15 C's P	
In 100 C's Fresh fruits: berries, currants, rhubarb	10 C's P	
Others	2 to 5 C's P	

Prewriting

RST Graphic Organizer

Topic:

My Thesis Statement:

Source A	Source B	Source C

Exactly how do the sources talk with each other?

Your Outline:

Write your Essay in your notebook or in your loose-leaf binder.

CHAPTER 9

Research Simulation Task Practice Questions

 Introduction

The following are a series of research simulation tasks that deal with a variety of subject areas. This is your opportunity to take the lessons you have been reading and writing about, and apply them in other disciplines.

The following questions are aligned with the common core standards listed below:

CCSS Alignment	
RL.1	Cite strong and textual evidence.
RL.5	Analyze how an author's choices contribute to its overall structure.
RL.7	Integrate and evaluate multiple sources of information presented in different media or formats (e.g., visually, quantitatively) as well as in words in order to address a question or solve a problem.
L.1	Demonstrate command of the conventions of standard English grammar and usage when writing.
L.3	Apply knowledge of language to understand how language functions in different contexts.
L.5	Demonstrate understanding of figurative language, word relationships, and nuances in word meanings.
W.1	Write arguments to support claims in an analysis of substantive topics or texts, using valid reasoning and relevant and sufficient evidence.

(continued)

CCSS Alignment	
W.2	Write informative/explanatory texts to examine and convey complex ideas, concepts, and information clearly and accurately through the effective selection, organization, and analysis of content.
W.5	Develop and strengthen writing as needed by planning, revising, editing, and rewriting.
W.6	Use technology to produce, publish, and update individual writing products.

Keep in mind the following steps as you work through:

Step #1	Read through the question carefully. Make sure to figure out if the question is asking you to give an opinion, or to provide information/research objectively.
Step #2	In the upper right-hand corner of your paper, simplify what the question is asking you to do. Put the question/task into your own words.
Step #3	Circle the minimum amount of sources that need to be addressed.
Step #4	Take notes with each of the sources. Address the source's main points. Underline actively.
Step #5	After you've addressed and highlighted the main point of the source, make separate notes on the reliability of these sources. Is the source reliable in general? Is it slanted in any way? Do logical fallacies or "holes in argument" exist?
Step #6	You've read through your sources. Choose the sources that you are most comfortable with, and put a star (*) in the upper right-hand corner of each source that you will be using in your research simulation task.
Step #7	In source chart, copy your notes from your sources into each.
Step #8	Now, look at the relationships of your sources. Do they agree with each other? Do they disagree? Use your source-relationship chart to begin thinking about how you will have your sources begin conversing or talking with one another.
Step #9	Complete the outline for your essay.
Step #10	Complete your essay, using the outline/framework as a guide.
Step #11	After you have completed your essay, go back to check that your sources have a conversation, and replace the verbs you've used to integrate these sources with the action verbs from the sheet provided.

Practice RST

Research Simulation Task — Art

85 minutes

The definition of art is blurred and unclear. Many feel that artwork, in both its process and product is an original form of expression, while others feel that little original thought is left, rendering all art forms to be nothing more than imitations of one another.

Please review the following sources as you articulate your response:

- **Source A:** "UK show puts Schwitters's 'Rubbish' Art Back in Frame"

- **Source B:** Photograph, Graffiti Art (Caroline Krueger)

- **Source C:** Article, "Why We Make Art"

Consider the perspective each source uses to demonstrate a viewpoint on art and its role in our society.

Is art a form of original expression, or does it serve as an experience that simply imitates previous thought? Write an essay that analyzes art's worth as a source for either original thought or imitation of ideas, using the three sources. Remember to use textual evidence to support your ideas.

Source A

"UK show puts Schwitters's 'Rubbish' Art Back in Frame" — article	My Thought Processes
January 29, 2013 Mike Collett-White | Reuters LONDON (Reuters) — Sheep bones, nails, pegs, a scrubbing brush, a metal toy — all, according to avant garde German artist Kurt Schwitters, are on a par with paint, and all appear in collages and sculptures in a London show dedicated to his time in Britain in the 1940s. Schwitters remains a relatively obscure figure in his adopted country, where he fled Nazi Germany and remained until his death, aged 60, in 1948. "Schwitters in Britain" at Tate Britain aims to bring his works to a wider audience, although he is already acknowledged in the art world as a major influence on Pop Art and on famous figures like Richard Hamilton and Robert Rauschenberg. He was also part of the Dada movement and a pioneer of both installation and performance art, most notably in his "Ursonate" poem which he developed between 1923 and 1932 and which consisted of repeated sequences of "pre-linguistic" sounds. Curators and journalists discussing the show, which opens on January 30, jokingly refer to Schwitters's art as "rubbish", and his use of everyday fragments was born out of a desire to create beauty from the ruins of German culture after World War One. In 1919 he created the radical new concept "Merz", a one-man movement and philosophy which he described as "the combination of all conceivable materials for artistic purposes, and technically the principle of equal evaluation of the individual materials . . ."	

(continued)

"UK show puts Schwitters's 'Rubbish' Art Back in Frame"—article	My Thought Processes
Works on display in the opening room of the show, designed to introduce visitors to his ideas and artistic career in Germany, include "Merzbild 46 A", or Merz Picture 46 A, a collection of wooden pegs and other objects stuck to cardboard. "DEGENERATE ART"	
His most famous work before fleeing Nazi Germany in 1937 was probably "The Merzbau", an architectural concept that took up several rooms in Schwitters's Hanover home. It was destroyed by a bomb in 1943.	
Schwitters was dismissed as "degenerate" by Hitler's Nazis and featured in an exhibition aimed at mocking modern art. He went first to Norway, and, when that was occupied by German forces, took the last boat out, arriving in Scotland in 1940.	
As an "enemy alien" in Britain, he ended up in a prison camp on the Isle of Man where he joined other eminent artists, musicians and academics and painted portraits of several of his friends which hang in the Tate Britain show.	
It was a prolific period for Schwitters, and included sculptures made out of porridge instead of plaster of Paris which produced an unpleasant smell and were covered in mildew. They have not survived, Tate curators confirmed.	
On his release he met and exhibited alongside leading figures in British abstract and surreal art, but always struggled to make a living from his art.	
In 1945 he moved to the picturesque Lake District in northwest England, where he sought to make ends meet by painting portraits of locals and landscapes in a period of his career looked down upon by some in the art establishment.	

(continued)

"UK show puts Schwitters's 'Rubbish' Art Back in Frame" —article	My Thought Processes
Several of his later collages featured brightly colored cuttings from magazines and food packets sent from the United States. One, "En Morn", features the printed words "These are the things we are fighting for", an apparent reference to the contrast between perceived post-war plenty in the United States and a rationing system still in place in Britain. His last sculpture and installation was the "Merz Barn", a continuation of his Merzbau project in which he attempted to transform a stone barn into a work of art by adorning its walls with natural materials from the surrounding area. Schwitters completed only one wall of the planned grotto by the time of his death in 1948, and nearly 20 years later it was moved to a permanent home at the Hatton Gallery in Newcastle. * Schwitters in Britain is organized in association with the Sprengel Museum in Hanover where it will tour in June. Tate Britain tickets cost 10 pounds, and the show ends on May 12. (Reporting by Mike Collett-White, editing by Paul Casciato)	

Source B

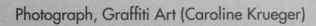

Photograph, Graffiti Art (Caroline Krueger)

My Thoughts

Source C

"Why We Make Art"	My Thought Processes
By Jeremy Adam Smith, Jason Marsh / Winter 2009 University of California, Berkeley Why do you make art? That's the simple question "Greater Good" posed to seven artists. Their answers are surprising, and very diverse. They mention making art for fun and adventure; building bridges between themselves and the rest of humanity; reuniting and recording fragments of thought, feeling, and memory; and saying things that they can't express in any other way. All their answers are deeply personal. In this issue of "Greater Good," we explore the possible cognitive and emotional benefits of the arts, and yet these artists evoke a more fundamental benefit: They are just doing what they feel they're born to do. **Gina Gibney: Giving power to others** *Gina Gibney is the artistic director of the New York-based Gina Gibney Dance Company, which was founded in 1991 to serve a dual mission: to create and perform contemporary choreography that draws upon the strength and insights of women and men, and to enrich and reshape lives through programs that give voice to communities in need, especially survivors of domestic abuse and individuals living with HIV/AIDS.* I make art for a few reasons. In life, we experience so much fragmentation of thought and feeling. For me, creating art brings things back together. In my own work, that is true throughout the process. At the beginning, developing the basic raw materials for the work is deeply reflective and informative. Later, bringing those materials together into a form—distilling and shaping movement, creating a context, working to something that feels cohesive and complete. That's incredibly powerful for me—something that really keeps me going.	

"Why We Make Art"	My Thought Processes
Interestingly, the body of my work is like a catalog of the events and thoughts of my life. For me, making work is almost like keeping a journal. Giving that to someone else—as a kind of gift through live performance—is the most meaningful aspect of my work. Dance is a powerful art form for the very reason that it doesn't need to explain or comment on itself. One of the most amazing performances I have ever seen in my life was of a woman—a domestic violence survivor—dancing in a tiny conference room in a domestic violence shelter for other survivors. She was not a professional dancer. She was a woman who had faced unbelievable challenges and who was living with a great deal of sadness. She created and performed an amazing solo—but to have described her performance as "sad" would have been to diminish what we experienced. That's the power of dance. You can feel something and empathize with it on a very deep level, and you don't have to put words to it.	

RST Graphic Organizer

Topic:

My Thesis Statement:

Source A	Source B	Source C

Exactly how do the sources talk with each other?

After you have written your essay, use the Scoring Checklist
and the Scoring Rubric found at the back of the book.

Research Simulation Task — Financial Literacy

85 minutes

In the United States, we currently live and work during some extremely trying economic times. As a result, it is not uncommon to hear about the "pinching of a penny" — or two — to get by. Many competing views exist regarding the importance of saving and budgeting. While many feel that saving and budgeting create a sense of security for us as citizens and consumers, others believe that the money we earn should be spent on luxuries and other things that make us immediately "happy."

You have reviewed three sources regarding the act of budgeting and saving. These three pieces provide information regarding some of the common benefits and disadvantages associated with each.

- **Source A:** "The Power of Money," from *Frenzied Finance* (Thomas Lawson).

- **Source B:** "The Importance of Saving Money: Hows and Whys" (*The News-Gazette* article)

- **Source C:** "Piggy Bank"

Are saving and budgeting necessary acts for all of us, as financial citizens? Write an informative piece that addresses the question and supports your position with evidence from at least two of the three *sources*. Be sure to acknowledge competing views. Give examples from past and current events or issues to illustrate and clarify your position. You may refer to the sources by their titles (Source A, Source B, Source C).

Source A

"The Power of Money," from *Frenzied Finance* (Thomas Lawson)	My Thought Processes
THE POWER OF DOLLARS At no time in the history of the United States has the power of dollars been as great as now. Freedom and equity are controlled by dollars. The laws which should preserve and enforce all rights are made and enforced by dollars. It is possible to-day, with dollars, to "steer" the selection of the candidates of both the great parties for the highest office in our republic, that of President of the United States. It is possible to repeat the operation in the selection of candidates for the executive and legislative conduct and control of every State and municipality in the United States, and with a sufficient number of dollars to "steer" the doings of the law-makers and law-enforcers of the national, State, and municipal governments of the people, and to "steer" a sufficient proportion of the court decisions to make absolute any power created by such direction. It is all, broadly speaking, a matter of dollars practically to accomplish these things. I must not be misunderstood as even insinuating that there are not absolutely honest law-makers and law-enforcers, nor that there arc not as many of them in proportion to the whole body as there were at the creation of our republic. I believe there is at the present time as large a percentage of honesty among Americans as ever there has been, but it is plainly evident to any student of the times that at no other period in the history of the United States has honesty been so completely "steered" by dishonesty as at this, the beginning of the twentieth century. *I shall go further and say that there to-day exists uncontrolled in the hands of a set of men a power to make dollars from nothing.* That function of dollar-making which the people believe is vested in their Government alone and only exercised under the law for their benefit, is actually being secretly exercised on an	

(continued)

"The Power of Money," from *Frenzied Finance* (Thomas Lawson)	My Thought Processes
enormous scale by a few private individuals for their own personal benefit. This, I am well aware, is a startling statement, but not more so than the facts which support it. Throughout the country we have all grown accustomed to the spectacle of men who, poor yesterday, to-day display more dollars than the kings and queens of olden times controlled. In flaunting this money these men proudly boast: "We made all this yesternight, and are going to multiply it five-or fifty-fold to-morrow night." The fact that there must be in this country some secret method of gaining vast fortunes gradually dawned on the minds of the people. This method, they argued, must be outside the laws of the land which they themselves had made, and they were confronted with the fact that the possessors of these fabulous fortunes were creating a power not recognized by their Government and which practically placed the Government in the hands of the fortune-owners. They realized that in some way the magic of this fortune-making was connected with, or seemed to be compounded in, institutions called corporations and trusts, and that among these the head and centre was a great affair called "Standard Oil." Wherever this "Standard Oil" was, all knew that strange wonders were worked. Within the sphere of its influence dirt changed to gold, liquids to solids, and what was, was not, and what was not, was. Whoever became a part of this mysterious "Standard Oil," at the same time was rendered "powerful"; as though touched by a fairy's wand, he changed from pauper to millionaire. But what was "Standard Oil"? The people knew that at the beginning it was only an aggregation of men, private individuals, who had accumulated much money by securing a monopoly of selling oil, and that these men were "Rockefellers," and that Standard Oil and "Rockefellers" had been cute and cunning in the conduct of their oil-selling to a degree greater than	

(continued)

"The Power of Money," from *Frenzied Finance* (Thomas Lawson)	My Thought Processes
had been rival sellers of oil or of other necessities. And as time wore on much more was heard of the cleverness of Standard Oil and "Rockefellers," as the victims of the cuteness and the cunning "hollered" in public places, and the newspapers and writers of books exclaimed against their practices and exactions. But many other things were happening simultaneously, and to the great bulk of the people it was interesting rather than portentous that there existed in the country a giant oil-thing whose owners were reputed the richest men in the world. It was not until the beginning of the twentieth century that the monster "Standard Oil" loomed up before the people as the giant of all corporate things and that its ominous shadow seemed to dwarf all other institutions, public or private. In multitudinous forms it was before the people. In awed whispers men talked of its mysterious doings and canvassed its extraordinary powers as though "Standard Oil" were a living, breathing entity rather than a mere business institution created by men and existing only by virtue of the laws of the land.	

SOURCE B

The following is an article on the importance of saving money and budgeting, from The News-Gazette, a central Illinois newspaper.

"The Importance of Saving Money: Hows and Whys"	My Thought Processes
By: Steve Bauer	
Saving is the "new spending."	
People are eating out less often, collecting their change or holding off on buying a new car.	
Savings have not been as much of a priority for most Americans in recent years, according to Steve Ayers, educator for the Champaign County unit of the University of Illinois Extension.	
But the economy in the past couple of years has everyone more aware of the need to take control of personal finances, he said. Rather than spending more than they have coming in, households are trying to figure out how to save.	
So, why should you save? And how do you do it?	
One reason, as the recent economy has shown, is that a "rainy day" or "emergency" fund can help you get through unexpected emergencies, including layoffs, illness or injury. The ideal is to avoid adding to debt through a loan, particularly a high-interest loan, Ayers said.	
Other reasons for savings vary according to the individual: one person may want to save for college, another for retirement.	
Ayers and other experts say tracking expenses, setting a budget and having savings goals are important for people at all income levels. The keys are to understand your income and spending and set aside some money for savings, he said.	
Saving is a conscious decision for one's long-term living and security, he said.	

(continued)

"The Importance of Saving Money: Hows and Whys"	My Thought Processes
"It is difficult with our 'immediate gratification' mind-set," Ayers said. So one strategy might be to "pay yourself first" through payroll deduction or start small with as little as $5 per week, he said. "Another small step is to save your change daily and it is amazing how fast that can add up," Ayers said. The economy in the last couple of years has made everyone more aware of the need to take control of personal finances, Ayers said. Champaign County organizations are participating in a national campaign called America Saves, which is designed to encourage people to "travel down the savings path." "Taking control of your finances ought to be the No. 1 New Year's resolution," Ayers said. "The whole thing is living within your means." Ayers said the first step in setting up a savings plan is to know where the money goes: Analyze how money is being spent. Comparing income and actual expenses makes developing a personal or household budget more meaningful, he said. "Getting in the habit (of saving) is as important as deciding how much to save," Ayers said. "Pay yourself first." Kathy Sweedler, consumer and family economics educator with the UI Extension program, said saving even $20 a week means more than $1,000 a year. "I believe that practicing saving money makes us better savers," Sweedler said. "Once we get in the habit of saving money, then I think it's likely that people will continue to save." She said one strategy is to have household members track their spending. That's even the $1-a-day coffee purchase on the way to work, which adds up to more than $300 per year.	

(continued)

"The Importance of Saving Money: Hows and Whys"	My Thought Processes
Having a goal is important to saving, and writing goals down is also important, Sweedler said.	
"If you know what your goal is, it's easier to save," she said. "Budgeting becomes an accomplishment tool rather than a punishment."	
Brian DeLaney, CEO for Consumer Credit Nationwide, with offices in Davenport, Iowa, and Champaign, said, "The most significant thing is to have a budget and build savings into that budget."	
Sometimes that means figuring out where your money is going now. Some things you're spending on now may better go into savings. Prioritize and make sure some goes into savings.	
He said for most people there are generally two types of savings: a "rainy day fund" and retirement fund. The rainy day or emergency fund should be five to six months' income, to be used just in case you lose your job or get sick or injured.	
DeLaney said most people can't put that much aside right away.	
"I tell people to first set aside one month and then two months, and so on," he said.	
Delaney said that savings for a "rainy day fund" should be simple and accessible, like a credit union account.	
Once people get a month or two of savings accumulated, they can think about putting some into a certificate of deposit, he said. For a larger savings goal, such as a retirement fund, people should talk to a professional financial adviser, Delaney said.	
Land of Lincoln, which is primarily known for providing legal services, also provides financial and debt management training for low-income households.	

(continued)

"The Importance of Saving Money: Hows and Whys"	My Thought Processes
Valerie McWilliams, managing attorney at Land of Lincoln Legal Assistance Foundation for over 25 years, said the agency has a foreclosure prevention program and also does financial education and credit counseling. Among her savings tips are to set up automatic debits from your paycheck or checking account into a savings account and making sure that you don't take that money back out every month. People qualifying for an earned income tax credit should consider using that money strategically to reduce debt and put some money aside for a "rainy day" account, McWilliams said. People need to educate themselves before making big spending choices—like cars, houses, insurance and retirement accounts. "And not just from someone trying to sell you something," she said. "Seek out help from someone good with money to help you look objectively at your income and expenses." McWilliams also said, "Never, never, never get a payday loan or title loan." Matt Reese, program manager for the Partnership Accounts for Individual Development at Land of Lincoln, said the program offers matched savings up to $2,000 for low-income participants. The office will also provide general budget counseling for anyone, he said. "The most important thing is to start saving now; start saving right away," Reese said. Reese said most financial advisers he has talked to stress the need for an emergency savings fund. That can generally be three-months worth of take-home pay, he said. That's the average amount of time most people who are laid off are out of work.	

(continued)

"The Importance of Saving Money: Hows and Whys"	My Thought Processes
Ideally, Reese said, the saver's emergency fund is separate from his goal savings fund.	
Reese said it's important for everyone to regularly assess his finances and make any necessary adjustments in spending or savings.	
Other agencies that will offer counseling include Central Illinois Debt Management and Consumer Credit.	

Source C

"Piggy Bank"	My Thought Processes

RST Graphic Organizer

Topic:

My Thesis Statement:

Source A	Source B	Source C

Exactly how do the sources talk with each other?

Once you have written your essay, check it with the Scoring Checklist and the Scoring Rubric found at the back of the book. (Be sure to go through your verbs to make them more lively and informative.)

Research Simulation Task — World Languages

85 minutes

Many feel that a culture is often defined by its language. With language being the communication method between members of a community and culture, words may be more significant than any other form of cultural norm.

You have reviewed three sources regarding cultural norms. These three pieces provide information on the role language has on groups that share a common culture.

- **Source A:** Speech, "The Disappearance of Literature" (Mark Twain)
- **Source B:** Photographs, "Vote Here," "Flying Flag"
- **Source C:** YouTube video, "The Importance of Speech and Language"

What role does language have on a culture? Write an informative piece that addresses the question and supports your position with evidence from at least two of the three sources. Be sure to acknowledge competing views. Give examples from past and current events or issues to illustrate and clarify your position. You may refer to the sources by their titles (Source A, Source B, Source C).

Source A

Speech, "The Disappearance of Literature" (Mark Twain)	My Thought Processes
Address at the Dinner of the Nineteenth Century Club, at Sherry's, New York, November 20, 1900 Mr. Clemens spoke to the toast "The Disappearance of Literature." Doctor Gould presided, and in introducing Mr. Clemens said that he (the speaker), when in Germany, had to do a lot of apologizing for a certain literary man who was taking what the Germans thought undue liberties with their language.	

(continued)

Speech, "The Disappearance of Literature" (Mark Twain)	My Thought Processes
It wasn't necessary for your chairman to apologize for me in Germany. It wasn't necessary at all. Instead of that he ought to have impressed upon those poor benighted Teutons the service I rendered them. Their language had needed untangling for a good many years. Nobody else seemed to want to take the job, and so I took it, and I flatter myself that I made a pretty good job of it. The Germans have an inhuman way of cutting up their verbs. Now a verb has a hard time enough of it in this world when it's all together. It's downright inhuman to split it up. But that's just what those Germans do. They take part of a verb and put it down here, like a stake, and they take the other part of it and put it away over yonder like another stake, and between these two limits they just shovel in German. I maintain that there is no necessity for apologizing for a man who helped in a small way to stop such mutilation. We have heard a discussion to-night on the disappearance of literature. That's no new thing. That's what certain kinds of literature have been doing for several years. The fact is, my friends, that the fashion in literature changes, and the literary tailors have to change their cuts or go out of business. Professor Winchester here, if I remember fairly correctly what he said, remarked that few, if any, of the novels produced to-day would live as long as the novels of Walter Scott. That may be his notion. Maybe he is right; but so far as I am concerned, I don't care if they don't. Professor Winchester also said something about there being no modern epics like Paradise Lost. I guess he's right. He talked as if he was pretty familiar with that piece of literary work, and nobody would suppose that he never had read it. I don't believe any of you have ever read Paradise Lost, and you don't want to. That's something that you just want to take on trust. It's a classic, just as Professor Winchester says, and it meets his definition of a classic—something that everybody wants to have read and nobody wants to read.	

(continued)

Speech, "The Disappearance of Literature" (Mark Twain)	My Thought Processes
Professor Trent also had a good deal to say about the disappearance of literature. He said that Scott would outlive all his critics. I guess that's true. The fact of the business is, you've got to be one of two ages to appreciate Scott. When you're eighteen you can read Ivanhoe, and you want to wait until you are ninety to read some of the rest. It takes a pretty well-regulated, abstemious critic to live ninety years.	
But as much as these two gentlemen have talked about the disappearance of literature, they didn't say anything about my books. Maybe they think they've disappeared. If they do, that just shows their ignorance on the general subject of literature. I am not as young as I was several years ago, and maybe I'm not so fashionable, but I'd be willing to take my chances with Mr. Scott to-morrow morning in selling a piece of literature to the Century Publishing Company. And I haven't got much of a pull here, either. I often think that the highest compliment ever paid to my poor efforts was paid by Darwin through President Eliot, of Harvard College. At least, Eliot said it was a compliment, and I always take the opinion of great men like college presidents on all such subjects as that.	
I went out to Cambridge one day a few years ago and called on President Eliot. In the course of the conversation he said that he had just returned from England, and that he was very much touched by what he considered the high compliment Darwin was paying to my books, and he went on to tell me something like this:	

(continued)

Speech, "The Disappearance of Literature" (Mark Twain)	My Thought Processes
"Do you know that there is one room in Darwin's house, his bedroom, where the housemaid is never allowed to touch two things? One is a plant he is growing and studying while it grows" (it was one of those insect-devouring plants which consumed bugs and beetles and things for the particular delectation of Mr. Darwin) "and the other some books that lie on the night table at the head of his bed. They are your books, Mr. Clemens, and Mr. Darwin reads them every night to lull him to sleep." My friends, I thoroughly appreciated that compliment, and considered it the highest one that was ever paid to me. To be the means of soothing to sleep a brain teeming with bugs and squirming things like Darwin's was something that I had never hoped for, and now that he is dead I never hope to be able to do it again.	

Source B

Photograph (Caroline Krueger)	My Thoughts
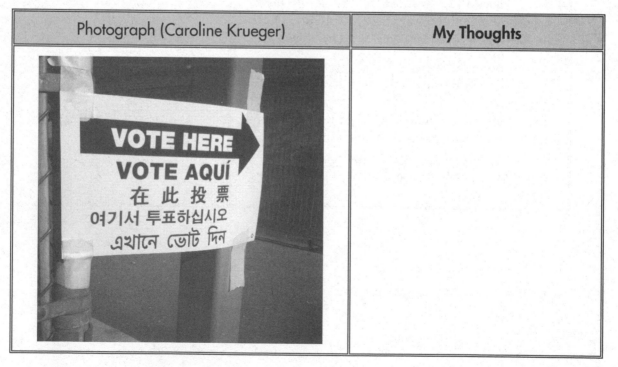	

(continued)

Photograph (Caroline Krueger)	My Thoughts

Source C

YouTube: "The Importance of Speech and Language"
http://www.youtube.com/watch?v=8wfpfLkEy-Y

Summary of "The Importance of Speech and Language"

In this video clip, CEO Kamini Gadhok of the Royal College of Speech and Language Therapists describes communication as the key 21st Century life skill. The video clips documents the "building blocks" of developing communication skills within children:

1. Are children in an environment that provides opportunity to communicate?

2. Eye contact, shared communication (turn taking), and other nonverbal communication skills.

3. Understanding of spoken language (vocabulary).

4. Expressive language: Talking.

5. Using accurate speech sounds.

It is these 5 areas that are essential to healthy communication from early childhood throughout all stages of life.

My Thoughts

RST Graphic Organizer

Topic:

My Thesis Statement:

Source A	Source B	Source C

Exactly how do the sources talk with each other?

Once you have written your essay look at it through the eyes of the PARCC test makers by using the Scoring Checklist and the Scoring Rubric found at the back of the book.

Research Simulation Task — Business

85 minutes

Our business culture is one where standards of dress exist. While the idea of business attire varies, expectations for appearance are a part of each businessman's or businesswoman's day.

You have reviewed three sources regarding the impact that employees' appearances have upon the supposed impression of a business or company. These three pieces provide information concerning the way in which employees' dress and appearance may or may not accurately reflect the impression of a business.

- **Source A:** Excerpt, *Psychology and Achievement* (Warren Hilton)

- **Source B:** Image ("Man in Business Suit")

- **Source C:** Excerpt, The Book of Business Etiquette (1922)

As time goes on, is society's perception of a successful business heightened based on established standards of dress and appearance? Write an informative piece that addresses the question and supports your position with evidence from at least two of the three sources. Be sure to acknowledge competing views. Give examples from past and current events or issues to illustrate and clarify your position. You may refer to the sources by their titles (Source A, Source B, Source C).

Source A

Excerpt, Psychology and Achievement (1914) (Warren Hilton)	My Thought Processes
Two Laws of Success-Achievement **The One-Man Business Corporation** As a working unit you are a kind of one-man business corporation made up of two departments, the mental and the physical. Your mind is the executive office of this personal corporation, its directing "head." Your body is the corporation's "plant." Eyes and ears, sight and smell and touch, hands and feet—these are the implements, the equipment. **Business and Bodily Activity** We have undertaken to teach you how to acquire a perfect mastery of your own powers and meet the practical problems of your life in such a way that success will be swift and certain. First of all it is necessary that you should accept and believe two well-settled and fundamental laws. I. *All human achievement comes about through bodily activity.* II. *All bodily activity is caused, controlled and directed by the mind.* Give the first of these propositions but a moment's thought. You can conceive of no form of accomplishment which is not the result of some kind of bodily activity. One would say that the master works of poetry, art, philosophy, religion, are products of human effort furthest removed from the material side of life, yet even these would have perished still-born in the minds conceiving them had they not found transmission and expression through some form of bodily activity. You will agree, therefore, that the first of these propositions is so self-evident, so axiomatic, as neither to require nor to admit of formal proof.	

(continued)

Excerpt, Psychology and Achievement (1914) (Warren Hilton)	My Thought Processes
The second proposition is not so easily disposed of. It is in fact so difficult of acceptance by some persons that we must make very plain its absolute validity. Furthermore, its elucidation will bring forth many illuminating facts that will give you an entirely new conception of the mind and its scope and influence.	

The Enslaved Brain

Remember, when we say "mind," we are not thinking of the brain. The brain is but one of the organs of the body, and, by the terms of our proposition as stated, is as much the slave of the mind as is any other organ of the body. To say that the mind controls the body presupposes that mind and body are distinct entities, the one belonging to a spiritual world, the other to a world of matter.

First Step Toward Self-Realization

That the mind is master of the body is a settled principle of science. But we realize that its acceptance may require you to lay aside some preconceived prejudices. You may be one of those who believe that the mind is nothing more nor less than brain activity. You may believe that the body is all there is to man and that mind-action is merely one of its functions.

If so, we want you nevertheless to realize that, while as a matter of philosophic speculation you retain these opinions, you may at the same time for practical purposes regard the mind as an independent causal agency and believe that it can and does control and determine and *cause* any and every kind of bodily activity. We want you to do this because this conclusion is at the basis of a practical system of mental efficiency and because, as we shall at once show you, it is capable of proof by the established methods of physical science.

Source B

Image ("Man in Business Suit")	My Thought Processes

Source C

Excerpt, The Book of Business Etiquette (1922)	My Thought Processes
The American Business Man The business man is the national hero of America, as native to the soil and as typical of the country as baseball or Broadway or big advertising. He is an interesting figure, picturesque and not unlovable, not so dashing perhaps as a knight in armor or a soldier in uniform, but he is not without the noble (and ignoble) qualities which have characterized the tribe of man since the world began. America, in common with other countries, has had distinguished statesmen and soldiers, authors and artists—and they have not all gone to their graves unhonored and unsung—but the hero story which belongs to her and to no one else is the story of the businessman.	

(continued)

Excerpt, The Book of Business Etiquette (1922)	My Thought Processes
Nearly always it has had its beginning in humble surroundings, with a little boy born in a log cabin in the woods, in a wretched shanty at the edge of a field, in a crowded tenement section or in the slums of a foreign city, who studied and worked by daylight and firelight while he made his living blacking boots or selling papers until he found the trail by which he could climb to what we are pleased to call success. Measured by the standards of Greece and Rome or the Middle Ages, when practically the only form of achievement worth mentioning was fighting to kill, his career has not been a romantic one. It has had to do not with dragons and banners and trumpets, but with stockyards and oil fields, with railroads, sewer systems, heat, light, and water plants, telephones, cotton, corn, ten-cent stores and—we might as well make a clean breast of it—chewing gum.	
We have no desire to crown the business man with a halo, though judging from their magazines and from the stories which they write of their own lives, they are almost without spot or blemish. Most of them seem not even to have had faults to overcome. They were born perfect. Now the truth is that the methods of accomplishment which the American business man has used have not always been above reproach and still are not. At the same time it would not be hard to prove that he—and here we are speak[Pg 3]ing of the average—with all his faults and failings (and they are many), with all his virtues (and he is not without them), is superior in character to the business men of other times in other countries. This without boasting. It would be a great pity if he were not.	

(continued)

Excerpt, The Book of Business Etiquette (1922)	My Thought Processes
Without trying to settle the question as to whether he is good or bad (and he really can be pigeon-holed no better than any one else) we have to accept this: He is the biggest factor in the American commonwealth to-day. It follows then, naturally, that what he thinks and feels will color and probably dominate the ideas and the ideals of the rest of the country. Numbers of our magazines—and they are as good an index as we have to the feeling of the general public—are given over completely to the service or the entertainment of business men (the T. B. M.) and an astonishing amount of space is devoted to them in most of the others. It may be, and as a matter of fact constantly is, debated whether all this is good for the country or not. We shall not go into that. It has certainly been good for business, and in considering the men who have developed our industries we have to take them, and maybe it is just as well, as they are and not as we think they ought to be. There was a time when the farmer was the principal citizen. And the politician ingratiated himself with the people by declaring that he too had split rails and followed the plow, had harvested grain and had suffered from wet spells and dry spells, low prices, dull seasons, hunger and hardship. This is still a pretty sure way to win out, but there are others. If he can refer feelingly to the days when he worked and sweated in a coal mine, in a printing shop, a cotton, wool, or silk mill, steel or motor plant, he can hold his own with the ex-farmer's boy. We have become a nation of business men. Even the "dirt" farmer has become a business man—he has learned that he not only has to produce, he must find a market for his product.	

(continued)

Excerpt, The Book of Business Etiquette (1922)	My Thought Processes
In comparing the business man of the present with the business man of the past we must remember that he is living in a more difficult world. Life was comparatively simple when men dressed in skins and ate roots and had their homes in scattered caves. They felt no need for a code of conduct because they felt no need for one another. They depended not on humanity but on nature, and perhaps human brotherhood would never have come to have a meaning if nature had not proved treacherous. She gave them berries and bananas, sunshine and soft breezes, but she gave them trouble also in the shape of wild beasts, and savages, terrible droughts, winds, and floods. In order to fight against these enemies, strength was necessary, and when primitive men discovered that two were worth twice as much as one they began to join forces. This was the beginning of civilization and of politeness. It rose out of the oldest instinct in the world—self-preservation. When men first organized into groups the units were small, a mere handful of people under a chief, but gradually they became larger and larger until the nations of to-day have grown into a sort of world community composed of separate countries, each one supreme in its own domain, but at the same time bound to the others by economic ties stronger than sentimental or political ones could ever be. People are now more dependent on one another than they have ever been before, and the need for confidence is greater. We cannot depend upon one another unless we can trust one another.	

(continued)

Excerpt, The Book of Business Etiquette (1922)	My Thought Processes
The American community is in many respects the most complex the world has ever seen, and the hardest to manage. In other countries the manners have been the natural result of the national development. The strong who had risen to the top in the struggle for existence formed themselves into a group. The weak who stayed at the bottom fell into another, and the bulk of the populace, which, then as now, came somewhere in between, fell into a third or was divided according to standards of its own. Custom solidified the groups into classes which became so strengthened by years of usage that even when formal distinctions were broken down the barriers were still too solid for a man who was born into a certain group to climb very easily into the one above him. Custom also dictated what was expected of the several classes. Each must be gracious to those below and deferential to those above. The king, because he was king, must be regal. The nobility must, *noblesse oblige*, be magnificent, and as for the rest of the people, it did not matter much so long as they worked hard and stayed quiet. There were upheavals, of course, and now and then a slave with a braver heart and a stouter spirit than his companions incited them to rebellion. His head was chopped off for his pains and he was promptly forgotten. The majority of the people for thousands of years honestly believed that this was the only orderly basis upon which society could be organized.	

(continued)

Excerpt, The Book of Business Etiquette (1922)	My Thought Processes
Nebulous ideas of a brotherhood, in which each man was to have an equal chance with every other, burned brightly for a little while in various parts of the world at different times, and flickered out. They broke forth with the fury of an explosion in France during the Revolution and in Russia during the Red Terror. They have smoldered quietly in some places and had just begun to break through with a steady, even flame. But America struck the match and gathered the wood to start her own fire. She is the first country in the world which was founded especially to promote individual freedom and the brotherhood of mankind. She had, to change the figure slightly, a blue-print to start with and she has been building ever since. Her material came from the eastern hemisphere. The nations there at the time when the United States was settled were at different stages of their development. Some were vigorous with youth, some were in the height of their glory, and some were dying because the descendants of the men who had made them great were futile and incapable. These nations were different in race and religion, in thought, language, traditions, and temperament. When they were not quarreling with each other, they were busy with domestic squabbles. They had kept this up for centuries and were at it when the settlers landed at Jamestown and later when the *Mayflower* came to Plymouth Rock. Yet, with a cheerful disregard of the past and an almost sublime hope in the future they expected to live happily ever after they crossed the Atlantic Ocean. Needless to add, they did not.	

(continued)

Excerpt, The Book of Business Etiquette (1922)	My Thought Processes
Accident of place cannot change a man's color (though it may bleach it a shade lighter or tan it a shade darker), nor his religion nor any of the other racial and inherent qualities which are the result of slow centuries of development. And the same elements which made men fight in the old countries set them against each other in the new. Most of the antagonisms were and are the result of prejudices, foolish narrow prejudices, which, nevertheless, must be beaten down before we can expect genuine courtesy.	
Further complications arose, and are still arising, from the fact that we did not all get here at the same time. Those who came first have inevitably and almost unconsciously formulated their own system of manners. Wherever there is community life and a certain amount of leisure there is a standard of cultivated behavior. And America, young as she is, has already accumulated traditions of her own.	
It is beyond doubt that the men who came over in the early days were, as a rule, better timber than the ones who come now. They came to live and die, if necessary, for a religious or a political principle, for adventure, or like the debtors in Oglethorpe's colony in Georgia, to wipe clean the slate of the past and begin life again. To-day they come to make money or because they think they will find life easier here than it was where they were. And one of the chief reasons for the discontent and unrest (and, incidentally, rudeness) which prevails among them is that they find it hard. We are speaking in general terms. There are glorious exceptions.	

(continued)

Excerpt, The Book of Business Etiquette (1922)	My Thought Processes
The sturdy virtues of the pioneers did not include politeness. They never do. So long as there is an animal fear of existence man cannot think of minor elegances. He cannot live by bread alone, but he cannot live at all without it. Bread must come first. And the Pilgrim Father was too busy learning how to wring a living from the forbidding rocks of New England with one hand while he fought off the Indians with the other to give much time to tea parties and luncheons. Nowhere in America except in the South, where the leisurely life of the plantations gave opportunity for it, was any great attention paid to formal courtesy. But everywhere, as soon as the country had been tamed and prosperity began to peep over the horizon, the pioneers began to grow polite. They had time for it.	
What we must remember—and this is a reason, not an excuse, for bad manners—is that these new people coming into the country, the present-day immigrants, are pioneers, and that the life is not an easy one whether it is lived among a wilderness of trees and beasts in a forest or a wilderness of men and buildings in a city. The average American brings a good many charges against the foreigner—some of them justified, for much of the "back-wash" of Europe and Asia has drifted into our harbor—but he must remember this: Whatever his opinion of the immigrant may be the fault is ours—he came into this country under the sanction of our laws. And he is entitled to fair and courteous treatment from every citizen who lives under the folds of the American flag.	
The heterogeneous mixture which makes up our population is a serious obstacle (but not an insuperable one) in the way of courtesy, but there is another even greater. The first is America's problem. The second belongs to the world.	

RST Graphic Organizer

Topic:

My Thesis Statement:

Source A	Source B	Source C

Exactly how do the sources talk with each other?

When you have completed your essay, use the Scoring Checklist and the Scoring Rubric found at the back of the book to verify that you stayed on track. Also check your verbs to be sure you chose the best ones for each instance.

CHAPTER 10

Final Thoughts

For all the students and educators who have used this book, we wish to impress upon you a thought as you take the PARCC and further your adventures both in and out of education. Aristotle, the great Greek thinker, once mused, ""We are what we repeatedly do. Excellence, then, is not an act, but a habit."

Through the habit of completing the exercises and repeated practices of this book, we are very confident that you will achieve excellence on the PARCC. There are some people in education who see testing as a negative—that testing interferes with the "real" education process. We, however, have a different viewpoint: The importance of the PARCC exam is not the test itself. It is not the research simulation task. It is not the literary analysis or the narrative essay. The importance of the exam is twofold: the authentic content that is used on the exam and the literacy skills that the exam requires of its takers. Our hope is that the PARCC exam spurs you on to continue reading literary works of great importance, especially those that give a broader and deeper perspective on the American experience and those that provide a wider landscape of the increasing global world in which we live. An excellent place to find a reading list would be to consult the reading list of the Common Core State Standards Initiative (CCSS). The Common Core is the national curriculum upon which the PARCC is based. Reading the literature suggested by the Common Core will give you a definite advantage when taking the exam. The reading list is reproduced for you in Appendix C.

Next, let's recap the skills you have gained in preparing for the PARCC:

- When this book asked you to "get your sources talking" on the research simulation task, we were actually asking you to synthesize information. After your first week in college or out in the workforce, you will see how important synthesis is—the ability to condense data and to formulate a working thesis based upon these sources. It is a skill that will set you apart from your peers as you go out into the world.

- When this book asked you to write the literary analysis, we were testing your ability to read texts critically. Critical reading can best be summed by the ability to ask the question "Why?" and to explore and verbalize divergent ways of thinking about both fiction and nonfiction. Thinking critically is a must in the 21st century world in which we live.

- Lastly, this book asked you to utilize your creativity and imagination when composing the narrative essay. Imagine how different our world would be if Steve Jobs, creator of the Macintosh computer, lacked imagination? We know that your imagination is one of the keys of success to your future.

If you followed this book well, we are confident that these three important skills— **synthesizing, critical thinking, creativity**—are ingrained within you. Good luck on the exam, and more importantly, best wishes to you in your future, regardless of what you decide to do. Remember Aristotle's words: *You are what you repeatedly do.*

BIBLIOGRAPHY

Chapter 2

Advertisement for Art Restoration Company (n.d.) *www.sierranevadaartrestoration.com/Blank.html*

Aron Art Prints (n.d.) The Art of Art Restoration: Montreal, Quebec *www.aaronartprints.org/theartofartrestoration.php*

Blake, William. "A Poison Tree." William Blake Archive, *www.poetryfoundation.org/poem/175222*

Chekov, A. "The Bet." *www.eastoftheweb.com/short-stories/UBooks/Bet.shtml*

Dickinson, E. "A Bird Came Down the Walk." Harvard University Press, *www.poets.org/viewmedia.php/prmMID/20949*

Fitzgerald, F.S. *The Great Gatsby.* Reprinted with the permission of Scribner Publishing Group from THE GREAT GATSBY by F. Scott Fitzgerald. Copyright © 1925 by Charles Scribner's Sons. Copyright renewed © 1953 by Frances Scott Fitzgerald Lanthan. All rights reserved.

Gillis, J. (2013). "An Alarm in the Offing on Climate Change" New York Times, *http://green.blogs.nytimes.com/2013/01/14/an-alarm-in-the-offing-on-climate-change/*

Keppler, Udo. (1904) Political Cartoon. "Benodellocinch."

Martinez, E.G. (2012). "Ecce Homo" fresco by artist Elias Garcia Martinez: Centro de Estudios Borjanos, *www.telegraph.co.uk/culture/art/9491391*

Poe, E.A. "The Raven." *www.bartleby.com/102/84.html*

Shakespeare, W. *Othello. http://shakespeare.mit.edu/othello/full.html*

"Something About Voting." 3/28/1903. *The Cleveland Journal.*

Chapter 3

Hawthorne, N. (1835). "Young Goodman Brown." *www.gutenberg.org/ebooks/512*

Kafka, F. (1915). *The Metamorphosis, www.gutenberg.org/ebooks/5200*

O. Henry. "The Gift of the Magi." *www.auburn.edu/~vestmon/Gift_of_the_Magi.html*

Chapter 4

Dickinson, E. "Because I Could Not Stop for Death." Harvard University Press, *www.poets.org/viewmedia.php/prmMID/15395*

Dickinson E. "I Felt a Funeral in My Brain." Harvard University Press *www.bartleby.com/113/4112.html*

Douglass, F. *The Articles of Frederick Douglass*. (1845).

Dunbar, P.L. "We Wear the Mask." *www.poetryfoundation.org/poem/173467*

Orwell, G. "Politics and the English Language." *www.orwell.ru/library*

Stewart, S. (2011) "A Language." *www.poetryfoundation.org*

Chapter 5

Brayton, R. (2012). "On Education and Technology." *http://watchmojo.com/video/id/7695/*

Brayton, R. (2012). "Challenges and Education." *http://watchmojo.com/video/id/7676/*

Cramer, P. (2011). Budget Cuts Graph. *http://gothamschools.org/tag/the-chopping-block/*

Hellman, Erik. (2011) "Should Kids Get e-Books in School?" *http://j.libraryjournal.com*

Lebert, M. (2009). *A Short History of eBooks*, www.gutenberg.org/cache/epub/29801/pg29801.html

Chapter 6

Ahlefeldt, F. (2012). Image, *www.hikingartist.com*

Bio True Story (n.d.) F. Scott Fitzgerald biography. *www.biography.com/people/f-scott-fitzgerald-9296261*

Bruccoli, Matthew J. "Fitzgerald, F. Scott." In Anderson, George P., Judith S. Baughman, Matthew J. Bruccoli, and Carl Rollyson, eds. Encyclopedia of American Literature, Revised Edition: Into the Modern: 1896–1945, Volume 3. New York: Facts On File, Inc., 2008. Bloom's Literary Reference Online. Facts On File, Inc. *www.fofweb.com/activelink2* (accessed February 8, 2013).

Darling, N. (2010). Teasing and Bullying, Boys and Girls *www.psychologytoday.com/blog*

Fitzgerald, F. S. *Tales from the Jazz Age*. *www.gutenberg.org/cache/epub/6695*

Hall, G.S. (2012). *Youth: Its Education, Regimen, and Hygiene*. *www.gutenberg.org/cache/epub/9173/pg9173.html*

Jones (2010). "Five Good Reasons Why You Can Believe Love at First Sight." *http://voices.yahoo.com/five-good-reasons-why-believe-love-first-5629642.html*. Reprinted with permission from Yahoo! Inc. 2013 YAHOO! and the YAHOO! logo are trademarks of Yahoo! Inc.

Shakespeare, W. *Romeo and Juliet*. *http://shakespeare.mit.edu/romeo_juliet/full.html*

Smolka, F. (2011). "History of Gaming." *http://vimeo.com/18743950*

Swan, A.S. (2012). "On Courtship and Marriage." *www.gutenberg.org/files/35963*

Chapter 7

Brayton, R. (n.d.) Franklin Delano Roosevelt Biography: New Deal, WWII: *www.watchmojo.com/index.php?id=10839*

Club, Marbella. (2013). "Puerto Rico Island." (advertisement)

George, M.M. (2011). "A Little Journey to Puerto Rico." *www.gutenberg.org/cache/epub/9995/pg9995.html*

Roosevelt, F.D. (1933). "Fireside Chats." *www.gutenberg.org/ebooks/5767*

Roosevelt, F.D. (1933) Franklin D. Roosevelt First Inaugural Address: *www.bartleby.com/124/pres49.html*

Icho, L. (2013). "The Great Depression." *http://vimeo.com/63867463*

Sandburg, C. (1914). "Chicago."

Van Middeldyk, R.A. (2004). "The History of Puerto Rico." *www.gutenberg.org/cache/epub/12272/pg12272.html*

Wright, O. (2008). "How We Made the First Flight." *www.gutenberg.org/files/25420/25420-h/25420-h.htm*

Chapter 8

Bazaar, Harper's (2006). "Are You Risking Your Health for Beauty?" Issue 3538, *http://web.ebscohost.com*

DeVries, "Species and Varieties," Their Origin by Mutation

Hunter, A. (2008). Cellulite Treatments: Do They Work? *http://abcnews.go.com/Health/SkinCare/story?id=4964279&page=1*

Knight, M.M. et al. "Taboo and Genetics," *www.gutenberg.org/files/14325*

Krueger, C. (2013). Newborn Child (Image)

Pelligrini, M. (n.d.) "Health Myths Debunked: Are Carbs Bad for You?" *http://watchmojo.com/video/id/10780/*

Peters, L. H. (2005). Diet and Health. *www.gutenberg.org/files/15069/15069-h/15069-h.htm*

Wheldon, R.H. (2007). No Animal Food. *www.gutenberg.org/files/22829/22829-h/22829-h.htm*

Chapter 9

Bauer, S. (2010). "The Importance of Saving Money: Hows and Whys" (*The News-Gazette* article) *www.news-gazette.com/news/business/economy/2010-01-24*. Reprinted by permission of The News-Gazette. Permission does not imply endorsement.

Collett-White, M. (2013). "UK show puts Schwitters's 'Rubbish' Art Back in Frame." *www.reuters.com/article/2013/01/29/entertainment*

Henney, N.B. (1922). The Book of Business Etiquette. *www.gutenberg.org/files/23025/23025-h/23025-h.htm*

Hilton, W. (2004). *Psychology and Achievement. www.gutenberg.org/files/13791/13791-h/13791-h.htm*

Krueger, C. (n.d.) Photograph, Graffiti Art. Caroline Krueger.

Krueger, C. (n.d.) Photographs, "Vote Here," "Flying Flag." Caroline Krueger.

Lawson, T.W. (2008). "The Power of Money." *www.gutenberg.org/files/26330/26330-h/26330-h.htm*

LBHounslow (n.d.) YouTube video, "The Importance of Speech and Language." *www.youtube.com/watch?v=8wfpfLkEy-Y*

Smith, J.A., & Marsh, J. (n.d.) "Why We Make Art." *http://greatergood.berkeley.edu/article/item/why_we_make_art*

Twain, Mark. (2006). "The Disappearance of Language." *www.gutenberg.org/files/3188/3188-h/3188-h.htm*

Chapter 10

Common Core State Standards (2013). Appendix B. *www.corestandards.org/assets/Appendix_B.pdf*

ACKNOWLEDGMENTS

Chapter 2

Excerpt on page 23 from "An Alarm in the Offing on Climate Change." *The New York Times*, January 14, 2013 © 2013, The New York Times. All rights reserved. Used by permission and protected by the Copyright Laws of the United States. The printing, copying, redistribution, or retransmission of this Content without express written permission is prohibited.

Poem on page 42, "A Bird Came Down the Walk," by Emily Dickinson. Reprinted by permission of the publishers and the Trustees of Amherst College from THE POEMS OF EMILY DICKINSON: READING EDITION, edited by Ralph W. Franklin, ed., Cambridge, Mass.: The Belknap Press of Harvard University Press, Copyright © 1998, 1999 by the President and Fellows of Harvard College. Copyright © 1951, 1955, 1979, 1983 by the President and Fellows of Harvard College.

Excerpt on pages 44–47 from "The Great Gatsby" by F. Scott Fitzgerald. Reprinted with the permission of Scribner Publishing Group from THE GREAT GATSBY by F. Scott Fitzgerald. Copyright © 1925 by Charles Scribner's Sons. Copyright renewed © 1953 by Frances Scott Fitzgerald Lanahan. All rights reserved.

Pages 75–76, "The Art of Art Restoration." Reprinted by permission.

Image on page 77, "Eco Homo." Reprinted by permission.

Chapter 4

Poem on page 146, "Because I could not stop for Death," by Emily Dickinson. Reprinted by permission of the publishers and the Trustees of Amherst College from THE POEMS OF EMILY DICKINSON: READING EDITION, edited by Ralph W. Franklin, ed., Cambridge, Mass.: The Belknap Press of Harvard University Press, Copyright © 1998, 1999 by the President and Fellows of Harvard College. Copyright © 1951, 1955, 1979, 1983 by the President and Fellows of Harvard College.

Poem on page 147, "I Felt a Funeral, in my Brain," by Emily Dickinson. Reprinted by permission of the publishers and the Trustees of Amherst College from THE POEMS OF EMILY DICKINSON: READING EDITION, edited by Ralph W. Franklin, ed., Cambridge, Mass.: The Belknap Press of Harvard University Press, Copyright © 1998, 1999 by the President and Fellows of Harvard College. Copyright © 1951, 1955, 1979, 1983 by the President and Fellows of Harvard College.

Chapter 5

Chapter 6

Chapter 8

Chapter 9

Commonly Used Action Verbs

Accept To receive; to regard as true, proper, normal, inevitable

Accomplish To execute fully; to attain

Adjust To make slight changes in something to make it fit or function better

Administer Manage or direct the performance of duties or actions

Adopt To take up and practice as one's own; to accept or carry out a plan

Advise Recommend a course of action; offer an informed opinion based on specialized knowledge

Analyze Separate into elements and critically examine, to study or determine relationship or accuracy

Answer To speak or write in reply to a request

Anticipate Foresee and deal with in advance, give advanced thought or consideration, remedy in advance

Apply To put to use for a purpose; to employ diligently or with close attention

Appraise Evaluate the worth or merit of

Approve Accept as satisfactory; exercise final authority with regard to commitment of resources

Arrange Make preparation for an event; put in proper order

Assemble Collect or gather together in a predetermined order from various sources

Assess Determine the value or accuracy of; evaluate

Assign Specify or designate tasks or duties to be performed by others

Assist To give support or aid

Assure Give confidence, to make certain, guarantee

Attain To gain or achieve

Attend To be present for the purpose of making a contribution

Articulate To give clear and effective communication

Audit To make a formal examination or review

Authorize Approve; empower through vested authority

Budget To plan the allocation, expenditure, or use of resources, especially money or time

Calculate Make a mathematical computation; judge to be sure or probable

Clarify Make something clearer by explaining in greater detail

Classify To arrange or assign to a category

Collaborate Work jointly with; cooperate with others, acts as liaison providing a close relationship, connection, or link

Communicate To impart a verbal or written message; to transmit information

Compare Determine if two or more items, entries are the same and if they are not, identify the differences

Compile Put together information; collect from other documents

Comply To conform to something for example, a rule, law, policy, or regulation

Compose To create or arrange in proper or orderly form

Conduct Guide; carry out from a position of command or control; to direct or take part in the operation or management of

Confirm Give approval to, verify

Consolidate To join together as one whole

Construct To form by combining or arranging parts

Consult Seek the advice of others; to give professional advice or services; to confer

Contribute To play a significant part in bringing about an end or result

Coordinate Combine the actions of others to bring to a common result

Correspond Communicate with in writing

Counsel To give advice or guidance, to consult with

Create To bring into existence; to produce through imaginative skill

Delegate Commission another to perform tasks or duties that may carry specific degrees of accountability

Design Conceive, create and execute according to plan

Determine Resolve; fix conclusively or authoritatively

Develop Disclose, discover, perfect, or unfold a plan or idea

Devise Come up with something new — perhaps by combining or applying known or new ideas or principles

Direct Guide work operations though the establishment of objectives, policies, practices and standards

Disseminate Spread or disperse information

Distribute Deliver to proper destinations

Document To support with written information and records

Draft Prepare papers or documents in preliminary form

Edit To revise and prepare material (written, film, tape, soundtrack) for publication or display

Endorse Support or recommend; express approval

Enhance Improve; make better

Ensure Guarantee or make certain

Establish Bring into existence; enact an agreement

Estimate Forecast requirements; appraise, judge approximate value

Evaluate Determine or fix the value of; assess, careful appraisal

Examine Scrutinize closely (as to determine compliance)

Execute Put into effect or carry out

Expedite Accelerate the process or progress of

Facilitate To make a process easier to perform

File To arrange in a methodical manner

Finalize To bring something to a point at which everything has been agreed upon and arranged

Forecast To predict; to estimate in advance

Formulate Develop or devise

Foster To promote the growth or development of

Generate To bring into existence; to cause to be; to produce

Greet To welcome in a cordial, professional manner

Guide To show or lead the way to; to manage the affairs of; to influence the conduct or opinions of

Gather To collect; to accumulate and place in order

Hire To employ

Identify To ascertain the origin, nature, or definitive characteristics of

Implement Carry out; execute a plan or program

Improve Make something better; enhance the value or quality of

Initiate Start or introduce

Inspect Critically examine for suitability; carries with it the authority to accept or reject

Instruct To teach; to coach; to impart or communicate knowledge

Insure To make certain by taking necessary measures and precautions

Interpret To conceive the significance of something; to explain something to others

Interview To obtain facts or opinions through inquiry or examination of various sources

Investigate Study through close examination and systematic inquiry

Issue Put forth or distribute officially

Lead To guide or direct on a course or in the direction of; to channel; to direct the operations of

Maintain Keep in an existing state; uphold

Manage Exercise administrative, executive and supervisory direction

Mediate To oversee an attempt to resolve a dispute by working with both sides to help them reach an agreement

Mentor To provide advice and support to, and watch over and foster the progress of a less experienced person

Modify To make changes to

Monitor Watch, observe, or check for a specific purpose; keep track of

Negotiate Confer with others for the purpose of reaching agreement

Notify To make known

Operate Perform an activity or function

Organize To set up an administrative structure; to arrange or form

Outline To make a summary of significant features

Oversee To supervise, to watch or survey

Participate To take part in

Perform Fulfill or carry out an action or function

Plan Devise or project the realization of a course of action

Prepare To make ready for some purpose, use or activity

Present To introduce; to bestow; to offer to view

Prioritize To order or rank things according to their importance or urgency

Proceed Begin to carry out an action

Process Handle in accordance with prescribed procedures

Promote Encourage growth and development; further something by arranging or introducing it

Proofread To read a text in order to identify errors and make corrections

Produce To give shape or form to, to make or yield something

Project To estimate something by extrapolating data

Propose Declare a plan or intention

Provide Supply what is needed; furnish

Purchase To buy something using money or its equivalent

Pursue Employ measures to obtain or accomplish

Recognize To perceive clearly; to acknowledge with a show of appreciation

Recommend Advise or counsel a course of action; offer or suggest for adoption

Recruit To seek out others to become new members, students or personnel

Refer To send or direct for aid, treatment, information, or decision

Register To enter in a record; to enroll formally or officially

Regulate To bring to order or method of

Report Give an account of; furnish information or data

Represent Act in the place of or for

Research Inquire into a specific matter from several sources

Resolve To find a solution

Respond To reply or to react to

Review Go over or examine critically; examine or re-examine

Revise Rework in order to correct or improve

Schedule Plan a timetable

Screen To examine and separate nature of importance; to filter

Secure Keep free from risk of loss

Select Choose the best suited

Serve To be of assistance to or promote the interests of; to act in a particular capacity

Sign Formally approve a document by affixing a signature

Solve To find a solution for

Specify State precisely in detail or name explicitly

Standardize To bring into conformity to something established by authority, custom, or general consent as a model or criterion

Submit Yield or present for the discretion or judgment of others

Summarize Succinctly present an abstract of the main points either orally or in writing

Supervise Personally oversee, direct or guide the work of others with responsibility for meeting standards

Support To promote the interests or cause of

Survey To examine as to condition, situation, or value

Track To observe and monitor the course

Train Teach or guide others in order to raise to a predetermined standard

Transcribe Transfer data from one form of record to another without changing the nature of the data

Update To bring current

Utilize To make use of

Verify Confirm or establish authenticity; substantiate

Write To author, to draft

Key Charts

Let's review some of the key charts that have remained integral throughout your reading of this test prep guide.

According to PARCC requirements, the following word counts apply to all reading selections:

Grade level	Word count
Grades 9–11	500–1,500 words

The PARCC requirements also deem a complexity rating for each text, which follows this protocol:

Grade level	PARCC "Complexity" Determination
Grades 9–10	1050–1335
Grade 11	1185–1385

The balance of texts on the Performance-Based Assessments and End-of-Year Assessments will shift by grade band.

Grade level	Types of texts
Grades 9–11	• Approximately thirty (30) percent literary texts • Approximately seventy (70) percent informational text

In order to be deemed "college and career ready," students must achieve at least a level "4" on the grade 11 PARCC ELA/literacy assessment. PLDs are further explained below:

Level	Policy-Level Performance Level Descriptor
5	Students performing at this level demonstrate a **distinguished command** of the knowledge, skills, and practices embodied by the Common Core State Standards assessed at their grade level.

(continued)

Level	Policy-Level Performance Level Descriptor
4	Students performing at this level demonstrate a **strong command** of the knowledge, skills, and practices embodied by the Common Core State Standards assessed at their grade level.
3	Students performing at this level demonstrate a **moderate command** of the knowledge, skills, and practices embodied by the Common Core State Standards assessed at their grade level.
2	Students performing at this level demonstrate a **partial command** of the knowledge, skills, and practices embodied by the Common Core State Standards assessed at their grade level.
1	Students performing at this level demonstrate a **minimal command** of the knowledge, skills, and practices embodied by the Common Core State Standards assessed at their grade level.

Lastly, it seems as if the shift of PARCC and the Common Core requires us to master a new language. We hope you found the acronym chart helpful as you moved from one task to the next.

Acronym	Actual Title	Explanation
PARCC	Partnership for Assessment of Readiness for College and Career	The name of this particular assessment's consortium
ELA	English Language Arts	This refers to the literacy skills used throughout these PARCC assessments.
CCR	College and Career Readiness	In order for you to be deemed as "college and career ready," you will have demonstrated the academic knowledge, skills and practices necessary to enter directly into and succeed in entry-level, credit-bearing courses in College English Composition, Literature, and technical courses requiring college-level reading and writing.
CCSS	Common Core State Standards	These standards are aligned with the PARCC assessment battery.

(continued)

Acronym	Actual Title	Explanation
OWG	Operational Working Group	The groups of professionals formed to work forward and to revise assessments
PLD	Performance Level Descriptor	Your level determined by your performance on each assessment
PBA	Performance-Based Assessment	This label is attributed to the three assessments you will take throughout the school year before the End-of-Year assessment. These include the narrative PBA, the literary analysis PBA, and the research simulation PBA.
MYA	Mid-Year Assessment	This assessment is taken in the middle of the school year.
EOY	End-of-Year Assessment	This assessment is taken at the end of the school year.
PCR	Prose Constructed-Response	The larger writing task that you will complete with each performance-based assessment.
EBSR	Evidence-Based Selected-Response	A second question on the PARCC that is dependent on your answer to a first question.
TECR	Technology Enhanced Constructed-Response	A task that requires you to use technology to capture your comprehension, including the following tasks: *drag and drop, cut and paste, shade text, move items to show relationships.*
WHST	Writing History, Science, and Technical Subjects	The interdisciplinary writing standard
RST	Reading Science and Technical Subjects	The interdisciplinary reading standard
RST	Research Simulation Task	The synthesis performance-based assessment that asks you to use information from a variety of sources to support your opinion.

Suggested Reading Titles from The Common Core State Standards Initiative

Stories

Achebe, Chinua. *Things Fall Apart*

Alvarez, Julia. *In the Time of the Butterflies*

Austen, Jane. *Pride and Prejudice*

Bellow, Saul. *The Adventures of Augie March*

Borges, Jorge Luis. "The Garden of Forking Paths."

Bradbury, Ray. *Fahrenheit 451*

Bronte, Charlotte. *Jane Eyre*

Chaucer, Geoffrey. *The Canterbury Tales*

Chekhov, Anton. "Home."

de Cervantes, Miguel. *Don Quixote*

De Voltaire, F. A. M. *Candide, Or The Optimist*

Dostoevsky, Fyodor. *Crime and Punishment*

Faulkner, William. *As I Lay Dying*

Fitzgerald, F. Scott. *The Great Gatsby*

Garcia, Cristina. *Dreaming in Cuban*

Gogol, Nikolai. "The Nose."

Hawthorne, Nathaniel. *The Scarlet Letter*

Hemingway, Ernest. *A Farewell to Arms*

Henry, O. "The Gift of the Magi."

Homer. *The Odyssey*

Hurston, Zora Neale. *Their Eyes Were Watching God*

Jewett, Sarah Orne. "A White Heron."

Kafka, Franz. *The Metamorphosis*

Lahiri, Jhumpa. *The Namesake*

Lee, Harper. *To Kill A Mockingbird*

Melville, Herman. *Billy Budd, Sailor*

Morrison, Toni. *The Bluest Eye*

Olsen, Tillie. "I Stand Here Ironing."

Ovid. *Metamorphoses*

Poe, Edgar Allan. "The Cask of Amontillado."

Shaara, Michael. *The Killer Angels*

Steinbeck, John. *The Grapes of Wrath*

Tan, Amy. *The Joy Luck Club*

Turgenev, Ivan. *Fathers and Sons*

Zusak, Marcus. *The Book Thief*

Drama

Fugard, Athol. *"Master Harold"...and the boys*

Hansberry, Lorraine. *A Raisin in the Sun*

Ibsen, Henrik. *A Doll's House*

Ionesco, Eugene. *Rhinoceros*

Miller, Arthur. *Death of a Salesman*

Moliere, Jean-Baptiste Poquelin. *Tartuffe*

Shakespeare, William. *The Tragedy of Hamlet*

Shakespeare, William. *The Tragedy of Macbeth*

Sophocles. *Oedipus Rex*

Soyinka, Wole. *Death and the King's Horseman: A Play*

Wilde, Oscar. *The Importance of Being Earnest*

Wilder, Thornton. *Our Town: A Play in Three Acts*

Williams, Tennessee. *The Glass Menagerie*

Poetry

Angelou, Maya. *I Know Why the Caged Bird Sings*

Auden, Wystan Hugh. "Musee des Beaux Arts."

Baca, Jimmy Santiago. "I Am Offering This Poem to You."

Bishop, Elizabeth. "Sestina."

Collins, Billy. "Man Listening to Disc."

Cullen, Countee. "Yet Do I Marvel."

Dickinson, Emily. "Because I Could Not Stop for Death."

Dickinson, Emily. "We Grow Accustomed to the Dark."

Donne, John. "A Valediction Forbidding Mourning."

Donne, John. "Song."

Dove, Rita. "Demeter's Prayer to Hades."

Eliot, T. S. "The Love Song of J. Alfred Prufrock."

Frost, Robert. "Mending Wall."

Hand, Learned. "I Am an American Day Address."

Henry, Patrick. "Speech to the Second Virginia Convention."

Houseman, A. E. "Loveliest of Trees."

Informational Texts: English Language Arts

Johnson, James Weldon. "Lift Every Voice and Sing."

Keats, John. "Ode on a Grecian Urn."

King, Jr., Martin Luther. "I Have a Dream: Address Delivered at the March on Washington, D.C., for Civil Rights on August 28, 1963

King, Jr., Martin Luther. "Letter from Birmingham Jail."

Li Po. "A Poem of Changgan."

Lincoln, Abraham. "Gettysburg Address."

Lincoln, Abraham. "Second Inaugural Address."

Neruda, Pablo. "Ode to My Suit."

Ortiz Cofer, Judith. "The Latin Deli: An Ars Poetica."

Poe, Edgar Allan. "The Raven."

Pound, Ezra. "The River Merchant's Wife: A Letter."

Quindlen, Anna. "A Quilt of a Country."

Reagan, Ronald. "Address to Students at Moscow State University."

Roosevelt, Franklin Delano. "State of the Union Address."

Shakespeare, William. "Sonnet 73."

Shelley, Percy Bysshe. "Ozymandias."

Smith, Margaret Chase. "Remarks to the Senate in Support of a Declaration of Conscience."

Tagore, Rabindranath. "Song VII."

Walker, Alice. "Women."

Washington, George. "Farewell Address."

Wheatley, Phillis. "On Being Brought From Africa to America."

Whitman, Walt. "Song of Myself."

Wiesel, Elie. "Hope, Despair and Memory."

Informational Texts: English Language Arts

Anaya, Rudolfo. "Take the Tortillas Out of Your Poetry."

Chesterton, G. K. "The Fallacy of Success."

Emerson, Ralph Waldo. "Society and Solitude."

Hofstadter, Richard. "Abraham Lincoln and the Self-Made Myth."

Jefferson, Thomas. *The Declaration of Independence*

Mencken, H. L. *The American Language, 4th Edition*

Orwell, George. "Politics and the English Language."

Paine, Thomas. *Common Sense*

Porter, Horace. "Lee Surrenders to Grant, April 9th, 1865."

Tan, Amy. "Mother Tongue."

Thoreau, Henry David. *Walden*

United States. The Bill of Rights (Amendments One through Ten of the United States Constitution)

Wright, Richard. *Black Boy*

Informational Texts: History/Social Studies

Amar, Akhil Reed. *America's Constitution: A Biography*

An Address Delivered in Rochester, New York, on 5 July 1852."

An American Primer. Edited by Daniel J. Boorstin

Bell, Julian. *Mirror of the World: A New History of Art*

Brown, Dee. *Bury My Heart at Wounded Knee, An Indian History of the American West*

Connell, Evan S. *Son of the Morning Star: Custer and the Little Bighorn*

Dash, Joan. *The Longitude Prize*

Declaration of Sentiments by the Seneca Falls Conference

Douglass, Frederick. "What to the Slave Is the Fourth of July?:

FedViews by the Federal Reserve Bank of San Francisco

Gombrich, E. H. *The Story of Art, 16th Edition*

Haskins, Jim. *Black, Blue and Gray: African Americans in the Civil War*

Kurlansky, Mark. *Cod: A Biography of the Fish That Changed the World*

Lagemann, Ellen Condliffe. "Education."

Mann, Charles C. *Before Columbus: The Americas of 1491*

McCullough, David. *1776*

McPherson, James M. *What They Fought For 1861–1865*

The American Reader: Words that Moved a Nation, 2nd Edition

Thompson, Wendy. *The Illustrated Book of Great Composers*

Tocqueville, Alexis de. *Democracy in America*

Informational Texts: Science, Mathematics, and Technical Subjects

Calishain, Tara, and Rael Dornfest. *Google Hacks: Tips & Tools for Smarter Searching, 2nd Edition*

Cannon, Annie J. "Classifying the Stars."

Devlin, Keith. *Life by the Numbers*

Euclid. *Elements*

Fischetti, Mark. "Working Knowledge: Electronic Stability Control."

Gawande, Atul. "The Cost Conundrum: Health Care Costs in McAllen, Texas."

Gibbs, W. Wayt. "Untangling the Roots of Cancer."

Gladwell, Malcolm. *The Tipping Point: How Little Things Can Make a Big Difference*

Hakim, Joy. *The Story of Science: Newton at the Center*

Hoose, Phillip. *The Race to Save Lord God Bird*

Kane, Gordon. "The Mysteries of Mass."

Kurzweil, Ray. "The Coming Merger of Mind and Machine."

Nicastro, Nicholas. *Circumference: Eratosthenes and the Ancient Quest to Measure the Globe*

Paulos, John Allen. *Innumeracy: Mathematical Illiteracy and Its Consequences*

Preston, Richard. *The Hot Zone: A Terrifying True Story*

Tyson, Neil deGrasse. "Gravity in Reverse: The Tale of Albert Einstein's 'Greatest Blunder.'"

U.S. Environmental Protection Agency/U.S. Department of Energy. *Recommended Levels of Insulation*

U.S. General Services Administration. *Executive Order 13423: Strengthening Federal Environmental, Energy, and Transportation Management*

Walker, Jearl. "Amusement Park Physics."

Charts Used in the Book

Narrative Graphic Organizer

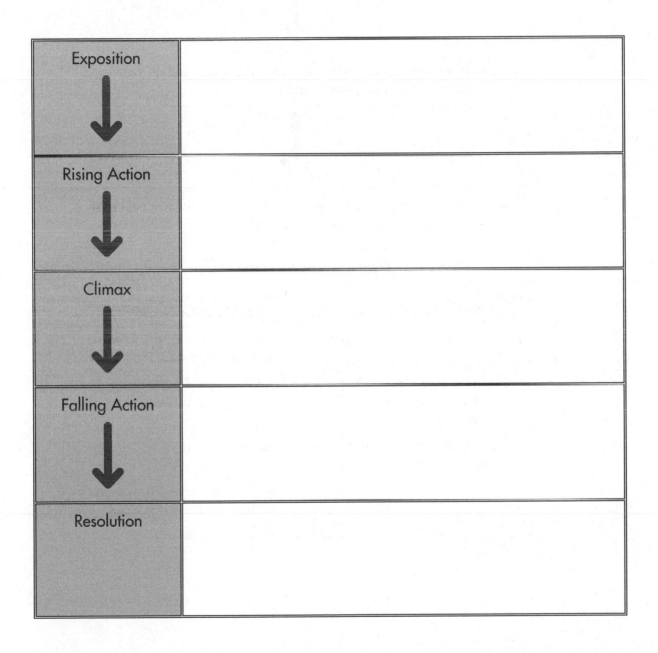

Literary Analysis Flowchart

> **Step 1:** Read the directions. Then, read the passage.

> **Step 2:** Note *some* literary and/or rhetorical devices as you read. And, write down the theme.

> **Step 3:** Ask yourself—Is the author conveying information to the reader or making an argument?

CONVEYING INFORMATION?	PRESENTING ARGUMENT?
1. Address theme in introduction.	1. Discuss, generally, the writer's purpose for making the argument.
2. Discuss the passage as a whole, involving a few devices, keeping in mind the overall theme of the passage throughout.	2. Address logical fallacies and the appeals when needed.
3. Close your essay with your final thought on the theme of the passage.	3. Do not forget to use common sense—How is the author trying to persuade his/her audience?
	4. Close your essay with your final thought on the theme of the passage.

Literary Analysis Top-Hat Graphic Organizer

Text 1	Text 2
Key Phrases:	
Analysis:	Analysis:

Common theme(s) in both works?

RST Steps

Step 1	Read through the question carefully. Make sure to decipher if the question is asking you to convey an opinion, or to convey information/research objectively.
Step 2	In the upper right-hand corner of your paper, simplify what the question is asking you to do. Put the question/task into your own words.
Step 3	Circle the minimum amount of sources that need to be addressed.
Step 4	Take notes with each of the sources. Address the source's main points. Underline actively.
Step 5	After you've addressed and highlighted the main point of the source, make separate notes on the reliability of these sources. Is the source reliable in general? Is it slanted in any way? Do logical fallacies or "holes in argument" exist?
Step 6	You've read through your sources. Choose the sources that you are most comfortable with, and put a star (*) in the upper right-hand corner of each source that you will be using in your research simulation task.
Step 7	In source chart, copy your notes from your sources into each.
Step 8	Now, look at the relationships of your sources. Do they agree with each other? Do they disagree? Use your source-relationship chart to begin thinking about how you will have your sources begin conversing with one another.
Step 9	Complete the outline for your essay.
Step 10	Complete your essay, using the outline/framework as a guide.
Step 11	After you have completed your essay, go back to check that your sources have a conversation, and replace the verbs you've used to integrate these sources with the action verbs from the sheet provided.

Video Clip Note-Taking Organizer

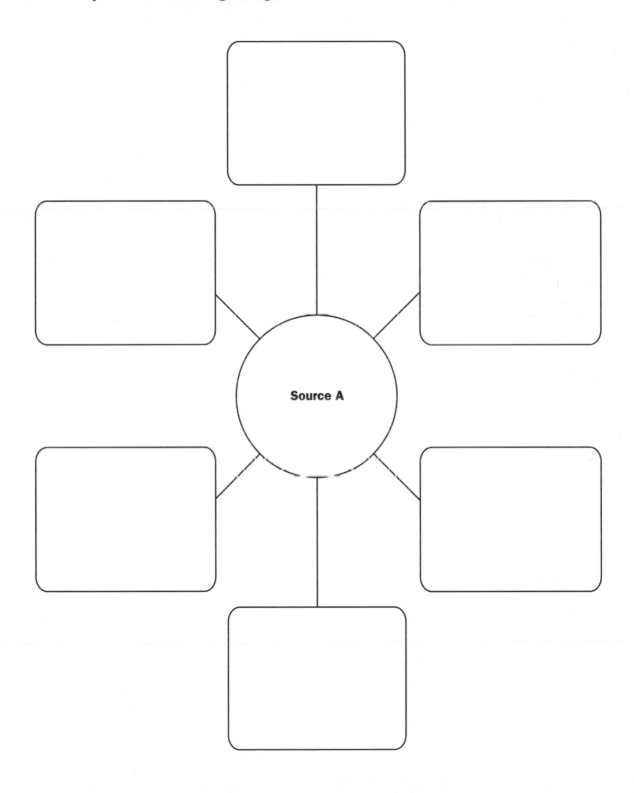

Source Relationships

Topic:

My Thesis Statement:

Source A	Source B	Source C

Exactly how do the sources talk with each other?

Scoring Checklist

Development of Ideas
❑ Did the author use evidence from the text?
❑ Did this evidence come from more than one source?"
❑ Did the author successfully have the two sources interact with each other?

Organization
❑ Is there a clearly expressed introduction, body, and conclusion?
❑ Does the introduction have an attention-grabber and a clearly stated thesis?
❑ Do each of the body paragraphs support the thesis?
❑ Does the conclusion successfully answer the So What? question?

Written Expression
❑ Does the author effectively use vocabulary, including content-specific words?
❑ Does the author utilize vivid and proper description?
❑ Does the author appropriately use transitional words throughout the piece?
❑ Is the style clear, concise, and to the point?
❑ Are any points in the essay ambiguous and unclear?

Knowledge of Language Conventions
❑ Were there any mistakes in grammar, mechanics, and usage?
❑ Did the author go back and edit the work?
❑ Does the work read effortlessly?
❑ Does poor grammar become a distraction or a nuisance?

Scoring Rubric for Analytic Writing

Construct Measured	Score Point 4	Score Point 3	Score Point 2	Score Point 1	Score Point 0
(Reading) Comprehension of Key Ideas and Details	Student cites convincing textual evidence to show a full understanding of his/her reading.	Student cites convincing textual evidence to show an extensive understanding of his/her reading.	Student cites textual evidence to show a basic comprehension of his/her reading.	Student cites textual evidence to show a limited comprehension of his/her reading.	Student cites little or no textual evidence; student does not exhibit close comprehension of his/her reading.
(Writing) Development of Ideas	Student response provides convincing reasoning and development that is appropriate to the task.	Student response provides clear reasoning and development that is largely appropriate to the task.	Student response provides some reasoning and development that is somewhat appropriate to the task.	Student response provides limited reasoning and development that is limited in appropriateness to the task.	Student response provides underdeveloped reasoning and development that is inappropriate to the task.
(Writing) Organization	Demonstrates purposeful cohesion, with well-executed progression of ideas.	Demonstrates a great deal of cohesion, and a logical progression of ideas.	Demonstrates some cohesion, and logically grouped ideas.	Demonstrates limited cohesion, making the writer's progression of ideas somewhat unclear.	Demonstrates a lack of cohesion.
(Writing) Clarity of Language	Establishes and maintains an effective style, including precise details and transitions.	Establishes and maintains an effective style, including mostly precise details and transitions.	Establishes and maintains a mostly effective style, including some precise details and transitions.	Establishes a limited effective style, including limited details and transitions.	Inappropriate style, with little to no precise language.
(Writing) Knowledge of Language and Conventions	While command of the language exists, few grammatical issues may exist.	While command of the language exists, distracting grammatical issues may exist.	While inconsistent command of the language exists, few patterns of grammatical issues may exist.	While limited command of the language exists, a series of grammatical issues may exist.	Demonstrates little to no command of language. Frequent and varied grammar and usage errors.